TRILINGUAL JOYCE

The Anna Livia Variations

PATRICK O'NEILL

Trilingual Joyce: The Anna Livia Variations

UNIVERSITY OF TORONTO PRESS
Toronto Buffalo London

Toronto Buffalo London
utorontopress.com

ISBN 978-1-4875-0278-2

Library and Archives Canada Cataloguing in Publication

O'Neill, Patrick, 1945–, author
Trilingual Joyce : the Anna Livia variations / Patrick O'Neill.

Includes bibliographical references and index.
ISBN 978-1-4875-0278-2 (hardcover)

1. Joyce, James, 1882–1941. Anna Livia Plurabelle. 2. Joyce, James, 1882–1941 – Translations into French – History and criticism. 3. Joyce, James, 1882–1941 – Translations into Italian – History and criticism. I. Title.

PR6019.O9A766 2018 823'.912 C2017-907226-9

This book has been published with the help of a grant from the Federation for the Humanities and Social Sciences, through the Awards to Scholarly Publications Program, using funds provided by the Social Sciences and Humanities Research Council of Canada.

University of Toronto Press acknowledges the financial assistance to its publishing program of the Canada Council for the Arts and the Ontario Arts Council, an agency of the Government of Ontario.

Canada Council for the Arts Conseil des Arts du Canada

Funded by the Government of Canada Financé par le gouvernement du Canada

For Trudi,
as always

Contents

Acknowledgments

For assistance, support, and encouragement of various kinds over the years, thanks are due to Marcelo Zabaloy in Argentina; Geert Lernout and Dirk Van Hulle in Belgium; Vitor Alevato do Amaral, Dirce Waltrick do Amarante, and Afonso Teixeira Filho in Brazil; the late Mark Boulby, Tim Conley, Beth Coward, Garry Leonard, and Margaret Maliszewska in Canada; Hervé Michel in France; Friedhelm Rathjen in Germany; Anne Fogarty and John Kearns in Ireland; Massimo Bacigalupo, the late Rosa Maria Bollettieri Bosinelli, Enrique Terrinoni, and Serenella Zanotti in Italy; Erik Bindervoet and Robbert-Jan Henkes in the Netherlands; Krzysztof Bartnicki and Tadeusz Szczerbowski in Poland; Marissa Aixàs and María Teresa Cabrera Caneda in Spain; Fritz Senn and his colleagues at the Zurich James Joyce Foundation in Switzerland; Christian Lloyd and Robert Weninger in the UK; and Kimberly Devlin and Derek Pyle in the USA.

Thanks are also due to the Faculty of Arts and Science at Queen's University in Canada for a generous research grant and also to Queen's University's Bader International Study Centre (BISC) at Herstmonceux Castle in the United Kingdom, where a term as Scholar in Residence afforded ideal conditions for producing a first draft of several chapters.

My best thanks are gratefully offered, as always, to my wife Trudi, who has been unfailingly supportive of my various literary enthusiasms over the years.

TRILINGUAL JOYCE

The Anna Livia Variations

Introduction

Latin me that, my trinity scholard, out of eure sanscreed into oure eryan! (*ALP* 34; *FW* 215.26–7)

It is well known that James Joyce, assisted to a greater or lesser degree by various collaborators, translated substantial excerpts from his *Anna Livia Plurabelle* (1928) into both French and Italian.[1] It has also been reported that in doing so he appeared in many instances to assign a significantly greater importance to sonority and rhythm, verbal effect, and linguistic flow, than to semantic fidelity to the original text. Surprisingly little consideration has been given, however, to how the three *ALP* variations, English, French, and Italian, each equally informed by Joyce's personal authority, compare in detail, both in stylistic and in semantic terms. Discussions of Joyce's translations have by and large confined themselves to a handful of particularly striking examples of the differences between the English and the French versions or between the English and the Italian versions. To my knowledge, no extended examination exists in either of these areas, and there likewise exists no sustained comparative examination of all three versions.[2] The present

1 *Anna Livia Plurabelle* the text will usually be referred to as *ALP*, Anna Livia Plurabelle the character will usually by referred to as ALP, unitalicized. For other abbreviations used in parenthetical references to Joyce's works, see section 1 of the bibliography.

2 For preliminary discussions, see O'Neill (2005, 194–219 passim; 2013, 237–62 passim); also O'Sullivan (2006). All three versions of *ALP*, English, French, and Italian, are reprinted by Rosa Maria Bosinelli (1996). They are also available online at http://www.rosenlake.net/fw/alp-III.php.

work aims to fill that gap, while comparing the corresponding portions of Samuel Beckett and Alfred Péron's preliminary (and long lost) French version, Ettore Settanni's (unauthorized) emendations of Joyce's own Italian, and C.K. Ogden's Basic English rendering of the closing pages, in which Joyce is also reported to have played some role.

ALP, separately published in book form in 1928, was subsequently incorporated as the eighth chapter of *Finnegans Wake*, and that chapter has frequently been described as the showpiece of that extraordinary text. Joyce himself famously wrote to Harriet Shaw Weaver that he "was prepared to stake everything" on *ALP* (*L* 3, 163). He claimed to Valery Larbaud in 1927 that he had already spent 1,200 hours of work on *ALP* (Ellmann 1982, 598) – and, as Walton Litz notes (1961, 100), this was while he was working on only the eighth of what would eventually amount to seventeen distinct revisions of the eventually twenty-page chapter between its inception in 1923 and its eventual appearance in the *Wake* in 1939. Louis Gillet reports that the writing of *ALP* up to its appearance in *transition* in 1927 took Joyce, by his own account, some 1,600 hours of sustained and meticulous work (1941, 67; Higginson 1960, 4; Litz 1961, 100–20).

ALP is now widely considered as "the most beautiful and the most famous section of *Finnegans Wake*" (Norris 1990, 166). That positive opinion was not necessarily shared by all astonished early readers. Seán O'Faoláin, for example, likened *ALP* to the mindless and "zany" doodles of bored schoolchildren (1928, 225). Arnold Bennett, only slightly less condemnatory, considered that *ALP* would "never be anything but the wild caprice of a wonderful creative artist who has lost his way" (1929, 7). Such negative views remained those of a distinct minority, however, even among early readers. "Joyce's inventions and discoveries as an innovator in literary form are more beautifully shown in it than in any other part of his work," Padraic Colum wrote (1928a, 318). Robert Sage, in a highly laudatory review in *transition*, wrote that the breathtaking complexity of the text was the rough equivalent of five movies playing simultaneously on the same screen, each accompanied by its own separate orchestra (1928, 172). The novelist Louis Golding found the final paragraph "an instance of sheer radiance in writing" (1933, 148), while the playwright John Drinkwater praised the work as "one of the greatest things in English literature" (*SL* 343). Joyce's fellow Dubliner James Stephens even considered *ALP* "the greatest prose ever written by a man" (*SL* 343). Richard Ellmann finds it the "most melodic chapter" of the *Wake* (1982, 602). For Patrick Parrinder, *ALP* "has been widely recognized as one of the most beautiful prose-poems in English" (1984, 205), coming, of all the chapters of *Finnegans Wake*, "closest to the genuinely magical use of language" (234), "an example of the Joycean grotesque celebration of life at its most magisterial" (235). For Tindall, *ALP* is "a triumph of sequence, rhythm, and sound" (1996, 140).

In addition to the 1,600 hours he spent on the original English text of *ALP*, it reportedly took Joyce and his collaborators more than fifty hours spread over seventeen three-hour meetings to translate the less than seven pages of the French *ALP*; it reportedly took Joyce and Nino Frank another fifty or so hours over a further twenty-four meetings to render the same lines into Italian. Given all this, it does not seem inappropriate to devote some detailed comparative attention to the results and resonances of the iconic endeavour.

1 English *ALP*

Shortly after the appearance of *Ulysses* in February 1922, Joyce started to make notes for what would seventeen years later become *Finnegans Wake*, and he put the first words of the new work on paper on 10 March 1923 (Ellmann 1982, 794). The opening words of *ALP* were penned some months later, in the fall of 1923 (Higginson 1960, 3); a longer draft, though less than half the length of the chapter that eventually appeared in the *Wake*, was produced by February 1924 (Hayman 1963, 302); and on 7 March 1924 he wrote to Harriet Weaver – very prematurely, as it turned out – that he had "finished the *Anna Livia* piece" (*L* 1, 212), famously describing it on that occasion as "a chattering dialogue across the river by two washerwomen who as night falls become a tree and a stone. The river is named Anna Liffey" (*L* 1, 213). The river is thus also ALP, and the washerwomen (who will eventually emerge also as aspects of ALP herself, the river talking to itself) are discussing her affairs (in all senses of the word) as well as washing her own and her husband's dirty linen (in all senses of the word). As Grace Eckley notes, *ALP* is composed entirely of this dialogue (1975, 130). Joyce was able to send Weaver the eleven-page typed manuscript of *ALP* on 15 March 1924 (*L* 3, 90).

ALP was in fact very far from finished, however. Joyce writes to Weaver on 8 July 1925 that he has been "getting into ever deeper Liffey water" (*L* 3, 121) and on 27 July 1925 that he has "added or changed about a hundred things in Anna Livia which I sent on to Miss Beach who is holding the MS" (*L* 1, 229). Four days later he asks Sylvia Beach to make "the few more changes enclosed" (*L* 3, 122). He had originally agreed to have *ALP* appear in a newly founded London review, *The Calendar of Modern Letters* (*L* 1, 228; *SL* 307), but when the English printer cautiously refused to set it (*L* 3, 127), Joyce withdrew it in September 1925 (*L* 1, 233; Ellmann 1982, 574). The first printed version of *ALP* thereupon appeared (under the title "From Work in Progress") on 1 October 1925 in Adrienne Monnier's likewise recently founded Paris journal *Le Navire d'Argent*.[3] This version of *ALP* also appeared in March 1926, without Joyce's permission, as "A New Unnamed Work," in Samuel Roth's New York journal *Two Worlds Quarterly*.[4] Roth had indeed asked Joyce for a contribution to the journal, but Joyce did not reply (*L* 1, 236, 237–8; *L* 3, 131), which Roth evidently considered sufficient licence to proceed.

Joyce – who habitually used the symbol Δ in his notes for both the character ALP and the text *ALP* – promptly began to work on further revisions of the text, and in September 1926 he sent Harriet Weaver a reworked version ("Δ2") of the *Navire d'Argent* text (*L* 3, 142), intended for Eugene Jolas's journal *transition*. When Weaver reacted with something less than the expected enthusiasm to the language of the future *Finnegans Wake*, Joyce wrote to her on 1 February 1927, "Either the end of Part I Δ [i.e., *ALP*] is something or I am an imbecile in my judgment of language" (*L* 1, 249). On 8 October 1927 he wrote to her that he was still "working very hard on the final revise of Δ [for *transition*] on which I am prepared to stake everything" (*L* 3, 163).

In mid-October 1927, still assiduously working away, he estimated to Valery Larbaud that the revision had so far taken him "1200 hours of work on 17 pages" and that the piece now contained about 350 river names of Anna Livia's "fluvial maids of honour from all ends of the earth" (*L* 3, 164). On 28 October 1927 he wrote to Harriet Weaver again, "I did not really finish with Δ till 6 yesterday evening. The final proofreading alone took me five hours. I do not know what to think of it. Hundreds of river names are woven into the text. I think it moves." He adds that he will postpone any further news for a day or so "until the singsong fades out of my addled head" (*L* 1, 259). The second authorized printed version of *ALP* appeared (as "Continuation of Work in Progress") in *transition* in October (though dated November) 1927 (Ellmann 1982, 795).[5]

---

3 "From Work in Progress," *Le Navire d'Argent* 1.5 (1 October 1925), 59–74.

4 "A New Unnamed Work," *Two Worlds Quarterly* 2.3 (March 1926).

5 "Continuation of Work in Progress," *transition*, no. 8 (November 1927), 17–35.

Nor was even this to be the final version of *ALP*, which was published in its various versions more often than any other chapter of the *Wake*. Joyce to Weaver on 29 October 1927: "I have not yet done with Mrs A.L. t.8 [the *transition* text] is out I believe but I am still working away on the final revise, as I am to read it to a group of 'critics' on Wednesday next. The stream is now rising to flood point but I find she can carry almost anything. Between t.8 which you will receive and [the newly revised] version there will be at most I suppose a difference of 50 or 60 words or expressions" (*L* 1, 260). That estimate was quite a bit too low, he writes to her in November, "I suppose you now have *transition* 8. Since it came out I have woven into the printed text another 152 rivernames and it is now final as it will appear in the book" – except, perhaps, for just one or two (or perhaps a small few other) minor details (*L* 1, 261).

In January 1928 the *transition* version was printed again as the last part of *Work in Progress Volume I*, a small edition published in New York by Donald Friede, in order to secure American copyright (Ellmann 1982, 587). In the spring Joyce continued to rework the text for publication in book form (Ellmann 1982, 795), and on 29 October 1928 the third authorized printed version of *ALP* was published in New York by Crosby Gaige as a slim volume, *Anna Livia Plurabelle*, in a deluxe limited edition of 800 copies in medium brown cloth, with a preface by Padraic Colum.[6] Ellmann reports Sylvia Beach's remark that the book "had to be published in a tea-colored cover because the Liffey was the color of tea" (603). In addition, fifty special copies were issued (on green paper), not intended for sale. Joyce himself did not seem to be particularly impressed with the overall result, referring to Crosby Gaige in a letter of 23 October 1928, based on an advance copy, as "the putter out of this (one cannot say it is published)" (*L* 1, 271) – though he seems to have been referring primarily to the small number of copies produced, and perhaps also to the price, unaffordable for many. He had written to Harriet Weaver on 30 September 1928 that he had promised to reserve a copy for someone, "though it is not easy to do this with such an edition" (*SL* 336).

Joyce reported to Weaver in July 1929 that T.S. Eliot, who had been an editor with Faber and Faber since 1925, seemed keen to bring out an

6 The 72-page volume sold for US$15, the equivalent in 2016 of approximately US$205. Colum's preface (1928b) had originally appeared in the American literary journal *The Dial* in April 1928.

English edition of *ALP* (*L* 1, 282; *SL* 343), and in June 1930 the fourth authorized printed version of *ALP*, differing only very slightly from the Gaige edition of 1928 (Higginson 1960, 18), was indeed published in London. It appeared both in brown cloth and as a two-shilling paperback (one of tne first paperbacks to appear, in fact) in Faber and Faber's Criterion Miscellany series. A mimeographed press release included a humorous piece of quasi-Wakean promotional doggerel by its author: "Buy a book in brown paper / From Faber & Faber / To see Annie Liffey trip, tumble and caper. / Sevensinns in her singthings, / Plurabelle on her prose, / Seashell ebb music wayriver she flows" (Ellmann 1982, 616–17). The much more affordable Faber edition, which sold very well, was reprinted in 1997, unchanged from 1930 other than in pagination, as number 25 in the Faber Library series.[7] Still by no means willing to leave well enough alone, Joyce wrote, for example, to Eugene Jolas, who was in Austria at the time, in late 1930 asking him to contribute the names of some further Austrian rivers (Maria Jolas 1949, 173). On 4 May 1939, however, the fifth and final authorized printed version of *ALP*, with just a small number of changes from and additions to the 1930 Faber text, appeared in London and New York as the eighth chapter of *Finnegans Wake*.[8]

The most widely-known eccentricity of *ALP* is its integration, punningly or otherwise, of an astonishing number of river names (and a considerable number of other water-related features). Joyce, continually and even obsessively increasing the number of river names with every revision of the text, once commented that *ALP* was "an attempt to subordinate words to the rhythm of water," on one occasion even confirming his own opinion of the validity of the fluvial principle by going down to the Seine to listen by one of the bridges to the sound of the waters (Ellmann 1982, 564).

The question as to exactly how many rivers may be said to be involved is itself an intriguing one. Should every occurrence of the pronoun *who* in Joyce's text be seen as also containing a Chinese *ho* ("river"), for example? Does every occurrence of the preposition *about* include

7 The text of the 1928 Gaige *ALP*, following Colum's preface (vii–xix), appears on pp. 3–61; the 1930 Faber text, without any preface, appears on pp. 5–32; the 1997 Faber text, likewise without preface, appears on pp. 3–35.

8 For stimulating discussions of the specific development of two different passages in *ALP* from inception to *FW*, see Fordham (2007, 66–86) on *FW* 203.17–204.05 and McCarthy (2007, 166–72) on *FW* 204.21–205.15.

reference to the South American Abou, the Nigerian Bou, and the Laotian Ou – not to mention the Old Irish noun *ab* ("river") and the Sardinian noun *aba* ("water")? One reasonable rule of thumb (however one might define "reasonable") would suggest that the presence of rivers may be discerned on the basis of three main criteria: undisguised mention, overt linguistic distortion, and linguistic serendipity. In the first case, an actual river name also stands in for a normal vocabulary item, as in "reppe" (the French river Reppe) for *rip* (*FW* 196.11) or "saale" (the German river Saale) for *soil* (*FW* 196.15). In the second case, a normal vocabulary item is deliberately deformed to enable punning access to a particular river name, as in "mouldaw" for *mouldy* and the Czech river Moldau (*FW* 196.17). In the third, a normal vocabulary item (like *about*) felicitously happens to include or imply the name of one or more or even several rivers or other aquatic features.

It is hardly surprising that different readers should arrive at very different calculations of the total number of rivers involved. Joyce himself suggested about 500 in the 1928 text (*L* 1, 261), but kept on adding more and more names. Fred Higginson suggests about 800 altogether (1953, 172–4; 1960, 13); Louis Mink identifies at least 980 (1978, xvii); John Bishop calculates that the total number exceeds 1,000 (1986, 455); Mario Grut extends the number to 1,022 (2001, 33–7); and Francisco García Tortosa suggests the figure may be as high as 1,200 (1992, 88).[9] As for the overall role of these proliferating river names, Higginson concludes that "the endless revisions and additions to this chapter very much complicate the text, but at the same time they sharpen its focus. In this respect the river names were structurally effective in the process of composition, not merely ornamental as they have often been taken to be" (1953, 174; qtd. Mink 1978, xvii).

Not all readers are persuaded that the inclusion of these multiple fluvial references amounts to more than a quirky obsession on Joyce's part. Edmund Wilson was an early sceptic on this point, asking "Has it really made Anna Livia any more riverlike to introduce the names of several hundred rivers?" (1952, 235). Anthony Burgess, on the other hand, is enthusiastic, "In prose

---

9 James Cerny establishes an areal ranking from 1 to 10 for the number of rivers evoked, with England heading the list, followed by Ireland, France, the former USSR, Africa, USA, India, Germany, South America, and, in joint tenth place, Canada and Scotland (1971, 220). Erik Bindervoet and Robbert-Jan Henkes, meanwhile, fluvially outjoycing Joyce, list 1,052 river names (from Aa to Zwin) worked into their Dutch rendering of *ALP* (2013, 137–48).

splashing with river-names, they celebrate in rich dream-Dublinese the water-mother who bears us forward gently to our next epoch of Viconian history" (1982, 216). Umberto Eco is humorously pragmatic: "If you catch the names of some rivers you know, you sense fluidity; if you do not, not to worry, it remains a private wager on the author's part, and a subject for a doctoral thesis" (2001, 112). Joyce himself whimsically observed to Max Eastman that he "liked to think how some day, way off in Tibet or Somaliland, some boy or girl in reading that little book would be pleased to come upon the name of his or her home river" (Eastman 1931, 99–100).

As far as a translation is concerned, however, the question is irrelevant: the river references, like them or not, are *there* (or may be seen to be there) as part of the text, and if some degree of fidelity to the original text is considered an appropriate goal for a translation, some method of transposing them into the target language needs to be devised. These methods will vary widely, including (or especially) when Joyce himself is the translator. Referring to the sheer number of punning fluvial references, Nathan Halper aptly observed that "these hundreds of puns – in a way – are a single running pun. As this flows through the chapter, it is a reflection of the flowing river itself. The translator may add or subtract without significantly changing the pervasive river-ness" (1967, 225). Louis Mink writes to similar effect that in *ALP* "the river-names cluster so thickly and are so artfully disposed that they virtually cease to bear any meaning as individual names. In this new language, they are more like phonemes than like morphemes. In his drafts of this chapter, Joyce returned again and again to the task of adding river-names to the expanding text, which in its final version flows without any sign of effort, like the river it celebrates" (1978, xvii). As with so much else in the *Finnegans Wake* universe, how and to what degree readers and translators (and *their* readers) should react to these apparent or possible fluvial prompts will very largely depend on the individual respondent and his or her sense of appropriate interpretive behaviour in the particular set of textual circumstances. The fact that no other reader may be in agreement on such finer points merely constitutes one more strand of the multifarious interpretive fun to be had in the encounter not only with Joyce's original text but also with its polymorphous continuations.

2 French *ALP*

"Everything Joyce wrote has to do with translation, is transferential," as Fritz Senn very aptly writes, and *Finnegans Wake* in particular, he adds, transforms "all of us into foreign readers" (1984, 39, 54). From his earliest years Joyce was fascinated by the textual possibilities of translation as one particular aspect of his lifelong fascination (or obsession) with language and languages and their interplay. A first volume of poems, hand-written as a fourteen-year-old, included, as Stanislaus Joyce later remembered, "perhaps half a dozen translations from Latin and French" (1958, 100).[10] Studying French and Italian at University College Dublin, he also began to learn Norwegian, as is well known, in order to read Ibsen in the original. He taught himself German in order to read Hauptmann (Ellmann 1982, 76), and as a nineteen-year-old translated two of Hauptmann's plays, *Vor Sonnenaufgang* (1889) and the then very recent *Michael Kramer* (1900). He also took Irish lessons from Patrick Pearse for about two years (O Hehir 1967, vii).

In 1904, having abandoned Ireland to its own devices, he briefly planned with Alessandro Francini Bruni, deputy director of the Pola Berlitz school, to undertake a joint Italian translation of George Moore's *Celibates* (*L* 2, 74; McCourt 2000, 19). Moving to Trieste in March 1905, he wrote newspaper articles in Italian for the *Piccolo della Sera*, Italian became the language of the home, he mastered and delighted in the Triestine dialect of that language, and he struck up an acquaintance with modern Greek (McCourt 2013). In early 1909 he wrote to a Milan publisher proposing an Italian translation of Oscar Wilde's *Dorian Gray*, but the offer was rejected (McCourt 2000, 133). He also considered translating Wilde's *The Soul of Man under Socialism* into Italian, but the pressure of other work prevented him from continuing with the project (Ellmann 1982, 274). Also in early 1909, his Italian lawyer friend Nicolò Vidacovich and he completed a joint translation of Synge's *Riders to the Sea*, which appeared in print in the Florentine journal *Solaria* twenty years later, in the autumn of 1929, as *Cavalcata al mare* (Frank 1979, 83).[11] He assisted Vidacovich in 1911 in an Italian translation of Yeats's *The Countess Cathleen* – which Yeats unfortunately refused to allow to be published or performed, since it was based on an earlier version of the play that he no longer liked (Ellmann 1982, 267; McCourt 2000, 175).

Spending five years in Zurich between 1915 and 1920, Joyce continued to work on his German and went on to acquire considerable fluency in that language (Budgen 1972, 182). During the 1920s in Paris he

10 Ellmann records one surviving example, namely the fourteen-year-old's translation of Horace's Ode 3.13 ("*O fons Bandusiae*") (1982, 50–1).

11 John McCourt speaks highly of the translation, calling it "a triumph of simplicity, naturalness and, most of all, rhythm" (2000, 135; 2008, 130–1).

became deeply involved in the progress and revision of both the French and the German translations of *Ulysses* as well as in the multilingual games of the *Work in Progress* that would eventually become *Finnegans Wake*. The later 1920s showed a particularly intense interest in new languages. He worked on Flemish in 1925 (Bowker 2011, 353), on brushing up his Danish in 1928 (Ellmann 1982, 603), took Spanish lessons from a tutor about the same time (Ellmann 1982, 607), and had Paul Léon, whom he met in 1928, give him lessons in Russian. Eugene Jolas reports that he also studied Hebrew, Japanese, Chinese, Finnish, "and other tongues" (1948, 13–14).

Joyce evidently began thinking about possible translations of *ALP* very shortly after its appearance in book form in October 1928. He must certainly have discussed the matter very soon with Georg Goyert, the German translator of *Ulysses*, who industriously set to work on a German *ALP* in early 1929 (Reichert and Senn 1970, 26). Joyce undoubtedly played a role in encouraging Goyert to undertake the translation, writing to him as early as 20 July 1929 to enquire about its progress and asking if Goyert could send him a few pages of it: "I would like to see if a translation of it is really possible."[12] Goyert very likely complied with this request from the master, and in so doing may well have confirmed Joyce's opinion that a translation was indeed a possibility.[13]

Four months later at any rate, on 22 November 1929, we find Joyce writing to Harriet Weaver that Léon-Paul Fargue and he were to meet the following day "to set to work to put Alp into French, the last eight pages" (*L* 1, 287).[14] The French poet and essayist Fargue (1878–1947), whom Joyce had known since the early 1920s, had been involved in the translation of some passages from *Ulysses* for Valery Larbaud's

12 "Können Sie mir ein Paar Seiten Ihrer Ubersetzung ALP schicken? ... [Ich] möchte sehen ob uberhaupt eine Ubersetzung davon möglich ist" (*L* 3, 191). See also Reichert and Senn (1970, 165).

13 The complete German *ALP* seems to have been ready by March 1933, and Joyce is reported to have given it his official seal of approval (Maria Jolas 1949, 173). Further involvement on Joyce's part is possible but remains uncertain, and in the political chaos of the times no part of Goyert's *ALP* appeared in print until 1946, while his complete German *ALP* was first published only in 1970 (Senn 1998, 188).

14 Joyce was referring to the final pages from the paragraph beginning "Well, you know or don't you kennet or haven't I told you every telling has a taling and that's the he and the she of it" (*FW* 213.11–12). He had recorded the same pages for C.K. Ogden's Orthological Institute in August 1929 and would later, in October 1931, collaborate with Ogden in rendering them into Basic English.

pre-publication promotional lecture on that novel in December 1921 (*L* 3, 55n2). Pressure of other commitments evidently caused Joyce to abandon the proposed collaboration, and no more is heard of any further involvement on Fargue's part.[15] The plan of a French translation was by no means abandoned, however, and at some point during the following month already (Bair 1978, 95) Joyce, "with his secondary passion for extending other languages as he had extended English" (Ellmann 1982, 632), invited his fellow Dubliner Samuel Beckett to undertake an experimental French translation of the opening pages (rather than the closing pages envisaged with Fargue).

Beckett had arrived in Paris on 1 November 1928, just days after the appearance of *ALP* in book form, and was quickly introduced to Joyce by Thomas MacGreevy (1893–1967), a fellow graduate of Trinity College, Dublin. The twenty-two-year-old Beckett had graduated with a first-class BA in French and Italian, the same subjects as Joyce, and had been selected by Trinity, as part of a standing exchange agreement with the École Normale Supérieure in Paris, to spend two years as MacGreevy's successor in the position of *lecteur d'anglais* at that institution. Beckett was understandably fascinated by the famous (or notorious) author of *Ulysses* and immediately became an enthusiastic member of the circle of admirers surrounding the master, who was by now deeply engrossed in the writing of what would eventually become *Finnegans Wake*. Beckett's first publication was devoted to that project: his "Dante ... Bruno . Vico .. Joyce" appeared in *transition* in June 1929 already.

Joyce's invitation to undertake a French translation of *ALP* was conveyed to Beckett by Philippe Soupault, acting as an intermediary. Soupault, then in his early thirties, was already a force to be reckoned with in French literary circles as one of the founders, together with André Breton, of the much publicized Surrealist movement. Their jointly composed experimental volume of automatic writing *Les champs magnétiques* had caused a considerable stir in 1920, and Soupault, whose later split with Breton in 1926 had likewise caused a considerable stir in Parisian literary circles, had gone on to publish four further volumes of poetry and half a dozen novels by 1929. Joyce and he had been acquainted, introduced by Ezra Pound, since shortly after Joyce's arrival in Paris

15 Willard Potts's mistaken assertion (1979, 85n) that Fargue assisted in the translation of *ALP* is evidently based on Joyce's letter to Harriet Weaver announcing the planned but eventually unrealized collaboration (*L* 1, 287).

in 1920 (Potts 1979, 106; Ellmann 1982, 491). Beckett had met Soupault on 2 February 1929 at Joyce's forty-seventh birthday party, and again at Adrienne Monnier's "Déjeuner Ulysse" on 27 June 1929, marking the publication of the French translation of *Ulysses* (Pilling 2006, 19).

The proposed translation was intended to appear in the recently founded avant-garde journal *Bifur*, with which both Joyce and Soupault were associated. Soupault's role in the matter was in fact a double one, acting on behalf of Joyce in soliciting the translation and on behalf of the journal in overseeing its progress (Knowlson 1996, 115). The first issue of *Bifur* had appeared just months before, in May 1929, founded and edited by Georges Ribemont-Dessaignes (1884–1974), a former Dadaist and, like Soupault, a former member of the Surrealist group. The young Italian writer Nino Frank (1904–1988), who would collaborate with Joyce a decade later on the Italian *ALP*, had been enlisted by Ribemont-Dessaignes as an assistant editor. Surprisingly, Joyce, who usually rejected all such invitations, had also been prevailed upon – Ellmann suggests by Frank (1982, 615) – to allow his name to appear on the title page of *Bifur* as one of its panel of international advisors (Ferrer and Aubert 1998, 179).[16]

According to Samuel Beckett's biographer Deirdre Bair, "Beckett was delighted by the opportunity, but still not sure of his command of French, and he asked Alfred Péron to assist him. He brought him to meet Joyce, and Péron passed Joyce's test and became Beckett's collaborator" (Bair 1978, 95). Péron had graduated in 1924 from the École Normale Supérieure – where he had studied Classics and English and shared a study with Jean-Paul Sartre (Ackerley and Gontarski 2006, 431) – and subsequently spent two years (1926–1928) as an exchange *lecteur* of French at Trinity College, Dublin, where Beckett, just two years younger than he, was one of his language students. The two young men quickly struck up a close and lasting friendship. Péron's two years at Trinity also had the significant advantage that they "had given an Irish cast to his English, which delighted Joyce" (Bair 1978, 95).

Beckett met with Soupault again on 2 February 1930, on the occasion of Joyce's forty-eighth birthday celebrations, when there was further

16 The title *Bifur* is said to have derived from the railway signal BIFUR (for *bifurcation*) which flagged up separating tracks and was thus felt to be indicative of the editorial team's belief in the importance of diversity (Holmes 2011). The 1930 Faber and Faber *ALP* and *Finnegans Wake* would later include a reference to the journal in the formula "Befor! Bifur!" (*FW* 215.18–19), replacing the "Before! Before!" of the 1928 *ALP*.

discussion concerning the proposed translation (Pilling 2006, 22–3). Beckett and Péron began work early in the spring of 1930 and continued to work with dogged (and sometimes grim) determination on the task during the summer, meeting several times a week, mostly in the evening, either in Beckett's room at the École Normale Supérieure (Cronin 1996, 109) or in a café in the Latin Quarter (Knowlson 1996, 115) to work on the dauntingly complex text (Bair 1978, 111).

The task began to seem insuperable as the work progressed. Beckett increasingly felt it was even impossible and considered telling Philippe Soupault that it simply could not be done (Cronin 1996, 119). Megan Quigley quotes a letter of 7 May 1930 to Soupault, in which Beckett, commenting on the translation so far, writes: "But I don't wish to publish this, not even a fragment, without the authorization of Mr. Joyce himself, who may well find this too badly done and too far off the original. The more I think about it, the more I find this unsatisfactory."[17] His initial enthusiasm for the project may well have been further diminished by Joyce's break with him in mid-June 1930 over what the latter, rightly or wrongly, saw as the younger man's objectionable treatment of his daughter Lucia (Pilling 2006, 25). In a further progress report of 5 July 1930, Beckett was nonetheless able to write to Soupault that two large single-spaced typed pages of the translation were ready (Aubert 1985, 417).[18]

Two days later, however, after Péron, in typical Parisian fashion, made arrangements to leave Paris for most of August, a disgruntled Beckett wrote to his friend MacGreevy on 7 July 1930 that he did not want to continue working on the translation alone, or to sign a contract with "that bastard Soupault." He continued to worry that Joyce might be disgusted "by the chasm of feeling and technique between his hieroglyphics and our bastard French" (Ackerley and Gontarski 2006, 13). Beckett wrote to MacGreevy again in early August that, with Péron now away, he found continuing with the translation quite impossible on his

17 Quigley's translation (2004, 486n33) of a letter held in the Beinecke Library at Yale. The original reads: "Mais je ne voudrais publier cela, pas même un fragment, sans l'au[t]orisation de Monsieur Joyce lui-même, qui pourrait très bien trouver cela vraiment trop mal fait et trop éloigné de l'original. Plus j'y pense plus je trouve tout cela bien pauvre" (Quigley 2004, 480).

18 "Un envoi de Samuel Beckett à Philippe Soupault en date du 5 juillet 1930 signale qu'un premier fragment de deux grandes pages dactylographiées sans interligne était prêt à cette date" (Aubert 1985, 417).

own. By mid-August a first draft was somehow nonetheless ready, and on 25 August 1930 Beckett, no doubt with great relief, was able to start work instead on the long postponed writing of a commissioned monograph on Proust (Pilling 2006, 26).

Beckett had to return to Dublin in mid-September for a 1 October 1930 start of term at Trinity, having successfully applied earlier in the year for a lectureship there in French (Pilling 2006, 25, 27). Deirdre Bair reports that when Beckett left, Péron was entrusted with the final polishing of the text, and since Beckett thought himself still persona non grata to Joyce "they agreed that Péron should present the manuscript to him. Joyce seemed satisfied with it and sent it to the printer" (1978, 112). The manuscript, rather extravagantly entitled "Anna Lyvia Pluratself," as prepared in late September 1930 (Pilling 2006, 26), translated the equivalent of the first six pages of *ALP* (*FW* 196.01–201.21), a total of 189 lines of that latter text.

By mid-October, Beckett and Péron's translation had reached the page-proof stage for *Bifur*, as attested by the printer's stamp of "16 oct 1930," and was already advertised in the journal as scheduled to appear in issue number 7 (10 December 1930). In early November, however, despite having initially encouraged Beckett and Péron to undertake the considerable task, Joyce, with very scant regard for the feelings of the two young translators after their months of assiduous labour, abruptly instructed them to withdraw their rendering.

Eugene Jolas reports that Ribemont-Dessaignes had been eager to publish Beckett and Péron's work in *Bifur*: "It had even been announced for appearance in a coming issue. I mentioned this fact to Joyce, who seemed disturbed. 'The translation is not yet perfect,' he said. 'It should be withdrawn.' To the great regret of our friend Ribemont-Dessaignes, this was done. In reality, this version was already quite remarkable, when one considers the almost insuperable difficulties involved" (Maria Jolas 1949, 172).

Several reasons have been suggested for what Beckett and Péron no doubt saw as a distressingly ruthless intervention on Joyce's part. First, the translation, in Joyce's opinion, presumably did still leave something to be desired – and it could very well be, as James Knowlson observes (1996, 728), that Beckett's own expressed lack of conviction, based perhaps largely on an excessive modesty, had been reported to Joyce and supported his decision. Second, Joyce very likely realized the desirability of a strategic move away from a small experimental journal whose continued survival was doubtful – and which did in fact cease publication after issue number 8, which appeared on 10 June 1931. Third, he very likely saw the commercial value of becoming involved himself and having his own name rather than those of two unknown young men associated with the translation (Quigley 2004, 479). Finally, and perhaps most important, a role was undoubtedly played by a significantly increased interest on his part in the possibilities of translation as related to the compositional process of *Finnegans Wake* itself. Daniel Ferrer and Jacques Aubert write that while Joyce had had a lifelong interest in translation, a new development in the twenties was that foreign languages, long a part of his private life, "invade, and become active in, his actual writing. How could he then fail to take part in such an experiment, just as, a few years later, he played a decisive part in the so-called Italian translation of the same *Anna Livia Plurabelle*? Was he not, after all, engaged in a 'Work in Progress' which was nothing less than generalized translation – translation raised to its ultimate power?" (1998, 180–1). Joyce, in short, decided to coordinate a team translation himself – and to extend it by including, in a partial return to the aborted earlier project involving Léon-Paul Fargue, those final paragraphs of *ALP* on which he had declared to Harriet Weaver that he was "prepared to stake everything" (*L* 3, 163).

Philippe Soupault, in an introduction to the resulting French translation that eventually appeared in the pages of the *Nouvelle Revue Française*, offers a detailed account of the complex process of its development. First of all, there was Beckett and Péron's "premier essai," their "first attempt," as Soupault rather slightingly called it.[19] A first revision followed, during which that version was reviewed by Paul Léon, Eugene Jolas, and Ivan Goll, under Joyce's own supervision (Soupault 1931, 633).[20] In a third stage, in Ellmann's words, paraphrasing Soupault, "it was decided that the French version must be revamped again, and at the end of November Philippe Soupault was enlisted to meet with Joyce and Léon every Thursday at 2:30 in Léon's flat on the rue Casimir Périer.[21] They sat for three hours at a round table ... and while

19 "Un premier essai a été tenté par Samuel Beckett, irlandais, lecteur à l'École Normale. Il a été aidé dans cette tâche par Alfred Perron [*sic*], agrégé de l'úniversité, qui avait séjourné pendant un an [*sic*] à Dublin" (Soupault 1931, 633).

20 "Une révision de cette première version fut exécutée sous la direction de l'auteur par Paul L. Léon, Eugène Jolas et Ivan Goll" (Soupault 1931, 633).

21 "A la fin de novembre 1930, nous nous réunîmes, M. Joyce, M. Paul L. Léon, et moi-même, rue Casimir-Périer, chez notre ami Léon" (Soupault 1931, 633).

Joyce smoked in an armchair Léon read the English text, Soupault read the French, and Joyce or one of the others would break into the antiphony to ask that a phrase be reconsidered. Joyce then explained the ambiguities he had intended, and he or one of his collaborators dug up an equivalent" (Ellmann 1982, 632).

In a statement that further infuriated Beckett, Soupault asserted that they "rejected, with Mr Joyce's approval, everything that seemed contrary to the rhythm, the meaning, or the transformation of the words and then tried to suggest a new translation."[22] In a fourth stage, the resulting draft, arrived at in early March 1931 after fifteen three-hour meetings, and which by that stage also included the rendering of the final pages, was sent to Eugene Jolas (who happened to be in Austria) and Adrienne Monnier, both of whom contributed further suggestions (Jolas in writing, Monnier in person), which were then considered at two further meetings, together with some additional translational points that Soupault and Joyce had already privately discussed.[23] "The completed version, published on May 1, 1931, in the *Nouvelle Revue Française*, is even more than the French translation of *Ulysses* a triumph over seemingly impossible obstacles" (Ellmann 1982, 633).

The team assembled by Joyce collectively boasted significant literary credentials. Philippe Soupault (1897–1990), French, and the star of the group, enjoyed a considerable literary reputation already, as mentioned, as a co-founder with Breton of the Surrealist movement. Eugene Jolas (1894–1952), an American, fluent in English, French, and German, was introduced to Joyce in December 1926, and the following year, with his wife Maria Jolas, he founded the influential Paris journal *transition*. Ivan Goll (1891–1950), likewise trilingual, was a German-born novelist, dramatist, and poet who wrote successfully in both French and German. Adrienne Monnier (1892–1955), a native Parisian, was a prominent and influential figure in avant-garde literary circles as the founder and owner of the bookshop and lending library *La Maison des Amis des Livres* and also as the recent founder of the literary journal *Le Navire d'Argent*. Paul Léon (1893–1942), fluent in English and French as

---

22 "Nous rejetions d'accord avec M. Joyce ce qui nous paraissait contraire au rythme, au sens, à la métamorphose des mots et nous essayions à notre tour de proposer une traduction" (Soupault 1931, 633; 1943, 74).

23 "Nous consecrâmes encore deux séances à discuter ces apports at à corriger différentes parties que nous avions revues M. Joyce et moi dans l'intervalle" (Soupault 1931, 634).

well as Russian, was a Russian émigré with a legal background and an advanced interest both in French literature and in Irish politics who had fled to Paris in 1918. Acquainted since 1928 with Joyce, he would prove to be his most devoted helper throughout the 1930s.[24] It has often been noted that none of the individuals involved in the collective French translation was a translator by profession. Beckett, meanwhile, confirmed to Jacques Aubert on 16 September 1983 that the final published version was arrived at by Joyce and his team without any further input from either Péron or himself.[25] For all his previously expressed lack of faith in the validity of his and Péron's rendering, and for all that their two names actually appeared first in the list of translators, Beckett was deeply disappointed with what in his view amounted to a rejection of their work on Joyce's part and "could not help but consider it a personal affront" (Bair 1978, 113).

Joyce's own enthusiasm for the team project was obvious. He reports to Harriet Weaver on 22 December 1930 that he has been "assisting at the seances of the French translation" (*L* 3, 209). On 10 January 1931 he sends Valery Larbaud "a few pages of the French A.L.P which may amuse you" (*L* 3, 212). He reports to Weaver again on 16 February 1931 that he has been "working a great deal" on the French translation with Léon and Soupault "and there is tremendous excitement about it, I believe," at the *Nouvelle Revue Française* (*L* 1, 300). Finally, on 4 March 1931, he informs her (possibly tongue in cheek, possibly not) that "the French translation of A.L.P. is now finished and I think it must be one of the masterpieces of translation" (*L* 1, 302).

A formal launch of the translation took place at a pre-publication *séance* in Adrienne Monnier's bookshop on 26 March 1931, with fifty persons or more in respectful attendance. Leon Edel has provided a lively account of the occasion, which he attended as a young man, fascinated by the overtones of a French *ALP* "rendered out of Joyce's liquid river-sounds into a strange, exotic Gallic equivalent" and declaimed in mantic fashion by Adrienne Monnier, clad in long flowing robes and chanting "in the accents of the Comédie Française, singsong, in her high musical voice" (1980, 473–4).

24 Arrested in Paris by the Gestapo in August 1941, Léon, who was Jewish, was murdered in April 1942 in a Silesian concentration camp.

25 The published version, Beckett wrote, "fut établie par un groupe d'écrivains sous la présidence de Joyce, en l'absence de Péron et de moi-même" (Aubert 1985, 417).

Beckett travelled from Dublin for the *séance*, during which he was much less than pleased to hear Soupault, in rehearsing the history of the translation, airily dismiss his and Péron's version as merely a rough first draft that required significant revision in terms of both sense and rhythm by the high-powered team assembled by Joyce. "Since Beckett considered what he and Péron had done as much more than a first draft, he keenly resented this but, in the company of Joyce and the other collaborators, felt obliged to hide his true feelings" (Knowlson 1996, 128). Beckett's smouldering resentment of Joyce's high-handed behaviour was woundingly compounded by Soupault's haughtily superior dismissal of their efforts, which Soupault later (1931, 1943) repeated in print. This casual dismissal contributes to the sense that relations between Beckett and Soupault had deteriorated sharply during the course of Beckett's work on the translation, recalling the reference to "that bastard Soupault" in Beckett's July 1930 letter to MacGreevy.

The list of translators – whom Joyce humorously dubbed "the Septante or Septuagint" in a letter of 23 April 1931 to Sylvia Beach (Banta and Silverman 1987, 167) – is given at the end of the translation as follows, "traduit de l'anglais par Samuel Beckett, Alfred Perron [*sic*], Ivan Goll, Eugène Jolas, Paul L. Léon, Adrienne Monnier et Philippe Soupault, en collaboration avec l'auteur" (Beckett et al. 1931, 646). While the two young men's names even occur as the first two names in the list, with the remaining five following in alphabetical order from Goll to Soupault, Péron's name, adding insult to injury, was misspelled as "Alfred Perron," as if ironically underlining the suggestion that his and Beckett's efforts were nothing more than a mere *perron*, a "flight of steps" leading to the real translation by the literary grown-ups.

While discounting Beckett's efforts, Soupault was careful to assert that Joyce's role in the experiment was crucial. "This text is not a translation," he wrote, "it is a reconstitution, in the sense that it is Joyce in French ... I have to say in all modesty that it was Joyce who was reconstituting, re-writing a portion of *Finnegans Wake* in French, and he alone is competent to do that. Of course I helped him, in finding the counterparts for names of rivers, for example: I helped Joyce, certainly, but in a sense Joyce re-did his text. If you compare the French text and the English text, you will see what an enormous difference there is between the two. It is a re-creation ... Joyce was extremely meticulous, sometimes spending an entire day on a single word" (1943; trans. Ferrer and

Aubert 1998, 181).[26] Soupault was evidently being diplomatically modest about his own contribution, for according to Eugene Jolas, "the most helpful collaborator was undoubtedly Soupault, who was inexhaustible in his invention of French equivalents for the Joycean neologisms" (Maria Jolas 1949, 172).

Soupault later wrote that the three-hour translation sessions were exhausting, "and Joyce was never satisfied with his successes. Yet, I have never met a man who was such a sure, such a faithful translator. He had to treat words like objects, stretch them out, cut them up, examine them under a microscope. He pursued his object obsessively and never yielded. It was not a matter of conscience or a mania, but the application of a pitiless method" (1979, 114–15).[27] Ellmann reports Soupault's later observation that "Joyce's great emphasis was upon the flow of the line, and he sometimes astonished them (as later, when he was helping Nino Frank with the Italian translation, he astonished him), by caring more for sound and rhythm than sense. But one or the other would insist upon rigor of this kind, too" (1982, 632–3). The rhythm of the language, Soupault wrote, "is like that of a river, sometimes rapid, sometimes sleepy, sometimes even swampy, then sluggish near its mouth."[28] W.V. Costanzo concurs: the French *ALP*, no less than the English *ALP*, he writes, is "lyric in its rhythms," and moreover, "whenever possible, the alliterative intensity is increased," while the "soft, wave-like flow" of the concluding lines in particular is obvious to any reader (1971, 234).

Beckett, however, did not share Joyce's opinion that the translation was a masterpiece. After its appearance in the *Nouvelle Revue Française*, Joyce sent Beckett, by then returned to Dublin again, an autographed

26 The original is quoted by Aubert (1967, 218–19): "Ce texte n'est pas une traduction, c'est une reconstitution, en ce sens que c'est du Joyce en français ... Je dois dire modestement que c'est Joyce qui reconstituait, qui ré-écrivait une partie de *FW* en français, et lui seul peut le faire. Evidemment je l'aidais, par example pour trouver des équivalences pour les noms de fleuves: j'ai aidé Joyce, c'est certain, mais en un sens Joyce a refait son texte. Si vous comparez le text français et le texte anglais, vous verrez quelle énorme différence il y a entre les deux. C'est une recréation ... Joyce était extrêmement scrupuleux, restant quelquefois une journée sur un mot."

27 Soupault's "James Joyce" (Potts 1979, 108–18) is a translation from his *Profils perdus* (1963, 49–70), an earlier version of which appeared in his *Souvenirs de James Joyce* (1943).

28 The rhythm, Soupault writes, "est comparable au cours d'une rivière tantôt rapide, tantôt dormante, tantôt même marécageuse, puis molle près de son embouchure" (1931, 635).

copy. "Characteristically," Beckett's biographer Anthony Cronin writes, "all that this mark of favour did for him was to fill him with doubts about the quality of the translation of *ALP*, for which he had been partially responsible," and he dashed off a note to Joyce to say "that it was impossible to read the text without thinking of the futility of the translation process" (1996, 154–5). As Ellmann writes, however, perhaps the most important thing about Beckett and Péron's contribution was that "although it was much changed in the course of revision by others, it demonstrated that a translation was feasible" (1982, 803).

Definitively sidelined by Joyce's "official" team translation, Beckett and Péron's version disappeared from general view for more than half a century, until it was printed for the first time in 1985 by Jacques Aubert under the title "Anna Lyvia Pluratself" (Aubert 1985, 417–22), making it available for comparison with the *Nouvelle Revue Française* version. And thereby hangs a tale; indeed more than one tale. Aubert reports in an introductory note that, according to information received from Alfred Péron's son Michel Péron, one set of the *Bifur* page proofs, corrected in pencil by Péron and in ink by Beckett, are deposited in "une université americaine" in a collection of Péron's personal papers (1985, 418). Aubert observes, however (1985, 418), that he was unable to consult the corrected proofs and consequently printed the text from an uncorrected set instead, provided by Maurice Saillet.[29] Working years later with access to the Péron papers, held in the Beinecke Library of Yale University, Megan Quigley made the dramatic assertion that those papers included a heavily revised version of Beckett and Péron's rendering that was in fact almost identical – with "fewer than a dozen small changes" (2004, 477) – with the version of the same pages eventually arrived at by Joyce and his team after more than fifty hours of detailed work.

The corrected "Anna Lyvia Pluratself" page proofs have now been made available online by the Beinecke Library and may be studied in close detail at various degrees of online magnification.[30] There

29 Maurice Saillet (1914–1990) was employed in Adrienne Monnier's bookshop from 1938, so the copy of the uncorrected proofs may very well have originally been hers. Aubert, without mentioning any involvement on Soupault's part, asserts (1985, 417) that it was Paul Nizan, recently appointed editor of *Bifur* and a personal friend of Péron's, who had invited Beckett and Péron to submit a translation of *ALP*. This information also appears to have been provided by Saillet.

30 James Joyce Collection, Beinecke Rare Book and Manuscript Library, Yale University, GEN MSS 112, Box 5, Folder 103. http://hdl.handle.net/10079/fa/beinecke.joyce.

are twenty-six corrections in ink, thus apparently by Beckett, made very clearly and carefully, as one would expect of an author correcting proofs. They are in general minor in nature, affecting only single misprinted letters, a dash corrected to a hyphen, a missing paragraph indent indicated, and the like. Only two significant changes are made in ink: the title "Anna Lyvia Pluratself" is changed back with meticulous care, letter by letter, to "Anna Livia Plurabelle," and the similarly exotic name "Husparey" is changed back to Joyce's original "Humphrey." The markings in pencil are similarly careful in a further five or six cases that are also of a relatively minor nature – and consist otherwise of a large number of carelessly scribbled marginal and interlinear notations, with underlinings and circlings of individual words and phrases. While the corrections in ink are clearly intended for a copy editor, those in pencil, other than the five or six exceptions noted, in fact give no such impression.

Megan Quigley, in a spirited attempt to show that Beckett and Péron's version was in fact incorporated into Joyce's final version to a very much greater degree than ever appropriately acknowledged, writes that the Péron papers in fact contain four versions of the Beckett-Péron translation: their initial typed version, evidently the one prepared for final submission in late September 1930; the *Bifur* proof pages, corrected "in pen by Beckett and in pencil by Péron"; and, very unexpectedly, two further typescripts labeled "Typescript of the second French translation by Beckett and Péron." The second of these two typescripts, Quigley asserts, "labeled 'Anne Livie Plurabelle,' includes a few pencil changes made in Joyce's hand, most of which (like the revised title) failed to be incorporated into the final published version of the text" – a fact that she understandably considers a seriously puzzling "conundrum" (2004, 474).

Accepting the evidence of the file that the two typescripts in question were the work of Péron, Quigley argues that "the most likely chronology of the translation is as follows: Beckett's first text was used for the *Bifur* page proofs, which were heavily revised by both Beckett and Péron. Péron incorporated these changes into his two typescripts that were at some later date shared with Joyce himself" (2004, 474). The implication here is that Joyce, having seen Beckett and Péron's September typescript, expressed some reservations, whereupon Péron in great haste (and in Beckett's absence in Dublin) revised the entire translation, resulting in a version almost identical with the final *Nouvelle Revue Française* version. The further implication is that Joyce still refused to allow even this heavily revised version to go to press. Instead, and again quite ruthlessly, not to mention quite unethically, he simply used Péron's typescript, rather than the "Anna Lyvia Pluratself" proofs, as a basis on which to begin his team's collaborative translation – though with most of the work having allegedly been already completed by Péron (Quigley 2004, 477). Given this scenario, one must further assume that Joyce, adding insult to injury, finally returned the typescript to Péron.

Quigley admits that "other scenarios are possible" (2004, 486n24) – and clearly they are. First of all, and most significantly, it is entirely unclear on whose authority the two typescripts in question were labeled as containing "the second French translation by Beckett and Péron"; nor is it clear that those typescripts were in fact typed by Péron (Quigley 2004, 485n15); nor is it at all clear that the more careless jottings on the proofs predated the two typescripts. Since we know from Soupault (1931, 634) that Joyce's team circulated typescripts among themselves, the two typescripts in question are in fact much more likely to have been among those produced by that team – and Joyce, unable as always to resist making further revisions to his own text, could certainly have jotted down a few last-minute alternatives on his own copy before, by accident or design, it reached Péron, thus explaining the "few pencil changes made in Joyce's hand" mentioned by Quigley (2004, 474). Péron, in other words, having initially made his few careful penciled corrections on the proofs (which he evidently retained after Beckett's departure), could at some quite indeterminate later date have acquired and read the two typescripts and, no doubt intrigued after his own months of work on the same text, have simply scribbled them down on the original corrected proofs purely for his own comparative interest.

The case Quigley makes – in a laudable effort to see justice done to Beckett and Péron's contribution, but almost certainly based on an original mistaken attribution of the typescripts – clearly rests on very shaky foundations. For after all, it is extremely unlikely that Joyce and his high-powered team, after meeting for more than fifty hours over a period of at least four months, could have succeeded only in translating the final forty-nine lines of *ALP*, while contenting themselves with making "fewer than a dozen" minor changes to the 189 lines of Beckett and Péron's version. Finally, of course, there is the letter of 16 September 1983 from Beckett to Aubert, already mentioned, in which Beckett unambiguously (though with considerable exaggeration) states that "practically nothing" of the rendering Péron and he submitted survived in the final published version.[31] It is surely also unlikely in the extreme that Péron would not have informed his friend and collaborator Beckett if he had indeed managed to arrive at a rendering almost identical with the version Joyce finally published.

The *Bifur* page proofs also play a role in another question, namely whether Beckett or Péron should be considered the primary translator of "Anna Lyvia Pluratself." Soupault wrote in his introduction to the *Nouvelle Revue Française* translation that "a first attempt" had been made by Samuel Beckett, "assisted by Alfred Perron [*sic*]" (1931, 633), and the published list of seven translators likewise gives Beckett in first and Péron in second place – though this could admittedly be merely alphabetical, since the remaining five translators involved do follow in alphabetical order, from Goll to Soupault. Ellmann clearly regards Beckett as the primary translator (1982, 632), as does Beckett's biographer James Knowlson (1996, 128). Aubert, on the other hand, identifies the translation as "traduit de l'anglais par M. [*sic*] Péron et S. Beckett" (1985, 421), but without giving any reason for listing Péron first or for using the wrong initial. A reason is suggested by the *Bifur* proofs, in which the attribution, at the end of the translation, actually reads "traduit de l'anglais par M. [*sic*] Perron [*sic*] et S. Beckett," with the two mistakes in Péron's name duly corrected in ink by Beckett. Given these two mistakes, the attribution was evidently added, most likely in haste, by some anonymous and less than reliable agent in preparing the proofs – and is thus clearly lacking in any authority, including as to the correct order of the two translators.[32] Beckett, for his part, possibly out of modesty once again, misplaced or otherwise, did not change the order in the corrected proofs.

Péron was later, in June 1939, to give the first radio talk on *Finnegans Wake*. By then a teacher of English at the Lycée Buffon in Paris, a noted centre of the French Resistance, he joined the Resistance movement in 1940 and recruited Beckett to it in September 1941, immediately after Paul Léon's arrest. Their cell was infiltrated and betrayed, Péron was arrested by the Gestapo in August 1942, and in February 1943 he was deported to the notorious Mauthausen concentration camp in Austria.

31 "De l'échantillon soumis par nous il ne reste pratiquement rien" (qtd. Aubert 1985, 417).

32 Rosa Maria Bosinelli's reprint of "Anna Lyvia Pluratself" as a "traduzione dall'inglese de A. Péron e S. Beckett" (1996, 153) follows Aubert without discussion in what is thus most likely a reversal of the correct order of names, as do Ferrer and Aubert (1998, 181).

Fatally weakened by his treatment there, he died in Switzerland on 1 May 1945, two days after his liberation from the camp by the Swiss Red Cross. Beckett had been warned in time by Péron's wife Mania about the betrayal of the cell and managed to escape arrest.[33]

3 Basic *ALP*

Within little more than a month of the appearance in May 1931 of Joyce's French *ALP*, we find him collaborating during the summer with C.K. Ogden on a Basic English rendering of the closing pages of *ALP*. Charles Kay Ogden (1889–1957), Cambridge-educated, was an English linguist, philosopher, and eccentric with a keen interest in literature and psychology. His translation from the German of Wittgenstein's *Tractatus Logico-Philosophicus* was published in 1922, and the following year he was co-author with I.A. Richards of *The Meaning of Meaning* (Richards and Ogden 1923). Ogden began working in the mid-1920s on the development of Basic English, a radically simplified subset of standard English with a vocabulary limited to 850 words, including only eighteen permissible verbs. The result was designed to be an international auxiliary language – ultimately in the idealistic but forlorn hope, following the catastrophe of the Great War, that international understanding might conceivably provide an eventual route towards world peace. His *Basic English: A General Introduction* was published in 1930.

One of Ogden's central concepts, to which he gave the name "orthology," involved the intersection and interaction of psychology, philosophy, and linguistics, and in 1927 he founded the Orthological Institute in Cambridge to promote Basic English and to train teachers of English who planned to employ the method for foreign learners. The Institute was equipped with sophisticated recording machines by the standard of the day, and part of Ogden's program was to organize recordings by contemporary writers as a further teaching tool. Joyce had made Ogden's acquaintance through Sylvia Beach and had agreed – after inviting Goyert and before inviting Beckett to undertake their respective translations – to record the closing pages of *ALP* (corresponding to *FW* 213.11–216.05) for Ogden's Institute. "The idea was Ogden's," Joyce later wrote (*L* 3, 203). The recording took place in Cambridge in August 1929. Joyce's sight was already so weak that the pages had been

33 Knowlson (1996, 314–15); Ackerley and Gontarski (2006, 431–2); Pilling (2006, 237).

prepared for him in half-inch letters, which he nonetheless had considerable difficulty in reading (Ellmann 1982, 617). Sales of the disc were disappointing (*L* 3, 203).

On the occasion of the recording Joyce reportedly indicated to Ogden that he would also be interested in seeing how the complex textual effects he had been aiming to achieve in *ALP* might transfer to the extremely strict confines of Basic English. During the Joyces' stay in London for matrimonial purposes from May to September 1931, Joyce collaborated with Ogden (to an indeterminable degree) on the experiment. The result appeared, with a very brief introductory note by Ogden, in *Psyche*, Ogden's own journal of experimental psychology, in October 1931 and was reprinted in Paris in Eugene Jolas's journal *transition* in March 1932.[34]

The purpose of the Basic English version, Ogden modestly wrote, was merely "to give the simple sense of the gramophone record made by Mr Joyce, who has himself taken part in the attempt; and the reader will see that it has generally been possible to keep almost the same rhythms." In some places, "the sense of the story has been changed a little, but this is because the writer took the view that it was more important to get these effects of rhythm than to give the nearest Basic word every time." Joyce also rejected the use of explanatory footnotes of any kind, and in this way "the simplest and most complex languages of man are placed side by side" (Ogden 1931, 95; 1932a, 259). The April 1932 issue of *Psyche* contained Ogden's further "Notes in Basic English on the *Anna Livia Plurabelle* Record" (1932b, 86–95), in the production of which Joyce himself also appears to have collaborated (McHugh 2006, 213n).

Basic English was never intended to be a literary language, and is thus, as Susan Shaw Sailer asserts, "a completely inadequate tool for translating *Finnegans Wake*" (1999, 866). Joyce's complex text necessarily suffers greatly in the highly reductive process of its transposition. Sailer identifies two major shortcomings in Ogden's procedure. First, "where multiple possibilities for signification arose, as they did continuously, Ogden decided what the passage's 'simple sense' was on the basis of the inflections that Joyce gave to his reading" – but, as Sailer points out, this was a very unreliable criterion to begin with, since Joyce, because of his by now extremely weak eyesight, had in fact "to be prompted in a

34 Ogden's *ALP* is also reprinted by Bosinelli (1996, 141–50).

whisper throughout" (Sailer 1999, 854). Second, and even more damaging, Ogden is "forced to combine silliness with distortion" (864) in his translation, because he sees the 'simple sense' of Joyce's language as merely one of transmitting semantic information, innocent of any literary or poetic connotations.

The two men's projects were in fact diametrically opposed: "Ogden tried to limit the vocabulary of the English language to 850 words, whereas Joyce kept pushing back all linguistic boundaries. But no matter how different their projects were, they both showed a keen interest in each other's extreme experiment" (Van Hulle 2004, 78). Van Hulle agrees with Sailer that Ogden's inevitably reductive and disabling aim was "to retrieve unambiguous, familiar meaning from Joyce's language," undoing in the process those aspects that do not strictly belong to its semantic communication, and thus constituting a rigorous – and a crippling – domestication of Joyce's text (81, 83). For Harry Levin, anticipating both Sailer and Van Hulle, Ogden's problem as a translator, as opposed to the challenges facing the French and German (and later the Italian) translations, "was not to imitate the suggestiveness of the original, but to reduce it to direct statement. Hence he is forced to ignore harmonies and conceits, and to rule out ambiguities, sometimes rather arbitrarily. There is not much left" (1960, 196). Despite that assessment of the translational results, however, Levin considers the juxtaposition of "Ogden's language of strict denotation and Joyce's language of extreme connotation" as being of considerable interest in that "both are reactions against our modern Babel" (1960, 197).[35]

Other than his central involvement in the French *ALP*, his involvement to at least some extent in the Basic English *ALP*, and his involvement in the German *ALP* to the extent at least of giving it his formal approval, Joyce was also personally involved in one further version, though in this case only to the extent of giving his permission to undertake the translation (*L* 3, 201). The result was a complete Czech *ALP*, the work of three translators, Maria Weatherall, Vladimír Procházka, and Adolf Hoffmeister, which appeared in Prague in 1932, the first complete version to be published in any language.[36]

35 See also Loukopoulou (2013); Quigley (2015, 138–46).

36 Hoffmeister reports that the three of them worked on the translation for "more than six months, and the book is barely over thirty pages long altogether" (1979, 136). The result, according to the Czech critic Josef Grmela, "represents one of the top creative performances in the whole history of Czech translation" (2004, 41).

Joyce's involvement in more minor translation projects continued unabated. In May 1932, in an exuberant *jeu d'esprit* in Wakean mode, he translated James Stephens's poem "Stephen's Green" into five different languages, including French, German, Latin, Norwegian, and Italian (Gorman 1941, 341–2; Ellmann 1982, 656). In more sober mood, after a visit to Zurich in 1934, he translated into English the Swiss writer Gottfried Keller's *Lebendig begraben*, a suite of fourteen German poems (Ellmann 1982, 669). Three years later, in 1937, he approached Nino Frank, rather to Frank's initial dismay, with the proposal that they should collaborate on an Italian *ALP*.

4 Italian *ALP*

Joyce first made the acquaintance of Nino Frank (1904–1988), who was introduced to him by Ivan Goll, in 1926. Born of Swiss parents in southern Italy, the twenty-two-year-old Frank had fled Mussolini's Italy for Paris earlier that year after developing politically dangerous antifascist views. Frank held a position as the Paris agent of the Italian journal *900: Cahiers d'Italie et d'Europe*, recently founded by Massimo Bontempelli and Curzio Malaparte. That journal published Auguste Morel's translation of "Calypso" in its first issue in autumn 1926, while Soupault, Ribemont-Dessaignes, and Ivan Goll would also all appear in its pages before its demise in June 1929. Frank, surprisingly, succeeded in persuading Joyce to add his name to its board of editors, just as, equally surprisingly, he repeated his success in 1929 in persuading Joyce to serve on a board of directors for *Bifur* (Frank 1979, 75–9, 87). After the demise of *Bifur* in 1931, Frank went on to become a well-known film critic. Joyce remained sporadically in touch with him throughout the 1930s (Ellmann 1982, 698).

In 1937, Joyce, presumably still pleased with the success of the French *ALP*, proposed to Frank, much to the latter's surprise, that they jointly undertake a matching Italian translation of *ALP*. Cheerfully ignoring Frank's protest that the task was impossible, since the Italian language did not lend itself to puns, least of all to Joycean puns, Joyce insisted, perhaps quizzically, "We must do the job now before it is too late; for the moment there is at least one person, myself, who can understand what I am writing. I don't however guarantee that in two or three years I'll still be able to" (Frank 1979, 96; Ellmann 1982, 700).[37]

37 Frank's "The Shadow That Had Lost Its Man" (1979) originally appeared in French in his *Memoire brisée* (1967), an expanded version of his "Souvenirs sur James Joyce" (1949) (Potts 1979, vi–vii).

Frank, no doubt impressed by the force of this argument, allowed himself, reluctantly, to be persuaded. As he reports, Joyce and he then met for fifty or so hours over some twenty-four meetings, "two afternoons a week for a good three months," completing "a dozen lines an afternoon, such was our harvest" (Frank 1979, 96). "I read and interpreted the text on my own, after which Joyce explained it to me word by word, revealing to me its various meanings, dragging me after him into the complex mythology of his Dublin. Then began the slow tennis of approximations, we tossed short phrases to each other like slow-motion balls through a rarefied atmosphere. In the end our procedure resembled incantation" (97). The resulting rendering, Rosa Maria Bosinelli writes, "seems to be based on the same 1928 'original' as the French translation, in that it rather consistently ignores additions and modifications that appeared in succeeding versions, including the 1939 final edition of *Finnegans Wake* " (Bosinelli 1998a, 175).[38]

The Italian *ALP* was completed early in 1938 (Bosinelli 1996, 54), and Frank reports that Joyce was once again delighted with the result. For his part, Frank was by now a complete convert: "Actually, it is perhaps richer harmonically, if I may say so, than the French. The Italian language is better suited than the others, even than English I sometimes think, to the at once colloquial and epic style that, along with a deliberate break from a certain Cartesianism, was sought by the writer" (Frank 1979, 97). A year later, and at Joyce's insistence, Frank gave a public reading of the Italian text on Joyce's fifty-seventh birthday, 2 February 1939 – the occasion on which Joyce, with an advance copy of *Finnegans Wake* already in hand, also publicly announced for the first time its long-withheld title. Frank reports (98) that Joyce was so pleased with the translation that he even insisted that Frank, somewhat to his embarrassment, since not everyone in the group understood Italian, should declaim it not just once, but twice.

The Italian *ALP* appeared in print in two parts, in two separate issues of the Roman journal *Prospettive*, edited by Curzio Malaparte (1898–1957) and Alberto Moravia (1907–1990). The first and longer part, entitled "Anna Livia Plurabella," corresponding to *FW* 196.01–201.21, appeared on 15 February 1940 – and it appeared with no mention at all of Nino Frank, but rather as a "traduzione italiana di James Joyce e

38 Eco suggests that the Italian version was in fact based on the 1939 text, but offers no evidence to support this view (2001, 131–2n21).

Ettore Settanni." And thereby hangs another translatorial tale, for the said Settanni played a decidedly shadowy role in the production of the Italian *ALP*.

Settanni, a native of Capri, probably came to Joyce's attention in 1933 with a short volume on modern novels and novelists, *Romanzo e romanzieri d'oggi*, which contained a brief chapter on Joyce's work, mainly *Ulysses*, celebrated as the work of an avant-garde writer. Having, like Frank, fled Mussolini's Italy for Paris, Settanni attracted favourable attention there in 1937 with a novel, written originally in Italian and published in French translation as *Les hommes gris*, with a preface by Valery Larbaud praising its sophisticated use of interior monologue. A collection of novellas, *Amour conjugale*, was to appear in 1939, while a number of popular travel books on Capri helped to pay the bills.[39] Settanni appears to have used his connections in Italy to help place the Italian *ALP* in Malaparte's journal – while taking the opportunity both to exclude any mention of Frank and to alter Joyce and Frank's translation, without any prior permission, by a number of textual emendations. The translation was preceded by an appreciative article on Joyce by Malaparte and an introductory note on *Finnegans Wake* by Settanni and followed by a short article on Joyce by Carlo Linati, who had translated substantial excerpts from *Ulysses* in the journal *Il Convegno* in 1926.

Both Frank's exclusion and Settanni's emendations seem to have been designed primarily to avert possible recriminations in Mussolini's Italy, including the risk of having the journal suppressed. Frank was still persona non grata with the authorities, while Settanni's emendations were clearly intended to defuse the potential charge of Joyce's more extreme sexual and political extravagances. *Prospettive* was already viewed with considerable suspicion by the fascist authorities (Risset 1973, 47). Its founder and editor Malaparte had been an early convert to fascism and one of the most powerful writers associated with the party, voicing his political views in *Prospettive*, of which he was a founder in 1937. His enthusiasm for fascism eventually waning, however, he was stripped of his party membership, and by 1940 he had already been arrested and jailed several times by Mussolini's regime. To this extent, as Bosinelli suggests (1998a, 175), Settanni's role as censor was, at least in principle, not an entirely unreasonable one.

39 Two of the latter have been republished as *Scrittore stranieri a Capri* (Naples: La Conchiglia, 1986, 62 pp.) and *Miti, uomini e donne di Capri* (Naples: La Conchiglia, 1989, 83 pp.).

In 1955, Settanni republished the *Prospettive* version of the Italian *ALP* together with a commentary by himself in which he very belatedly revealed Frank's role as translator, while claiming at the same time to have in fact also been involved himself, together with Nino Frank and Benjamin Crémieux, in the translation of the opening pages (1955, 27).[40] Frank's version of events, however, rejects this claim, vigorously asserting instead (with no mention of Crémieux) that Settanni arrived on the scene only after the translation had already been completed. Frank's own version of Settanni's alleged involvement is emphatic. "Having made the acquaintance of an Italian writer, Ettore Settanni, who did not lack talent, Joyce had given him our attempt at translation to read. Settanni was enraptured, but added immediately that it might be improved here and there. Joyce then summoned me to explain the affair and to introduce me to the young Italian ... Settanni promptly cited two or three changes, which we easily showed him to be unsuitable because they failed to capture the meaning of the original ... Let me say in his defense that he was no more familiar with the English original than with the English language as a whole" (Frank 1979, 101). As for Settanni's published emendations, Frank reports that "a dozen slight modifications, most of them absurd, had been made in our text," modifications which, he says, neither Joyce nor he liked (102).

Frank also reports Settanni's assertion that "as a result of his militant antifascism he had taken refuge in Paris, where he was nearly dying of hunger because his part time job in an Italian bookstore earned him a pittance" (1979, 101). Frank, "although he struck me as a dubious character," helpfully found him someone to translate one of his travel books on Capri – but the unfortunate translator, Frank asserts, received not a penny for her work, for "Settanni made off with the money, having decided in spite of his supposed antifascism that the momentous events under way since Munich required his presence in Italy" (101–2). Frank also darkly surmises that the omission of his own name may very well

---

40 Bosinelli observes that this is the only extant reference to any possible involvement on Crémieux's part (1996, 57). Crémieux (1888–1944), a French novelist, scholar of Italian literature, and translator of Pirandello into French, figured among Joyce's Paris acquaintances and published one short article on his work (1929). Joyce had enlisted his assistance in 1924 in his successful bid to bring Italo Svevo's novel *La coscienza di Zeno* (1923) to world notice (*L* 1, 211; Ellmann 1982, 560). Like Péron and Beckett, Crémieux became actively involved in the French Resistance. Arrested in 1943, he was murdered in Buchenwald concentration camp in 1944.

have had something to do also with the personal enmity of Malaparte, "another well-known 'anti-Fascist,'" who, according to Frank's version of events, "hated" him and was in fact largely to blame for his own hurried departure from Italy (102) – the implication presumably being that Malaparte, at that time still a convinced fascist, had denounced Frank's antifascist sympathies to the political authorities.

While Frank was thus understandably furious with Settanni's actions, whatever their motivation might have been, Joyce, obviously delighted by the appearance of *ALP* in Italian (Frank 1979, 102), remained very uncharacteristically tolerant of Settanni's meddling with his text – and serenely undisturbed by the lack of recognition of Frank. He writes very blandly to Frank on 13 March 1940: "Settanni writes me from Capri that he thought it as well to soften certain passages. Please obtain a copy of the review and note the variants in the margin. In that way I will have our original text. Settanni writes me that your name does not appear for reasons you will understand at once. But it will not always be kept hidden, I trust" (*L* 3, 469; Ellmann's translation). A postcard to Victor Sax in the same month refers to "an Italian version I made with 'E. Settanni' of the river piece" (*L* 3, 471). He writes to Settanni himself in very cordial terms on 26 March 1940, conveying his gratitude to Malaparte for the courtesy of his pages and thanking Settanni – "grazie sopratutto a lei" (*L* 3, 473), "thanks above all to you" – for his part in the publication of the Italian *ALP*: "I have had much pleasure in learning that my little lady from Dublin ["la mia piccola donnicciuola, quella di Dublino"] has completed her pilgrimage and has so tactfully made her modest curtsy before her august uncle Tiber" (*L* 3, 473–4; Ellmann's translation).[41] Settanni promptly arranged to have the letter, written in Italian, appear in the April 1940 issue of *Prospettive*.[42]

The second instalment of the Italian *ALP*, the final paragraphs, corresponding to *FW* 215.11–216.05, appeared in *Prospettive* on 15 December 1940 under the title "I fiumi scorrono" (literally, "the rivers run").[43] This time the translation was attributed to "James Joyce, Nino Frank e Ettore

41 The "curtsy" of Ellmann's translation suggests a pun, conscious or otherwise, on editor Malaparte's (assumed) given name, Curzio. Of German origin on his father's side, his real name was Kurt Erich Suckert, *Malaparte* being conceived as a pun on *Buonaparte*.

42 "Una lettera di Joyce," *Prospettive* 4.4 (15 April 1940), 11.

43 "I fiumi scorrono di James Joyce (Da 'Anna Livia Plurabella')." *Prospettive* 4.11–12 (15 December 1940), 14–16.

Settanni," suggesting that Frank may have meanwhile had the opportunity to convey his thoughts on the matter to Settanni in suitably blunt terms. The journal, which continued to appear until 1943, does not seem to have suffered any negative political consequences. Joyce himself was never to see this second part in print, since the December issue did not in fact appear until a few weeks after his death in January 1941 (Bosinelli 1998b, 197). Just nine days before he died, in a postcard of 4 January 1941, Joyce mentions Settanni to Stanislaus as one of several persons who might be able to help him in those difficult days, describing Settanni as having "made with me (or rather revised) the translation of a passage from *Anna Livia*" (*L* 3, 507; Ellmann's translation). For almost forty years, from 1940 until 1979, the only published version of the Italian *ALP* was the version as emended by Settanni. Jacqueline Risset, in an article in *Tel Quel* in 1973, republished that version, whereupon Nino Frank, to set the record straight, sent her the original, unamended version (Risset 1984, 5), which Risset subsequently published in 1979 in a volume of Joyce's writings in Italian, *Scritti italiani* (*SI* 197–214).

The Italian *ALP* has attracted considerably more critical attention than its French counterpart. Ellmann, surprisingly, implies that the Italian *ALP* is essentially Frank's rather than Joyce's work, referring to Joyce's role merely as "helping Nino Frank with the Italian translation" (1982, 633). This is presumably based on Frank's report that Joyce "asked me to try to transpose into Italian, with his help," the same excerpts translated in the French *ALP*. Frank goes on, however, to recount Joyce's obvious subsequent delight in playing with the Italian language as he had already done with English: "thus I can say without any false modesty that Joyce is responsible for at least three-quarters of the Italian text; for the most part I served as guinea pig and fellow worker" (1979, 96). Joyce, for his part, seems to have been in no doubt at all as to the importance of his own contribution, repeatedly referring with obvious pleasure in correspondence during March and April 1940 to the translation as *his* own achievement. Thus while in a letter to Nino Frank he collegially refers to "our translation" ("la traduzione nostra"; *L* 3, 468); a letter to Frank Budgen refers to "my Italian version " (*L* 3, 469), as do other missives to Jacques Mercanton ("ma version italienne"; *L* 3, 470), to James Johnson Sweeney ("the ... Italian version I made"; *L* 1, 410), and to Mary Colum ("the Italian translation I made of Anna Livia"; *L* 1, 412).

As for the original progress of that translation, and Joyce's specific role in it, Frank reports having quickly been struck by the fact "that the rhythm, the harmony, the density and consonance of the words were more important to him than the meaning, and that, for example, having written one thing [in English], Joyce scarcely hesitated to put down something completely different in Italian, as long as the poetic or metrical result was equivalent" (1979, 97). Ellmann records Frank's comments in a later interview that "Joyce's whole emphasis was again on sonority, rhythm, and verbal play; to the sense he seemed indifferent and unfaithful, and Frank had often to recall him to it" (Ellmann 1982, 700). Any suggestion that Joyce was less interested in "sense" is of course debatable. As John Bishop puts it, "reading 'Anna Livia' suggests quite the opposite of what is generally assumed from accounts like [Frank's]. Because the chapter is about a kind of sense and [meaning] that fills the ear in the absence of literal sense and meaning, Joyce knew quite well what he was doing" (1986, 457). As for rhythm, when Frank on one occasion objected that Joyce's proposed version sacrificed the original rhythm, Joyce reportedly replied nonchalantly that he liked the new arrangement better (Ellmann 1982, 700).

Jacqueline Risset asserts that the Italian *ALP* "cannot really be called – in the usual sense of the word – a translation at all; for what takes place is a complete rewriting, a later elaboration of the original, which consequently does not stand opposite the new version as 'original text,' but as 'work in progress'" (1984, 3) – and, she adds, "a more daring variation on it" (1984, 6). Serenella Zanotti similarly writes that the Italian translation was done when Joyce "was out of the writing process and thus tended to recreate rather than to reproduce the original text" (2001, 422). A primary focus of interest for students of Joyce in translation, indeed, has been that Joyce, especially in the Italian version, emerges as being much less interested in producing a translation aiming at fidelity to the original than in providing a parallel original text. Bosinelli argues that Joyce functions essentially as author of the Italian *ALP* while he is rather a collaborator and supervisor of the French version (1996, 46). The Italian *ALP*, she argues, should more properly be regarded as an autonomous parallel text, a recreation or rewriting rather than a translation in any traditional sense.[44]

The specifically Italian nature of the translation has been emphasized by several Italian critics. "Joyce recast his text for readers of Italian

44 Settanni similarly defined the Italian *ALP* as a "ricreazione più o meno approssimativa, in una lingua eufonicamente parlando italiano" (1955, 27), "an approximate recreation in a language that sounds pleasingly like Italian."

culture (multilingual elements are drastically reduced) and additionally abandoned most of the fluvial allusions which abounded in the original because he was more interested in exploring the musicality and the creative potential of the Italian language" (Zanotti 2001, 422).[45] "The ideal reader of this text is undoubtedly an Italian reader," writes Bosinelli. "Joyce privileged a pragmatic attitude to translation as a cross-cultural transferral of the reverberations of meanings inscribed in the original composition. He wanted to trigger associative chains for Italian readers according to a principle of equivalence, not of 'faithfulness'; in other words, the Italianized text aims to provide a similarity of reading experience even at the expense of semantic equivalence" (Bosinelli 1998b, 195). Joyce's Italian version, in short, is not so much a translation in any traditional sense as "the last page of great prose that Joyce left us shortly before dying" (197).

Umberto Eco calls Joyce's Italian version "a most particular case of rewriting, taken to extremes" (2001, 107). He describes *Finnegans Wake* as "a plurilingual text written as an English-speaker conceived of one. It seems to me therefore that Joyce's decision to translate himself was based on the idea of thinking of the target text (French or Italian) as a plurilingual text the way a French- or Italian-speaker might have conceived of one" (108). In the Italian version, Joyce "found himself having to render a language that lends itself to pun, to neologisms, and agglutination, as well as English does (which has the advantage of an abundance of monosyllabic terms) into a language like Italian, which resists the formation of agglutinative neologisms" (108–9). Noting Joyce's rejection in Italian of many of the originally included river names, Eco observes: "No longer playing with the idea of rivers (perhaps the oddest and most punctilious idea in this punctilious and extravagant book), he was playing with Italian instead" (115).

The Italian *ALP*, Jacqueline Risset writes, is "an exploration of the furthest limits of the Italian language," a sustained play on "the essentially plural quality" of Italian, in which the multiple intersecting layers of the language are "understood not as fixed stratifications, but

45 Settanni reports Joyce's comment on the musicality of the Italian *ALP*, "io sono partito da questa tecnica della deformazione per raggiungere un'armonia che vince la nostra intelligenza, come la musica" (1955, 29–30). "I took this technique of deformation as my point of departure in trying to achieve a harmony that vanquishes our intelligence as music does" (trans. Reynolds 1981, 203–4).

as moving planes" (Risset 1984, 3, 4). In Joyce's Italian, "viewed as an aggregate of strata, of reservoirs, polyglottism is transformed into 'plurilinguism,' ... dialects, tones, lexical levels merging together in a contradictory co-presence," a technique that Joyce himself suggested, as reported by Settanni (1955, 29–30), that he had learned from Dante.[46]

This play with the rich plurality and multiple levels of the Italian language itself, written and spoken, from its highest literary expression in the work of Dante to its multiple and competing local and regional dialects and colloquial usages, involves especially Triestine, Venetian, and Tuscan idioms and turns of phrase (Risset 1973, 48, 52). Corinna del Greco Lobner is particularly struck by the number of Tuscan idioms and sayings (1989, 38). Serenella Zanotti claims that the language Joyce wanted his washerwomen to speak is closer to Triestine than it is to any other dialect (2001, 423), and she aptly observes that his continued predilection for the Triestine form of Italian is similar to his predilection for the Dublin form of English (2002, 303–4). Lobner adds Friulian and Roman dialects to the list, while observing that idiomatic and humorous turns of phrase, popular sayings and word plays, proverbs, and tongue-twisters are all welcome grist to Joyce's linguistic mill (1986, 84). The cumulative result, as Risset writes, is nonetheless "a *poetic language* with three levels: rhythm, syntactic structure, phonic texture" (1984, 7; emphasis in original).

From the very first words of his Italian rendering, in which the opening "O" of the English original, so carefully and significantly positioned, is simply ignored, it is clear that fidelity to the letter of the original text is far less important for Italian Joyce than the *authorial* rather than *translatorial* impulse, not so much to make the original text helpfully available in another language as to *continue* the original text by other means, in other words, in another language (Risset 1984, 6). For Bosinelli, there are even points where "one might formulate the hypothesis that it was the Italian version that influenced the 'original' [*Finnegans Wake*] rather than the other way round" (1998a, 175). Louis Gillet, writing in 1941, goes even further, so impressed by the Italian *ALP*, "an outstanding *tour de force*," which Joyce had shown him shortly before his death, that he

46 Mary Reynolds demonstrates convincingly that Joyce "saw himself as Dante's disciple particularly in the area of linguistic innovation" (1981, 202) – and Beckett pointed out as early as 1929 the similarities between Dante's and Joyce's use of language (1972, 18). On Dante in *ALP*, see Reynolds (1981, 203–5) and Risset (1984, 9).

even prefers it to the original and "cannot too strongly advise beginners to read *Finnegans Wake* in the Italian text" (1941, 156; 1979, 193).

5 Text and Macrotext

There is a sense in which every translation, whatever its quality, may be said to extend rather than merely attempt to replicate its original text, with that original and its various translations constituting in combination a multilingual macrotext (O'Neill 2005, 5–12). Nowhere is this contention more obviously apt than in the case of Joyce's trilingual *ALP*, its triple iterations at once three separate and authorially validated individual texts and in combination one single Annalivian macrotext. That macrotext is further enhanced, and the original further extended, by Beckett's French, Settanni's Italian emendations, Ogden's Basic English, and each of the numerous later renderings in a whole range of languages.[47]

Translation is always and inevitably a process of what *Ulysses* calls "almosting it" (*U* 3.366–67). Translators of *Finnegans Wake* in particular, like any other reader of the *Wake*, may frequently have very little idea of what is "really" going on – but the text, whatever it means, is *there* and demands translation. In Joyce's case, since he functions both as translator and as original author, one may assume that he has a reasonably good idea of what is going on – though even he, as he suggests himself, may begin to become a little vague as to finer details over the years. His comment to Nino Frank, already mentioned, that the Italian translation of *ALP* needed to be undertaken sooner rather than later suggests as much (Frank 1979, 96).

That comment may of course have been intended jocularly – but not necessarily entirely jocularly. And even if the translator Joyce did understand very well what the author Joyce had intended to be translated, he quite frequently (as we shall see) decided to substitute instead something subtly or distinctly or even flamboyantly different. The resulting relationship between Joycean original and Joycean translation, and between his French translation and his Italian translation, juggling elision and substitution, is oddly similar to that linking the terms of a pun, as succinctly defined by Umberto Eco in *The Aesthetics of Chaosmos*. "The

47 For a chronological listing of these later renderings, see the Appendix; for comparative discussion of some of them, see O'Neill (2005, 194–219; 2013, 153–77).

pun," Eco writes, "is a continuity produced by reciprocal elisions so that one word can stand for another word, even if no word appears in its entirety" (1989, 65). The range and relationship of Joyce's translatorial responses – and their contribution to an Annalivian macrotext – are the central concern of *Trilingual Joyce*.

Hugh Kenner observes that *Finnegans Wake* "leaves us forever uncertain what possibilities we can safely discard" (1992, 150). "There are no nonsense syllables in Joyce," Campbell and Robinson write (1961, 360), and, as Michael Begnal observes, "nothing, no matter how small, is without its underlying function and significance" (1975, 120). By the time he got to *Finnegans Wake*, Kenner continues, "Joyce's unit of attention had narrowed down to the single letter" (1992, 151). At the same time, he warns, as others had warned before him, that over-interpretation is a constant danger. The danger, clearly, is all the greater when one is dealing with three different versions of what simultaneously is and is not the same text. Grand narratives and overarching interpretive schemes are therefore unapologetically avoided in what follows, in favour of what Finn Fordham calls "burrowing down into the work at ground or underground level" (2007, 21), and what Fritz Senn has humorously dubbed "pedestrian semantic rummaging" (1995, 226). The result is a series of comparative microanalyses of roughly fifty selected short excerpts, organized into chapters merely for ease of presentation and reading, and examining altogether slightly more than half of Joyce's French and Italian renderings of the English *ALP*, along with the corresponding portions of Beckett and Péron's French, Settanni's Italian, and Ogden's Basic English variations.[48]

48 The complete English *ALP* is 870 lines long in the pagination of the 1997 Faber reprint of the 1930 text. Beckett and Péron translated 193 lines of the 870 (22 per cent); Joyce's team translated a further 37 lines, thus altogether 230 of the 870 (26 per cent). *Trilingual Joyce* works with 124 of the 230 lines (54 per cent) of Joyce's French and Italian renderings (as well as with Settanni's emendations of the latter); with 91 of the 193 lines (47 per cent) of Beckett's French rendering; and with just 33 of the 130 lines (25 per cent) of Ogden's Basic English rendering of the closing pages.

1 All about Anna

O / tell me all about / Anna Livia! I want to hear all about Anna Livia. Well, you know Anna Livia? Yes, of course, we all know Anna Livia. Tell me all. Tell me now. You'll die when you hear. (*ALP* 3; *FW* 196.01–6)[1]

[1] O / tell me all about / Anna Livia! I want to hear all about Anna Livia. (*ALP* 3; cf. *FW* 196.01–4: "I want to hear all / about Anna Livia")

Edna O'Brien considers that Anna Livia "is the most accessible and indeed beloved character ever conceived by Joyce" (2000, 143). But ALP, the Anna Livia Plurabelle of Joyce's title, is by no means just a woman. She is also "the female principle of flux and continuity" (Hart 1962, 202) – and, most important of all, she is a river, specifically Dublin's River Liffey but more generally any river, anywhere, anytime. Joyce, as Margot Norris puts it, "as surely rivermorphized the woman as he anthropomorphized the river" (1982, 197). ALP's male counterpart, who in *Finnegans Wake* is assigned the name Humphrey Chimpden Earwicker, is simultaneously her erring husband (and certainly one by all accounts no better than he should be), a corresponding male principle, a mountain peak or rocky headland, and both the builder of a city and the city itself, specifically the city of Dublin, and more generally any city, anywhere, anytime. *ALP*, as the title suggests, is

1 Page numbers preceded by *ALP* in parenthetical references are to the more easily accessible 1997 Faber reprint of the 1930 Faber edition of *Anna Livia Plurabelle*.

centrally about ALP; and in *ALP*, as opposed to *Finnegans Wake*, Earwicker's role is largely but by no means entirely limited to that of erring husband. ALP, as the title suggests, is central and omnipresent; her husband will from time to time be evoked through some combination of his initials (HCE, CHE, ECH, HEC), which will occasionally even be identifiable in the initial letters of words in phrases such as "*h*er *e*rring *c*hief."

The opening "O" of *ALP* suggests for readers of *Finnegans Wake* the circular structure of that extraordinary 628-page text as a whole, which, famously, ends with the first half of a sentence and begins with the second half of the same sentence. No such insight was yet available to readers of the 1928 *ALP*, though many will no doubt have noticed that that "O" is also readable not only as French *eau* ("water") and as Greek omega, but also as a symbol of female sexuality and fertility. Francisco García Tortosa notes that the letter "O" is a widespread symbol of birth and new life (1992, 98), and Patrick McCarthy observes in similar vein that in *ALP* "the text emerges through the 'O,' suggesting birth through the vagina as well as the emanation of words from the mouth" (2007, 175).

The name Anna Livia, meanwhile, appears on old maps, a corruption of the Latin *Amnis Livia* (River Liffey) but evocative also of the Irish *Abha na Life* /'auə nə 'lɪfə/ ("River Liffey"), which in turn, and invitingly, looks as if it should be referring to the Heraclitean "river of life."[2] Etymologically, at least, though certainly offering a tempting interlingual pun, it is doing nothing of the sort, the Irish name *Life* /'lɪfə/, pronounced approximately like its English variant "Liffey," being an entirely unrelated place name – but only, of course, if one accepts that *Finnegans Wake* allows for the concept of unrelatedness in the first place. The river appears in fact to have acquired its present name from the place name *Magh Life* /'mɑ: 'lɪfə/, which refers to the fertile plain (*magh*) of what is now County Kildare. It has been suggested (O Hehir 1967, 392) that *Life* is related to the modern Irish noun *luibh* /lɪv/, whose various meanings include "vegetation, grass, herb, leaf." The original *Magh Life* might therefore be taken to mean "the fertile plain" – and *Life*, entirely appropriately for Anna Livia, to mean "fertility." Anna Livia's additional name, Plurabelle, not yet mentioned in the text, attests

2 In a linguistic coincidence of a kind that particularly appealed to Joyce, the Maori word for "river" is *awa*.

primarily to her multiplicity and her beauty. Robert Sage in 1929 saw it also as "added to designate the numerous tiny tributaries of the stream" (1972, 159).

Throughout his multitudinous notes for *Finnegans Wake*, Joyce, as mentioned, used the Greek uppercase delta, Δ, as a shorthand symbol for Anna Livia – a symbol that reappears in the typographical delta formed by the opening lines of *ALP*, suggesting not only the gradual broadening of the streamlet that becomes the river but also, in anticipation, the mouth of the river as it flows into the sea. Patrick McCarthy notes (2007, 174–5) that the triangular block of text is missing in both the *Navire d'Argent* and the *transition* versions: the typographical delta first appears in the 1928 Crosby Gaige *ALP* as just two lines ("O / tell me all about"), expanding to three lines in the 1930 Faber and Faber *ALP*, as also in *Finnegans Wake*. It is a preliminary indication of the complexity of Joyce's text that the delta symbol for the river that is ALP has a shape, Δ, that also suggests the mountain that is HCE (Eckley 1975, 148).

The very first word of the opening sentence in Joyce's English, as the river springs from an "O" readable as *eau*, underlines the textual omnipresence in *ALP* of water – and invites the water itself to tell us all about Anna Livia, suggesting immediately that the two gossiping washerwomen are also a dual manifestation of ALP, "alter egos of ALP" (Begnal 1975, 41), and that the entire narrative is therefore also an implied soliloquy, with a monologizing ALP following in the literary footsteps of Molly Bloom. The opening "O" also already opens a pervasive series of punning references to rivers and waterways and to water in general, while the opening six-word invitation in perfectly plain English to "tell me all about Anna Livia" may be read, by readers prepared to play Joyce's hydronymous game, as contributing additional references, some obvious and others less so, to more than a dozen other sister rivers of Anna Livia – namely, and in succession, the Indian Tel, American Elm, Ugandan Alla, South American Abou, Nigerian Bou, Laotian Ou, Norwegian Tana, American Ana, Scottish Annan, Thai Na, the Nali of Bangladesh, the Lyvia of New Zealand, and the Ugandan Ivi. Even the Old Irish noun *ab* ("river") and the Sardinian noun *aba* ("water") are present.

The colloquial simplicity of the language in these opening phrases limits, with only one or two exceptions, the degree to which renderings in other languages are likely to introduce striking translation effects – other than in the potential generation of river names. References to rivers, streams, lakes, ponds, wells, springs, bays, inlets, and other water-related features not to be found in the original text can be expected to put in an appearance. The precise geographical location of these multiplying waterways and water features, though potentially interesting in its own right, is (or at any rate appears to be) essentially irrelevant (if the concept of relevance has any relevance in the universe of *Finnegans Wake*), since the most immediately overt role of the multiple river references especially is clearly to function as fluvial representatives and emanations of Anna Livia, the river of all rivers, wherever they themselves may flow.[3]

> BECKETT: Ô dis-moi tout d'Anna Livia! Je veux tout savoir d'Anna Livia!
> JOYCE: O, dis-moi tout d'Anna Livie! Je veux tout savoir d'Anna Livie!

Beckett's translation (shorthand from now on for Beckett and Péron's translation) originally bore the title "Anna Lyvia Pluratself," as already mentioned, a title that gestures reflexively towards the act of translation itself by transposing "Livia" into "Lyvia," as well as augmenting the Liffey by adding not only New Zealand's river Lyvia but also, by the suggestion of a lengthened vowel, the Irish Lee, English Lea, and Chinese Li. The flaunted strangeness of the translated title also suggests ALP as a problematically fractured personality, sometimes almost "plural," sometimes almost (but only almost) "itself," no doubt a continuing puzzle (German *Rätsel*) even to itself, the flow of the river paralleled by the flow of tears (Latin *plorat* "she weeps"), tears no doubt over many things (Latin *plura*), specific and unspecific, past and present, singular and cumulative, Virgil's tears of things and for things in general, *lacrimae rerum* (*Aeneid* 1.462). Joyce opted in French for the considerably less baroque title "Anna Livie Plurabelle." Whether in Beckett's "Pluratself" or Joyce's "Plurabelle," the Belgian Our, Mongolian Ur, and Russian Ura are sympathetically present. Serendipitously, moreover, the Basque noun *ura* means "the water."

Beckett's and Joyce's French renderings of this opening sentence are almost but not quite identical. Both of them dispense with the opening typographical suggestion of a delta in the 1928 *ALP*. One might conceivably object to the very first word of Beckett's version on the grounds that his opening "Ô," with its circumflex, is rather too literary for the generally quite untutored diction of the two washerwomen.

3 In 1982, in an appropriate act of onomastic homage to ALP, and to mark the centenary of Joyce's birth, the former Chapelizod Bridge, in the western suburbs of Dublin, was renamed the Anna Livia Bridge.

Such a potential quibble, however, is far outweighed by the fact that this opening "Ô" not only contains Joyce's opening "O" and its conflated symbolic potential but also strikingly succeeds, by means of the strategically placed circumflex, in conveying with exemplary concision a humorously minimalist suggestion of a fluvial delta. Serendipitously, moreover, in at least one variety of Chinese *ô* means "lake." Oddly, however, this admirably aquatic Beckettean strategy is in fact not Beckett's at all, but rather an unstated editorial contribution on the part of Jacques Aubert, since the *Bifur* proofs read, as in Joyce's English and French, simply "O."

Beckett's Anna Livia remains unchanged in name from Joyce's English, the form "Lyvia" occurring only in the title submitted to *Bifur*, but Joyce's French goes to some pains to remind us that Anna Livia is also "Anna Livie," the river of life (French *la vie*) itself, perhaps not entirely without a certain translingual evocation of the Irish *uisce beatha*, literally the "water of life," otherwise whiskey – and thus allowing for a complementary reference to Tim Finnegan's fortuitous resurrection after inadvertent aspersion with whiskey, a baptism of firewater. A trilingual pun on Irish *Life* /'lɪfə/, English *life*, and French *la vie* is of course also perceptible.

While Joyce's English wants to "hear" all about Anna, Beckett and Joyce himself both opt instead in French for the verb *savoir*, wanting to "know" all rather than just hear all. The semantic variation is evidently introduced primarily in order to accommodate the Croatian Sava (or Save) and the eastern African Save (or Sabi) rivers, a very early indication of Joyce's (but also Beckett's) willingness as translator to abandon literal fidelity in a good cause. The original note of potential scepticism, readable as implying that hearing all rather than knowing all about Anna Livia is the only likely option, disappears in French.

Both renderings, given the game rules of Joyce's original hydronymy, offer their readers the opportunity to discover a punning fluvial evocation ("dis-moi") of the Scottish Dee and the Irish Moy, while "Je veux tout savoir d'Anna" ("I want to know all about Anna") not only suggests the African Save and the Croatian Sava, but also the American Ana and the Irish Lough Dan.

JOYCE: Raccontami di Anna Livia. Tutto sapere vo' di Anna Livia.
SETTANNI: Raccontami di Anna Livia. Tutto vo' sapere di Anna Livia.

Joyce's English is at obvious pains to locate the opening "O" exactly on the page and in the text, while his French retains the "O" but abandons the typographical symbolism of the delta. It is all the more noticeable, therefore, that in Italian he chooses simply to omit both, opting instead for the more immediately urgent rhythm of an unadorned "Raccontami di Anna Livia" ("Tell me about Anna Livia").[4] That formulation, moreover, asks more modestly merely to be told about Anna Livia, rather than to be told *all* about her. The formulation "Tutto sapere vo'" once again indicates a desire, as in his French, to "know" (*sapere*) rather than to "hear" (*sentire*) all about her, and the departure from the original is once again fluvially motivated. While the invitation "Raccontami" ("tell me") succeeds in evoking the Raccoon River of Iowa, the Irish Lough Conn, the Welsh Teme, and the English Thames (*Tamigi* in Italian), the declaration that "Tutto sapere vo' di Anna Livia," now clarifying that "I want to know *all* (*tutto*) about Anna Livia," contributes the Indian Tut once again, the Japanese Tosa, and the Sape River of the Solomon Islands.

Settanni emends "tutto sapere vo'" to "tutto vo' sapere" – possibly on the grounds that the latter is a rather more normal word order in colloquial Italian, namely the linguistic level suggested by the colloquial *vo'* for the formal *voglio*. The change, retaining the Tut and the Sape, but abandoning the Japanese Tosa in favour of the English Tove, also succeeds in introducing what to the ear of an English speaker is a double dactyl, "*tut*to vo' | *sa*pere." By the rules of Italian metrics, meanwhile, both renderings consist of an octosyllabic line followed by a decasyllable. This is a very early example of one striking stylistic feature of Joyce's renderings in both French and Italian, namely the composition of metrical lines or partial lines by the particular prosodic rules of French or Italian, while his ear obviously also remains that of an English speaker, informed by the very different rules of English prosody. There are numerous examples of this kind of play on interlingual metrical effects.

[2] Well, you know Anna Livia? Yes, of course, we all know Anna Livia. (*ALP* 3; *FW* 196.04–5)

The question "Well, you know Anna Livia?" operates at first reading merely as a rhetorical effect, serving to heighten narrative anticipation. But there is of course a sense in which we *don't* know Anna Livia, whose

4 Bosinelli makes the point that while Joyce and Frank appear to have worked with what would become the 1939 text, they very largely ignored any changes made since 1928 (1996, 40). Joyce's Italian version is therefore in effect based once again on the 1928 *ALP*.

essence is her mutability and indefinability, simultaneously woman, river, female principle, and goddess.

> BECKETT: Eh bien, tu connais Anna Livia? Évidemment, tout le monde connaît Anna Livia.
>
> JOYCE: Eh bien! tu connais Anna Livie? Bien sûr tout le monde connaît Anna Livie.

The question-and-answer sequence produces no significant divergences on a semantic level in either Beckett's or Joyce's French. The aquatic overtone of Joyce's original "Well" remains without any echo in either version. The verb *connaître,* "to know" in the sense of being acquainted with, employed in both renderings, includes aquatic access to Ireland"s Lough Conn and the Japanese river Onna. Both versions evoke in addition the Peruvian Río Tuco in opting for "tu connais Anna Livia?" While Joyce's English "Yes, of course" serendipitously invokes the Chilean Yeso and Belgian Our as well as the "course" of any river or other waterway, Beckett's "Évidemment" ("obviously") contributes the Swiss river Emme instead, at least visually, while Joyce's "bien sûr" ("of course") concisely evokes the two homonymous Luxembourg rivers Sûre and Syr as well as the Central Asian Syr. Joyce's rendering colloquializes Beckett's version both in vocabulary and in punctuation, the omission of the comma suggesting the listener's impatience to hear all the gossip as soon as possible.

> JOYCE: Beh, conosci Anna Livia? Altro che, conosciamo tutte Anna Livia!
>
> SETTANNI: Beh, la conosci Anna Livia? Altro che, conosciamo tutte Anna Livia.

On a semantic level, Joyce's Italian specifies that the "we" who "all know Anna Livia" is feminine, "conosciamo tutte" rather than "conosciamo tutti." Fluvially, his "Beh, conosci Anna Livia? Altro che" ("Well, you know Anna Livia? Yes, of course, what else?"), contributes evocations of the Behy of County Kerry, the Philippine Baco (if only as pronounced by an American), Lough Conn again, the Japanese Uno, and two English rivers, the Alt and the Roch. Settanni's emendation to "Beh, la conosci Anna Livia?" ("Well, you know Anna Livia?") is able to add the English Bela and substitute the Philippine Laco for the Baco. For a reader of today, blessed with hindsight and familiarity with *Finnegans Wake* as opposed to just *ALP*, the colloquial "altro che" allows for a serendipitous early glimpse of ALP's consort HCE, lightly disguised as CHE.

[3] Tell me all. Tell me now. You'll die when you hear. **(*ALP* 3; *FW* 196.05–6)**

Two further sentences in plain English repeat the opening "tell me," but plain English now already begins to give way to the more normal idiom of *Finnegans Wake*. "You'll die when you hear," a final introductory flourish for the ensuing narrative, means no more in colloquial Irish English usage than "you'll think it hilarious." Joyce's English does not actually mention hilarity, however, and – for today's reader at least, if not necessarily for early readers of *ALP* – in the overall context of the *Wake*'s circular patterning the phrase thus also already evokes cycles of death and resurrection, whether the watery death of the river that dies as it flows into the sea towards a rainy rebirth or the fiery death and rebirth of the phoenix who will put in an at least implied appearance within a few lines in the likewise implied name of Dublin's Phoenix Park. "Ironically, the river-chapter begins with a delta, which we would expect to find at its end, where the river 'dies.' Yet the chapter's opening includes a premonition of death, 'You'll die when you hear'; moreover, the idea of the circular return is encapsulated in the 'O' with which the chapter opens" (McCarthy 2007, 174). The American Elm flows quietly in "tell me."

The sequence of eleven monosyllables and the strongly anapestic rhythm of the three sentences are striking, "Tell me *all.* | Tell me *now.* | You'll *die* | when you *hear.*" If the palindrome "Anna," readable in either direction, already reflects, in a first-level conceptual pun, the fact that certain stretches of the tidal Liffey may be seen to flow sometimes forwards and sometimes backwards, the marked anapestic rhythm arguably constitutes a second-level conceptual pun, the Greek *anapaistos* literally meaning "struck back" (*ana* "back"; *paiô* "I strike"), which is to say, "reversed," with the anapest conceived of as a reversed dactyl. While seeing cretics rather than anapests in a less urgent "*Tell* me *all.* | *Tell* me *now,*" Tadeusz Szczerbowski observes that the two sentences each consist of three elements, thus suggesting the triangular form of the Greek delta that is the symbol of ALP (2000, 90). By the same token, that triangle suggests the three female figures that populate this chapter, ALP and her two commentators, alias the river and its two banks, alias (eventually) river, tree, and stone.

BECKETT: Dis-moi tout. Dis-moi vite. [*text omitted*]
JOYCE: Dis-moi tout, dis-moi vite. C'est à en crever!

Joyce's "Tell me all. Tell me now" is rendered in French as "Dis-moi tout. Dis-moi vite" by both Beckett and Joyce himself, preserving the anapestic urgency of the original and increasing the urgency by substituting "vite" ("quickly") for the original "now." Beckett, presumably inadvertently, offers no translation of the phrase "You'll die when you hear." The phrase is effectively rendered in Joyce's version as "C'est à en crever!," combining a hyperbolically literal "It would make you burst" and a colloquial "It would make you die," while introducing (less for a French speaker's ear than an English speaker's eye) fluvial hints of the Canadian Cree and Eve and the English Ver to accompany the already present Scottish Dee and Irish Moy ("dis-moi").

JOYCE: Dimmi tutto, e presto presto. Roba da chiodi!
SETTANNI: Dimmi tutto, e presto presto. Roba d'altro mondo!

The anapestic rhythm of "Tell me all. Tell me now" changes in Joyce's Italian to the likewise urgent trochees of "Dimmi tutto, e presto presto," with the urgency increased, as in French, by the substitution of a colloquial "presto presto" ("quickly, quickly") for the English "now." The Turkish Dim, Scottish Dee, Dutch Diem, Sudanese Immi, and Indian Tut, meanwhile, are all suggested in "dimmi tutto" ("tell me all").

In the most radical departure so far from the English text, "You'll die when you hear" loses both its overt reference to death and its implied reference to laughter. Joyce's vigorous and idiomatic Italian ejaculation "roba da chiodi," introducing a change of tone, translates roughly as an exclamatory "incredible!" or "unbelievable!" while evoking the Nigerian river Bada and, visually, the Thai river Chi. Joyce no doubt encountered the idiomatic expression during his Triestine years: Serenella Zanotti notes the Triestine variant *roba de ciodi* (2001, 424). Settanni, presumably concerned that Italian readers other than northerners may not understand the idiosyncratic exclamation, opts for a more generally understandable but still idiomatic "roba d'altro mondo," invoking the "other world" ("altro mondo") to suggest "unreal, unheard of," and likewise evoking the Nigerian Bada, dropping the Thai Chi, but adding the English Alt and Nigerian Ndo. Both expressions evoke the Russian Ob and Nigerian Oba, while italianizing the name of the Irish river Robe, which flows near the eastern boundary of that part of Connacht known as Joyces' Country.

[4] Comments and Contexts

The washer at the ford is a familiar figure in Irish oral tradition. Like the banshee (*bean sidhe* "fairy woman"), she is a death omen, in this case foretelling impending death, washing bloody garments at the ford of a river and informing the beholder, usually a warrior, that the garments are his (MacKillop 1998, 428). Here there are two of them, rather less ominous, two "salty old gossips who complain of back pains and varicose veins" (Eckley 1975, 135). Szczerbowski notes the conventional cultural connection between washerwomen and gossiping: German *schwatzen wie ein Waschweib* and Italian *parlare come una lavandaia* both mean "to chatter like a washerwoman" (2000, 89).

ALP, as Margot Norris writes, is constructed of "metaphors that create multiple frames." The chattering women are thus simultaneously "two washerwomen gossiping about a Dublin neighbor, the Celtic banshees washing the bloody shirts of the soon-to-die heroes, the opposite banks conversing about the river, and the rival sons [Shem and Shaun, whom we meet only in the concluding sentences of *ALP*] airing the family's dirty linen as they probe ... into the mystery of their parentage." The metaphors, however, "will not allow for a reduction into levels of meaning; the 'reality' of Anna Livia Plurabelle is suspended forever at a conjunction of images, from which she cannot be extricated" (1976, 109).

The relationship of the two women has struck different critics rather differently over the years. For Robert Sage, in 1929, they were just "two garrulous old washerwomen" (1972, 161). For Edmund Wilson, they are also just "two old washerwomen" (1952, 224), but where "one of the parties, like the stone, is always hard-boiled, immobile and prosaic, while the other is sensitive, alive, rather light-mindedly chattering or chirping" (244). For Campbell and Robinson (who call *FW* I.8 "The Washers at the Ford" rather than "Anna Livia Plurabelle"), one of the washerwomen is old, while the other "is something of the young temptress." The two are evoked, "like spirits, from the countryside, the elder from a stone, the younger from a whispering elm, and as the dusk thickens they will melt back again into their elemental forms" (Campbell and Robinson 1961, 132–3). For Wilson, the stone and the elm "represent the death principle and the life principle (Ygdrasil)" (1952, 224). John Gordon and Philip Kitcher both return to Wilson's assessment. For Gordon, the washerwomen are just a pair of "old women": "one is the educator and tale-teller, the other an alternately fascinated and indignant listener" (1986, 165); for Kitcher, they are just "two old women who have done their wash together for many years" (2007, 127). Finally, as mentioned, we do not in fact need to distinguish two voices at all, rather than just one voice, Anna's voice, the voice of the river, talking to itself. The river of water that is ALP is recreated in the stream of words of the washerwomen, the fluidity of whose own being is revealed by their eventual transformation into tree and stone on the banks of that river (Norris 2015, 135).

An experiential impulse for the particular structure may have involved women Joyce claimed several years later to have seen on a trip to Chartres washing clothes on both banks of the French river Eure (Ellmann 1982, 563; Norris 1990, 167). A second impulse may relate to the fact that Joyce wrote to Ettore Schmitz (better known as Italo Svevo) on 20 February 1924 that he had borrowed the name of Schmitz's red-haired wife, Livia, for his female protagonist (*L* 1, 211).[5] Margot Norris speculates that the structure of the chapter may thus be the result of an overheard conversation (real or imagined) between Joyce's sisters Eileen and Eva, when they were both living with Joyce in Trieste, concerning the beauty of Livia Schmitz's red hair, "thus perhaps creating for him the interlocutory structure of the chapter, that of a male eavesdropping on the gossip of two women discussing another of their sex" (1990, 166–7). As Norris observes, "the gossip of the washerwomen is never allowed to form a coherent story, however, because the red-haired woman they talk about keeps dissolving into the river, the waves of her hair become the waves of the water ...; her freckles the dappled light on the water surface ...; her dress the topological features of the water and its surrounding land ...; and her possessions and gifts the flotsam and jetsam riding the seafoam ... of her tides" (1990, 167).

The attempt to identify narrative lines in the *Finnegans Wake* universe, meanwhile, is a readerly activity that, implicitly, is continually encouraged – and continually thwarted. To the extent that one can identify a central narrative thread in *ALP*, however, the washerwomen's conversation, as we shall see, quickly turns to various indeterminate acts of real or imagined wrong-doing on the part of ALP's consort, HCE.

---

5 David Hayman considers it likely, however, based on manuscript evidence, that Joyce is retrospectively embellishing the truth here (1990, 169). John McCourt suggests that Anna Livia's hair may also owe something to that of the Austro-Hungarian empress Elisabetta (Sissi), who appears in period photographs with hair flowing to her heels (2000, 255).

ALP's centrality is already reflected in the opening typographical delta of Joyce's English: her symbol throughout *Finnegans Wake* continues to be "Δ," also representing (topsy-turvy) the female genitalia. It is typical of the pervasive blurring of identities, including (or especially) the identities of ALP and HCE, that if the text of *ALP* begins with the river's delta, the remainder of the text would thus "logically" have to represent the open sea – and thus be representative of HCE rather than ALP. Along similar lines, we may note Brendan O Hehir's observation (1965, 165) that in Irish the term *alp* means, inter alia, "a protuberance, a huge lump, a high mountain" – attributes, that is to say, consistently evocative of HCE rather than ALP. The two washerwomen on their opposing banks will likewise blur towards the end of the text, as night falls, not only into aspects of ALP herself, but also into tree and stone, emanations of ALP *and* HCE respectively, as of their twin sons Shem and Shaun.

The opening sequence of excerpts examined in the present chapter, presented in plain English in Joyce's original, understandably does not yet provide a great deal in the way of comparative translational excitement. Certain incipient trends may already be distinguished, however. There is some early indication of Joyce's and also of Beckett's willingness as translators to abandon literal fidelity in a good cause when both of them translate "to hear" as "savoir" ("to know") [1.1].[6] No significant differences between Beckett's and Joyce's renderings are to be found, with the exception of Joyce's "Anna Livie" for Beckett's "Anna Livia" [1.1], his colloquializing of Beckett's "évidemment" to "bien sûr" [1.2], and Beckett's failure, presumably the result of an oversight, to translate "You'll die when you hear!" [1.3]. All three renderings – Beckett's and both of Joyce's – enter into Joyce's original evocation of rivers with some enthusiasm. One striking stylistic feature of Joyce's renderings in both French and Italian, namely the composition of metrical lines or partial lines by the relevant prosodic rules of those languages, is already discernible. His Italian "Roba da chiodi!" [1.3] for "You'll die when you hear" as opposed to his more literal French "C'est à en crever!" is a definite sign of the degree of translational freedom Joyce will flamboyantly demonstrate in his Italian rendering.

Settanni undertakes three stylistic emendations in this sequence. He changes Joyce's "tutto sapere vo'" to "tutto vo' sapere," arguably a more

6 Parenthetical references in square brackets are to chapter and individual excerpts of the present work; thus "[1.1]" refers to the first excerpt in chapter 1.

likely formulation for a relatively untutored speaker [1.1]. His emendation of "Beh, conosci Anna Livia?" to "Beh, la conosci Anna Livia?" is able to evoke an additional river, the Philippine Laco [1.2]. His change of "Roba da chiodi!" to "Roba d'altro mondo!" substitutes a perhaps more generally understandable version of Joyce's colourful regional exclamation [1.3]. This is an early example of Settanni's practice of frequently toning down what he apparently sees as unnecessary excesses on Joyce's part.

2 The Old Cheb

Well, you know, when the old cheb went futt and did what you know. Yes, I know, go on. Wash quit and don't be dabbling. Tuck up your sleeves and loosen your talktapes. And don't butt me – hike! – when you bend. Or whatever it was they threed to make out he thried to two in the Fiendish park. (*ALP* 3; *FW* 196.06–11)

[1] Well, you know, when the old cheb went futt and did what you know. Yes, I know, go on. Wash quit and don't be dabbling. **(*ALP* 3; *FW* 196.06–8)**

Despite their stated intention to tell all and hear all about ALP, the washerwomen turn almost immediately to her renegade husband. ALP's consort, never far away, and even more productive of dirty linen than she is, enters the washerwomen's eager dialogue within the first few lines as the "old chap," his identity discreetly concealed and simultaneously revealed by the first three letters of the distorted version, CHE standing in (as on many subsequent occasions) for HCE. This washing of dirty linen in public also recapitulates on one narrative level, as Bernard Benstock puts it, "the adventure of a young Earwicker, a Scandinavian navigator, sailing up the river (between the legs of the young maiden) as a Viking invader, and settling down in Ireland, converting to Christianity and marrying Anna" (1985a, 167).

The language of the first sentence poses few translational difficulties in principle. To go "futt" or "phutt" variously suggests fizzling out like a damp firework, suffering a short circuit, blowing a fuse, going bust, losing it – some or all of which HCE here reportedly does, or might have done if given the chance. What exactly his alleged failing was, or is, or might have been, however, is never unambiguously revealed, though there are strong suggestions at various points in *Finnegans Wake* that voyeurism of some kind may (or might) at least have been involved, perhaps along the lines of Leopold Bloom's self-satisfying spectatorial activities in "Nausicaa."

Many good stories begin with an introductory "well," and this one is no exception, while the phatic "well" doubling as an aquatic well reminds us that we are still reading a text awash in water references. The appearance of HCE, "you know," as the "old cheb" is accordingly accompanied by evocations of the Japanese Yuno, the Old River of Louisiana, and the Cheb, a river flowing formerly in the Austro-Hungarian Empire and nowadays in the Czech Republic. The Cheb even does double duty, not only standing in for a concealed and perhaps voyeuristic HCE as CHE but also providing, as a river, another fluvial reference to ALP. The old cheb in question, meanwhile, will reveal himself as an old chap of many parts. Fritz Senn already detects the visual presence of the Swiss-German noun *Cheib* in "the old cheb," meaning, Senn observes, approximately "the old bugger" (1967, 108) – though "the dirty old shagger" would be closer to Irish English idiom. Whatever the details of his disreputable character may be, when HCE "went futt," the event is likewise fluvially marked by the simultaneous appearance of the English Went and South American Futa.

The first sentence relating to HCE begins and ends with "you know": the issue, in other words, is less that HCE did what he did (if he did) than that he "did what you know," which is "you know what," whatever it is you think you know – where "you," of course, includes the reader as well as the washerwomen. What we think we know can quickly become what he did.

"Yes, I know, go on" is a plain English phrase, though still managing to harbour the Italian Esino, New Zealand Ino, English Noe, Australian Nogo, and Nigerian Ogun rivers. "Wash quit and don't be dabbling," however, in best Wakean idiom, suggests variously "wash quietly and don't splash," "wash quickly and don't just dabble," or "for goodness' sake quit just dabbling." The Wash is a large English bay on the coast of East Anglia, and the Ash is an English river; and if "quit" is taken as the principal verb, then "wash" also suggests the common Irish English interjection *wisha* (Irish *mhuise*), loosely translatable as something like "for goodness' sake." Rose and O'Hanlon's *Restored Finnegans Wake*, meanwhile, substitutes the phrase "Wash away and quit dabbling" (*FW2* 154.07), a restoration that reduces the Wakean idiom to plain English and emphasizes the relationship of "dabbling" and Dublin. The Scottish river Ling flows quietly in the background.[1]

> BECKETT: Alors, tu sais, quand le vieux gaillarda fit krach et fit ce que tu sais. Oui, je sais, et après? Lave tranquillement, et ne bats pas l'eau comme ça.
> JOYCE: Alors, tu sais, quand le vieux gaillarda fit krach et fit ce que tu sais. Oui je sais, et après, après? Lave tranquillement ton linge et ne patauge pas tant.

Joyce follows Beckett relatively closely here, though with some telling embellishments. Both versions begin with "Alors, tu sais" ("Well, you know"), evoking the Irish Allow and Indian Sai. For both, the old cheb is a "gaillarda," a "dirty old brute" who is apparently not only a "sly customer" (*gaillard*) but also still a "strapping character" (*gaillard*), doubtless with a taste for *gaillardises* ("dirty stories, dirty jokes"). Three separate rivers named Arda are evoked in passing, flowing respectively in Italy, Portugal, and Bulgaria. In both versions too, the old cheb's problems are ironically treated as if they were in fact market-related, for in each he "fit krach" ("went bust"), as if a victim of financial disaster (French *krach* "crash"), while the French river Krach is added to our already burgeoning collection of waterways. Beckett's "Oui, je sais, et après?" ("Yes, I know, and then?") becomes more urgent in Joyce's "Oui je sais, et après, après?" ("Yes, I know, and then, and then?"). Beckett's washerwoman admonishes her companion, "Just carry on washing, and don't keep thrashing the water like that." Joyce's admonition, "Just carry on washing your washing and don't splash so much," improves on the salutary advice by the addition of an alliterative and assonantal word play ("patauge pas tant"). Beckett's "ne bats pas l'eau" evokes the New Caledonian Neba and the Irish Allow as well as the Romanian noun *apă* ("water"). Joyce's fluvial references include the Portuguese Ave (visually in "lave"), Indian Ang, French Ill, and German Ilm ("tranquillement"), English Lin, Scottish Ling, and Dutch Linge (visually

1 In the 1925 *Navire d'Argent* text the sentence reads simply "Wash away and don't be dabbling" (Higginson 1960, 60). Higginson asserts that Joyce emended the sentence on the Gaige galleys to read "Wash away and quit be dabbling," but the emendation – possibly intended to read either "Wash away and quit dabbling" or "Wash away and quit the dabbling"– was ignored in all three of the Gaige, Faber, and *FW* texts (109).

in "linge"), and French Tauge ("patauge") and Korean Patong ("pas tant"). The implied pun on "dabbling" and Dublin disappears in both versions.

> JOYCE: Beh, sai quando il messercalzone andò in rovuma e fe' ciò che fe'? Si, lo so, e po' appresso? Lava pulito e non sbrodolare!
>
> SETTANNI: Beh, sai allorché il messercalzone andò in rovuma e fe' ciò che fe'. Sí, lo so, e po' appresso? Lava, sbrigati e non sbrodolare.

Joyce's Italian rendering of this sequence is far more exuberantly baroque than his French rendering. "Well," exclaims his Italian washerwoman, approximately, "you know when the old so-and-so went crazy and did what he did?" More specifically, the old cheb is now "il messercalzone," an epithet combining *mascalzone* ("wretch, scoundrel") and the archaic Florentine *messere* ("master") while simultaneously invoking all of *calzone* ("trouser leg"), *calzoni* ("trousers"), and *calzare* ("to try something on"), and thus suggesting a combination of "Master Scoundrel" and "Mister Trousers," hinting strongly at misdemeanours unspecified but evidently involving trouser-related derelictions. While the original old cheb went futt, his Italian counterpart "andò in rovuma," suggesting with exemplary compactness that he went to the dogs (*andò in rovina*), that he suffered a bad fall (*rovina*), that he came to his ruin (*rovina*), and that all of this was connected in some likewise unspecified way with a bush (*rovo*) of some sort as he notoriously "did what he did" ("fe' ciò che fe'"), the identity of the miscreant now discreetly adumbrated in the ostensibly innocuous relative pronoun *che*. Settanni's emendation of the opening "Beh, sai quando" to "Beh, sai allorché" leaves the surface meaning unchanged ("Well, you know when") while pointedly managing to include the incriminating letters CHE one more time.

That streams of some sort may also have been involved is amply evident from the subliminal presence of the Irish Behy (an italianized Irish river flowing from an English-language "well"), the Indian Sai, the Ando of the Solomon Islands, the Romanian Şercaia ("mes-sercalzone"), the German Alz, the Rovuma of Mozambique (embedding the Arabic *ma* "water"), and the American Santa Fe. Settani's emendation of "quando" to "allorché" abandons the Ando in favour of the German Aller and its English namesake, while the impatient response "Si, lo so, e po' appresso?" ("Yes, I know, and what then?") contributes the Italian Po.

Joyce's Italian washerwoman's poetically phrased professional advice "Lava pulito e non sbrodolare" might initially seem to mean no more than "Do your washing neatly and quickly," with *pulito* suggesting "cleanly" in standard Italian, "properly" in Triestine (Zanotti 2001, 423), and *sbrodolare* a colloquial term for "to prolong, to drag out." Since the likewise colloquial phrase *dare una pulita* means "to give a lick and a promise," however, while the primary meaning of *sbrodolare* is actually "to soil," the sober advice is simultaneously undermined by an implied and rather less professional "Give it a quick lick and a promise – and at least don't get it any dirtier." Settanni's emendation of "Lava pulito" to "Lava, sbrigati" reduces the advice to an unambiguously sober "Just do your washing and hurry up." The punning presence of "Dublin" in "dabbling" once again disappears, for both Joyce and Settanni.

The consciously poetic effect, meanwhile, in two languages simultaneously, of "Lava pulito e non sbrodolare" is striking. For an anglophone reader it constitutes a line of dactylic tetrameter: "*La*va pu- | *li*to e | *non* sbrodo- | *la*re." By the rules of Italian prosody it playfully approximates a *decasillabo*, defined as consisting of ten syllables (allowing for such elisions as "pulit*o e*") with emphasis on the third, sixth, and ninth syllables – while the emphasis here is adjusted to fall on the first, fourth, sixth, and ninth syllables.

[2] *Tuck up your sleeves and loosen your talk-tapes. And don't butt me – hike! – when you bend.* (*ALP* 3; *FW* 196.08–9)

"Tuck up your sleeves" is once again a plain English phrase, though also managing to embed a reference to the English Uck and Canadian Eve; "Loosen your talk-tapes" ("talktapes" in *FW*) implies a surface meaning of "get ready for a good chat," while providing glimpses of the Russian Loo, German Oos, and French Eure. The term "talk-tapes" both evokes vocal cords and to some extent echoes the consonantal sequence of "tuck up," while an action of tightening is followed by one of loosening. Hints of the Irish Tolka and Russian Tap may be detected.

"And don't butt me – hike! – when you bend," extending the consonantal sequence (*tuck, talk, hike*), may be read as referring to the washerwomen's heads banging together over the river, still narrow so near its source, as they bend forward, their butting evoking historical and mythological battles over Irish rivers, while "butt" as noun also suggests their posteriors colliding when they bend over to pick up the piles of washing behind them on their respective riverbanks. A double reference to Liffey bridges is also suggested: Butt Bridge (named for Isaac Butt, a prominent nineteenth-century Irish politician), as any map of Dublin will show, is "butted" by a noticeable "bend" in the railway line that likewise crosses the river by way of the immediately adjacent Loopline Bridge. Meanwhile, "butt" here echoes the "futt" of a few lines earlier. The political fall of Isaac Butt is also invoked, Butt's career having gone dramatically futt at the hands of the rising young star Charles Stewart Parnell – whose childhood nickname because of his obstinate character, very appropriately for the present context, was "Butthead" (Glasheen 1973, 80), and whose own career would soon enough go even more dramatically futt. The fall of fathers at the hands of sons – as in a Butthead headbutting a Butt – is a theme that will later resound throughout *Finnegans Wake*.

BECKETT: Retrousse les manches et délie ta langue. Et ne me bouscule pas – ho! – quand tu te penches.
JOYCE: Retrousse tes manches et délie ton battant. Et ne me cogne pas avec ta caboche, hein!

Beckett's rendering, evoking the English Channel, *La Manche*, translates literally as "Roll up your sleeves and untie your tongue." Joyce's "Retrousse tes manches et délie ton battant" repeats the evocation of the English Channel but complicates "untie your tongue" with "untie the tongue of your bell," *battant* literally meaning the clapper or tongue of a bell but also suggesting *battoir*, a washerwoman's beater or battle, while completing a wordplay on *pataugе / pas tant / battant*. Joyce's phrase also reads as a perfect French hendecasyllable.

Beckett's "Et ne me bouscule pas ... quand tu te penches" translates relatively neutrally as "And don't bump into me when you bend over," leaving it up to the reader to decide whether heads or tails are primarily involved. Joyce is more crisply specific, with "Et ne me cogne pas avec ta caboche," roughly, "And don't bang into me with your big fat head," ignoring the business of bending, but rescuing the alliteration of "butt / bend" with "cogne / caboche," while adding the Norwegian Ogne and American Abo. The colloquial French *caboche* ("head, nut") is enhanced by Norman French *caboche* ("cabbage"). Beckett's exclamation "ho!" invokes the Chinese noun *ho* ("river"), while Joyce is content with an all-purpose French "hein!" ("okay?"), which allows at least a visual reference to the Chinese river Hei.

JOYCE: Rimboccamaniche e sciogliliinguagnolo. Ma la zucca per te se mai ti pieghi!
SETTANNI: Rimboccamaniche e sciogliliinguagnolo. Se mai ti pieghi la zucca è per te.

The phrase "Rimboccamaniche e sciogliliinguagnolo" shows the Italian Joyce at his most exuberantly baroque. Umberto Eco has argued (1996, xvi) that since Italian, as compared to English, is relatively lacking in monosyllabic forms, Joyce here and elsewhere deliberately opts for the other extreme of inventing extravagant polysyllables – in which Italian, if anything, is even more lacking. The first example of this produces two sesquipedalian monsters at once. "Rimboccamaniche," however, rather less than monstrous, is in fact merely a humorously telescoped version of a standard Italian *rimbocca le maniche* ("tuck up your sleeves"). "Sciogliliinguagnolo," as Bosinelli observes (1998b, 196), is a more complex creation, a portmanteau word arguably combining *scioglilingua* ("tongue twister"), *lingua* ("tongue"), *linguaggio* ("language"), and, incorporating an aquatic touch, *rigagnolo* ("stream"). The literal implication, entirely appropriate for our Wakean washerwomen, is thus something like "Roll up your sleeves and wring out the stream of language." "Rimboccamaniche," meanwhile, also serendipitously contains the element *-bocca-*, a homophone of Italian *bocca* ("mouth") and thus immediately anticipating *lingua* ("tongue").

The phrase also plays on the effects of poetic language in both English and Italian. An English reader, adjusting the normal spoken Italian accent of the word *rimbocca*, may well read the phrase as a line of dactylic tetrameter, "*Rim*bocca | *ma*nich(e e) | *scio*glilin- | *gua*gnolo." By the rules of Italian metrics, meanwhile, as Risset observes (1984, 7), the phrase constitutes a dactylic hendecasyllable. In accordance with those rules, the thirteen actual syllables of the phrase are reduced to the obligatory eleven first by the elision in "manich*e e*" and then by the special rule for lines ending with an accent on the third last syllable, where the final three syllables count as only two. This particular type of line, moreover, with its dactylic ending, is technically called a *sdrucciolo*, a term that envisages the line slipping (*sdrucciolare* "to slip, to slide") down a "steep slope" (*sdrucciolo*). The verb *sdrucciolare*, meanwhile, may also refer specifically to water, meaning "to flow down" – and thus allowing also for a splendidly cryptic aquatic reference. Other aquatic overtones are also not lacking, meanwhile, represented by both the Vietnamese river Cam and the English Channel, known in Italian as the *Canale della Manica,* the word *manica* meaning both an "inlet" and a "sleeve." The plural *maniche,* meanwhile, allows another fugitive glimpse of HCE as CHE. The Chinese Li, English Lin, Scottish Ling, Corsican Guagno, Philippine Agno, and Portuguese Olo all flow in the tongue-twisting "scioglilinguagnolo."

Risset also observes that "Rimboccamaniche e scioglilinguagnolo," unlike Joyce's English and French versions of the relevant phrase, is a striking first example of a recurrent element of poetic organization throughout the Italian text, namely of "the large number (much larger than in the original) of nominal constructions pulled out of the normal, that is to say verbal narrative structure," constructions that thus combine to set up "a sort of perpendicular axis on the narrative plane" (1984, 8). In narratological terms, they demonstrate the radical priority of discourse over story, of *how* over *what,* temporarily displacing the horizontal axis of narrative on "*what* happens" by the vertical axis of *how* what happens is told.

An Italian *zucca* is a "pumpkin," meanwhile, and the jocular warning "Ma la zucca per te se mai ti pieghi!" – another Italian hendecasyllable (Risset 1984, 7) – evoking in passing the Romanian Mala and Lazu and the English Uck and Sem as well as the Arabic *ma* ("water"), translates roughly as "But keep your big fat head to yourself when you're bending over!" Settanni achieves one of his occasional stylistic improvements by rearranging the order of these two clauses, abandoning the Mala, and turning the hendecasyllable into a decasyllable in order to accentuate the rhythm of what in English prosody is a truncated dactylic dimeter, "*Se* mai ti | *pie*ghi la | *zucc*(a è) per | *te.*" Joyce's Italian omits any rendering of the exclamation "hike!" and there is no reference either to Isaac Butt or to Liffey bridges.

[3] Or whatever it was they threed to make out he thried to two in the Fiendish park. (*ALP* 3; *FW* 196.09–11)

Whatever it was that HCE did or did not do or might have done if given half a chance, the report of it gives rise to the most complex utterance we have so far encountered, even though its surface meaning appears to be relatively clear, namely, "Or whatever it was they tried to make out he tried to do in the Fiendish park." The first extant draft, indeed, reads only minimally differently, namely, "Or whatever it was they try to make out he tried to do in the Phoenix park" (Higginson 1960, 23).

The "Fiendish park" is of course a humorous distortion of the Phoenix Park, the fictional location of HCE's fall from grace, whatever form that may or might have taken. The English name of the park derives from that of a residence named *The Phoenix,* built by one Sir Edward Fisher about 1615 on the site of the future Magazine Fort. The property was later greatly extended to form a viceregal demesne and deer park, and by 1700 it was already known as the Phoenix Park. The association of the phoenix and the park is etymologically spurious, as it happens, for the name chosen for Sir Edward's residence is merely a serendipitous corruption of an earlier Irish place name involving the term *fionnuisce* /fjʌn'ɪʃkə/ ("clear water"), referring to a natural well of clear water that once existed near the present Zoological Gardens (de Courcy 1996, 297–8).

Spurious or not, however, the phoenix's mythological connotations enable it to function as a symbol both of death and of resurrection, and also as a broad hint that HCE's alleged misdemeanour may have involved risings and fallings of a more earthy nature. One possible version of HCE's misdemeanour is that he seized an opportunity to spy on two girls surreptitiously relieving themselves in the park (and thus also contributing to the general water level of the chapter). Whether he "tried to do" anything further is unclear. Whatever he did, he himself was possibly observed doing so by three soldiers, who at any rate, whatever they might or might not have seen, appear to have subsequently spread various colourful versions of the story around Dublin. One piece of "evidence" for this particular version of the story is the present sentence fragment, with its pronounced play, conflating concealment and revelation, on the numbers three and two, which may be construed in more extended fashion as also implying "whatever it was the three in the trees tried to make out he tried to do to the two in the Fiendish park." Both groups are doubly present, the one as "threed" and "thried," the other as "to" and "two."

The two girls and three soldiers, whatever their degree of fictional reality, may be read as corresponding to the five members of Earwicker's own family, mother and daughter as the perennially watched, father and sons as the perennially voyeuristic watchers (Tindall 1959, 241). Alternatively, the two (witting or unwitting) temptresses may be read as two versions of his daughter Issy, who suffers from (and perhaps at least sometimes enjoys) a split personality; while the three soldiers can be read as his sons Shem and Shaun individually, and, as a joint threat to a father all too uneasily conscious of the passing years, combined.

One possible pictorial source of the whole incident, meanwhile, as has been variously observed, is the Dublin city coat of arms, which shows two demure maidens holding aloft olive branches of peace – and in at least some representations also the hem of their virginal garments – while three warlike escutcheoned castles burst impetuously into flame.

The location of Earwicker's fall from grace in the "Fiendish park," meanwhile, whether it really took place or not, not only underlines the irredeemably diabolical nature of his offence, whether actual, alleged, or hypothetical. The name simultaneously suggests the possibility of encountering an enemy (Old English *fēond*) in such a location, thus also suggesting the Phoenix Park as a Dublin garden of Eden, an abode of primeval innocence shattered by the irruption of the fiendish tempter of Genesis. The biblical Eden also has appropriately fluvial associations, being the source of the four great rivers of the then known world, the Pishon, Gihon, Tigris, and Euphrates (Genesis 2:11–14), while the name Eden itself, at least according to one theory, may derive from the Akkadian *edinu* ("plain"), referring to the alluvial plain of Mesopotamia, the "land between the rivers" (McKenzie 1965, 211). The biblical garden is also amply provided with trees (Genesis 2:9), out of which a fiendish serpent might well emerge, or among which, translated to Dublin, three concealed watchers might well be able to witness a latter-day Adam falling prey to temptation.

BECKETT: Ou quel quel que fût le tréfleuve qu'il aurait trouvé dans le parc de l'Inphernix.

JOYCE: Ou quelque fut le tréfleuve que le triplepatte qu'on dit qu'il trouva dans le parc de l'Inphernix.

In French, Beckett's rendering departs quite radically from Joyce's original with something like "or what whatever the triple stream or three-leaved clover was that he was supposed to have found," where the initial "quel quel" may be read as hinting at the presence of the two temptresses, while the stuttering sequence "quel quel que" provides an example of HCE's stammer, a recurring reference to his guilty conscience. The *tré-* of "tréfleuve" may similarly be read as hinting at the three watchers in the trees.There now also appears to be the hint of a quite unexpected reference to St Patrick, however, whose reputation, long since sanctified, was also once subject to malicious rumour, and the three-leaved shamrock or clover (French *trèfle,* from the Latin *trifolium* "three-leaved") he reportedly used to demonstrate the unity of the Trinity. But the portmanteau coinage "tréfleuve" is at least as much *fleuve* ("river") as it is *trèfle*, so we do still seem after all to be talking also about the less strictly theological concerns of HCE and the forbidden "river" (or rivers) he may, his interest piqued, have peeked at in the park. Appropriately for the context, the past participle "trouvé" ("found") duly evokes the French river Ouve and the Laotian Ou.

Joyce's own French provides a further elaboration of Beckett's rendering that is even less amenable to linear back-translation, "Ou quelque fut le tréfleuve que le triplepatte qu'on dit qu'il trouva." One possible reading of this would be "or whatever the triple stream or three-leaved clover or triple whatever it was they say he found." The new term "triplepatte" plays on the verb *tripatouiller*, which means both to fiddle about with something and, not without a certain relevance in the context, to grope somebody sexually. The element "-patte," for good measure, now doubly refers to St Patrick, both as a hypocoristic Saint Pat and as a legendary evangelizer whose short-armed heraldic cross is technically known as a *croix pattée*, a "footed cross." Perhaps the implied parallel of HCE and the sainted predecessor is all too pat, however, for HCE's guilty conscience still appears to play an even more noticeable role in the stuttering "quelque ... que ... qu' ... qu'" that runs through Joyce's French. Joyce's rendering, in which the Ouve and Ou still flow ("trouva"), dispenses with overt reference to the two temptresses, and thus obscures the details of the alleged misdeed, focusing instead on the perceived threat posed by the three observers of what may or may not have happened.

Any trace of Eden disappears in French. Rather the "infernal" setting of the encounter, whatever it may have been, is stressed by both Beckett's and Joyce's versions, "le parc de l'Inphernix" and "le parc d'Inphernix" respectively, combining phoenix and inferno to hint ominously at the appropriateness of Dantesque retribution. Readers are invited both by Beckett's "quel quel" and by Joyce's "quelque" to detect an underlying translingual aquatic pun on German *Quelle* ("spring, well").

JOYCE: O cosa mai fece bifronte o triforo in quel'infenice di porco nastro?
SETTANNI: O cosa mai fece bifronte o triforo in quell'infenice di porco nastro?

Joyce's Italian introduces watchers and watched with a crisp formulation that once again deviates flamboyantly from his original English. The first phrase, "o cosa mai fece," simply means "or whatever it was he did"; the second plays much more polyvalently on the Italian architectural terms *bifronte* ("double-fronted") and *triforo* ("having three openings"), evoking the Tanzanian river Foro while suggesting HCE's two-faced (*bifronte*) behaviour relating to two girls as observed from three vantage points. Sexualized details of female anatomy are also discreetly adumbrated. The phrase also adroitly plays once again on interlingual metrical effects, an English dactylic tetrameter – "O | *co*sa mai | *fe*ce bi- | *front*(e o) tri- | *fo*ro" – comfortably sharing space with an Italian dodecasyllable, composed according to standard metrical rule of two hexasyllables, each with an accent on its second and fifth syllable, "O *co*sa mai *fe*ce | | bi*front*(e o) tri*fo*ro."

Joyce's description of the location of the encounter as "quel'infenice di porco nastro," playing on *infelice* ("unfortunate") and *fenice* ("phoenix"), suggests "that unfortunate phoenix park of ours," while evoking the Chinese Fen and Indian Feni as well as the watery English noun *fen*. The phrase *parco nostro* ("our park"), however, is humorously rearranged into "porco nastro," which not only invokes the Romanian Porcu, Italian Orco, Scottish Cona, and Canadian Nass rivers, as well as the German adjective *nass* ("wet"), but also roundly characterizes HCE's offence as that of a complete swine (*porco*). The trace of an Edenic fiend in the English *ALP* and of a Dantesque inferno in the French metamorphoses into the hint of a blasphemous *pater noster* ("our father") – which suggestively contributes a perceptible hint of incest in the affair. Settanni slightly emends Joyce's "quel'infenice di porco nastro" to "quell'infenice di porco nastro, the change from "quel'" to "quell'" emphasizing the translingual reference to German *Quelle* ("spring, well") while hinting at the English river Ellen.

[4] Comments and Contexts

Joyce follows Beckett's French exactly regarding the "vieux gaillarda" who "fit krach," thus adopting the humorous suggestion of a financial component in the old cheb's fall from grace; emphasizes the listener's impatience once again by intensifying "et après?" to "et après, après?"; and improves Beckett's "ne bats pas l'eau comme ça" by substituting the much more pleasing (and hydronymously enhanced) play "ne patauge pas tant" [2.1]. Beckett's "délie ta langue" becomes a more complex "délie ton battant," introducing a translingual play on the double meaning of the English *tongue*, human and campanular, and Beckett's more literal "ne me bouscule pas ... quand tu te penches" is altered to "ne me cogne pas avec ta caboche," less strictly literal but rescuing the alliteration of the original while once again colloquializing the washerwoman's language [2.2]. Beckett moves away from semantic fidelity with his boldly complex "Ou quel quel que fût le tréfleuve qu'il aurait trouvé dans le parc de l'Inphernix," a challenge to which Joyce gleefully responds with an even more elaborately inflated "Ou quelque fut le tréfleuve que le triplepatte qu'on dit qu'il trouva dans le parc de l'Inphernix," thus also adopting Beckett's introduction of the stuttering motif and the cryptic allusions to both St Patrick and Dante [2.3].

Joyce's Italian waxes extravagant with the statement that "il messercalzone andó in rovuma e fé' cio che fé'," while the play on the different meanings of *pulito* in Triestine and in standard Italian is another early indication of Joyce's enthusiastic deployment of regional and dialect forms [2.1]. The bravura construction "Rimboccamaniche e scioglilinguagnolo" [2.2] already shows the Italian Joyce at one of his more exuberantly baroque moments. It also exemplifies a tendency in his Italian *ALP*, identified by Jacqueline Risset (1984, 8), to replace syntagmatic by paradigmatic constructions, privileging the vertical axis of discourse over the horizontal axis of story. The echo of Dublin in "dabbling" disappears in all translated versions, including both of Joyce's renderings.

Several interesting examples of Joyce's interlingual play on English, French, and Italian metrics occur in the present sequence. Our opening chapter also had a number of examples of consciously or unconsciously poetic lines as defined by the prosodic rules of the relevant language. While English metric lines are determined by the distribution of accented and unaccented syllables, French and Italian metric lines are determined primarily by the number of countable syllables, allowing for elision of vowels under certain conditions. A phrase like "O, dis-moi tout d'Anna Livie!" [1.1] thus constitutes a French octosyllable; "Dimmi tutto, e presto presto" [1.3] similarly (with vocalic elision linking *tutto* and *e*) constitutes an Italian octosyllable. The application of such labels may or may not be of any particular interest purely for its own sake. What is certainly of interest, however, is the play of metrical effects that can be identified between and across the relevant languages.

Settanni arguably achieves three small but not insignificant stylistic improvements in this sequence. His emendation of the opening "Beh, sai quando" to "Beh, sai allorché" improves on Joyce's version in that it includes ("allor*ché*") an initial incriminating reference to HCE [2.1].

He arguably improves Joyce's "Ma la zucca per te se mai ti pieghi!" by rewriting it as "Se mai ti pieghi la zucca è per te" in order to accentuate the dactylic rhythm [2.2]. His one-letter alteration of "quel'infenice di porco nastro" to "quell'infenice di porco nastro" emphasizes the translingual reference to German *Quelle* and adds a river, the English Ellen [2.3]. His emendation of "Lava pulito" to "Lava, sbrigati," on the other hand, reduces the complexity of Joyce's version by eliminating the play on *pulito* [2.1].

3 Steeping and Stuping

He's an awful old reppe. Look at the shirt of him! Look at the dirt of it! He has all my water black on me. And it steeping and stuping since this time last wik. How many goes is it I wonder I washed it? I know by heart the places he likes to saale, dudduurty devil! Scorching my hand and starving my famine to make his private linen public. Wallop it well with your battle and clean it. My wrists are rwusty rubbing the mouldaw stains. And the dneepers of wet and the gangres of sin in it! (*ALP* 3–4; cf. *FW* 196.11–18)

[1] He's an awful old reppe. Look at the shirt of him! Look at the dirt of it! **(*ALP* 3; *FW* 196.11–12)**

Talktapes duly loosened and inhibitions abandoned, our washerwomen warm up to their enthusiastic demolition of the old cheb's character, further discussion of ALP herself temporarily and pleasurably postponed. She nonetheless continues to be very much present in the proliferating fluvial series, which begins here with the German Repe and French Reppe. The overt meaning of the next few sentences, with their binary opposition of clean and dirty, is entirely clear: HCE is totally depraved, an awful old reprobate, and physically as well as morally very literally a dirty old man. A strongly marked dactylic rhythm establishes itself once again, found here already in "*Look* at the | *shirt* of him ! | *Look* at the | *dirt* of it!"

BECKETT: C'est un beau salaud. Regarde-moi sa chemise! Regarde-moi cette saleté.

JOYCE: C'est un beau saalaud! Vois sa chemise à lui! Vois-moi cette saleté.

For Beckett's French, the "awful old reppe" is "un beau salaud," a "right bastard (*salaud*)," a sentiment echoed by Joyce's, which makes the reference to the German river Saale more obvious ("saalaud") by doubling a vowel – and thus also adding the French Aa. Just how dirty (*sale*) HCE and his shirt and his affairs in general are motivates a verbal repetition in both versions. Rhythmically (if not metrically), Beckett's "Regarde-*moi* | sa che*mise*! | Regarde-*moi* | cette sale*té*," changes the dactyls of the original to anapests, while Joyce's French restores the original dactyls, "*Vois* sa che- | *mise* à lui! | *Vois*-moi cette | *sa*leté."

JOYCE: Oibò, quel lughero malandrone! Che sudiciume di camiciaccia!
SETTANNI: Oibò, quel lughero malandrone. Che sudiciume di camiciaccia.

The "awful old reppe" is introduced in Joyce's Italian with, roughly, "For shame (*oibò*), what an extraordinary ruffian (*malandrino*)!" The Triestine noun *lùghero* corresponds to the standard Italian *lucherino* ("siskin"), characterizing our man as both a distinctly queer bird and something of a dullard who is moreover clearly "dishonest" (*malandrino*), even very dishonest indeed (*malandrone*). Supplementary overtones generated by the combination suggest a ruffian not only "ghastly" (*lugubre*) and with a distinctly "queer look" (*luchera*), but one very possibly also infected with syphilis (*lue*). Zanotti (2001, 423) also suggests a play on *lugaro* ("silly"). The introduction simultaneously evokes five foreign rivers, the Philippine Ibo, Welsh Lugg, Romanian Mala, Indian Malan, and American Andro.

The shirt of him and the dirt of it are concisely rendered. The noun *sudiciume* literally means "dirt, filth," but in the overall fluvial context also suggests the Neapolitan *ciume* ("river, stream"), while *camicia* ("shirt") acquires the pejorative ending *-accia*, suggesting, roughly, "What a disgusting old shirt, with rivers of filth on it!" As in many other cases, the surface meaning is of less interest than the means by which it is obtained. Here, for example, the disgust implied by the triple occurrence of the affricate /tʃ/, the final occurrence even strengthened to /ttʃ/, is palpable. Settanni limits himself to substituting periods for Joyce's exclamation marks – as he (or a *Prospettive* copy editor similarly averse to this particular stylistic effect) will continue consistently to do thoughout.

[2] *He has all my water black on me. And it steeping and stuping since this time last wik.* (*ALP* 3; *FW* 196.12–13)

The blackening of the water reflects the fact that the name Dublin derives from the Irish *dubh* ("black") and *linn* ("pool"). The dactylic rhythm continues in "*steep*ing and | *stup*ing since | *this* time last | *wik*," the effect strengthened by the marked alliteration in "steeping and stuping." Fluvial references continue unabated with the Irish Blackwater, English Steeping, Polish Stupia, and Russian Upa, followed by the Scottish Wick and Russian Ik conflated with "week."

BECKETT: Il a noirci toute mon eau. N'empêche que ça fait déjà une samamaine que ça trempe et boit.
JOYCE: Il m'a noirci toute mon eau. Et ça trempe et ça traîne toute une sommamaine!

"He has all my water black on me" becomes "Il a noirci toute mon eau" for Beckett, improved as "Il m'a noirci toute mon eau" in Joyce's French, both versions hinting at the Canadian Rivière Noire, with Joyce also allowing access to the German Ilm.

Beckett's French suggests, roughly, "He has blackened all my water. Even though it's been a week now of it steeping (*trempe*) and soaking (*boit*)," a formulation permitting reference to the Rivière Noire, the river Pech of Afghanistan, the introduction of the stuttering motif, and the conflation of the French Maine, Irish Maine, Russian Samara, and, at a further remove, the French Somme, whose Romano-Celtic name was also the Samara. The alliteration on "steeping and stuping" is abandoned.

Joyce's own crisper version suggests, roughly, and alliteratively, "He has blackened all my water on me. And it lying around (*traîner* 'to lie around') soaking for a whole week!" Joyce's rendering introduces the German Ilm, retains the Rivière Noire, abandons the Pech and the Samara, makes the presence of the Somme more obvious, and otherwise captures the same effects as Beckett. Dactyls give way to anapests in "Et ça *trempe* | et ça *traîn-* | e toute *une* | somma*maine*!" – a formulation that also replicates the original alliteration and introduces an internal rhyme on "traîne" and "-maine."

JOYCE: Guarda un po', tutta l'acqua ne ho sporca. Bagno di qua, bagno di là, otto giorni di bucato.
SETTANNI: Guarda un po', tutta l'acqua ne ho sporca. Bagno di qua, bagno di là, son otto giorni di bel bucato.

Joyce's Italian suggests, roughly, "Just look, all my water is filthy from him," the adjective *sporco* ("filthy") concisely implying that the old reppe is also an old pig (*porco*). Aquatic associations include the

Italian Lago di Garda,the Scottish Loch Ard, the Italian, Portuguese, and Bulgarian rivers Arda, the Italian Po, the French noun *lac* ("lake"), and the Chinese noun *ho* ("river").

The filthy shirt "steeping and stuping since this time last wik" is rendered as "Bagno di qua, bagno di là, otto giorni di bucato," suggesting "Soaking it here, soaking it there, a whole week of washing it." The first six words, as Zanotti notes (2002, 298), humorously evoke Figaro's operatic patter – "Figaro qua, Figaro là" – in Rossini's *Barber of Seville*, similarly complaining of unreasonable and excessive labours demanded. Settanni adjusts the final words to "son otto giorni di bel bucato," roughly, "it's been a whole week of nothing but washing and washing." Both versions allow glimpses of the New Zealand Otto, Fijian Buca and English Uck, while Settanni adds the Japanese Ono ("son otto") and hints at the German Elbe ("bel bu-").

***[3] How many goes is it I wonder I washed it? I know by heart the places he likes to saale, duddurty devil!* (*ALP* 3; *FW* 196.13–15)**

The opposition of clean and dirty is firmly established as the opposition also of ALP and HCE, the latter crisply described as "duddurty devil," all too easily identified by the old dud's guilty stammer and the implied initials of "dear dirty Dublin," while washed (if to little apparent avail) by the French Onde and the English Ash and Wash, not to mention the American Heart, German Saale, American Dirty Devil, English Duddon, and Alaskan Dudd Creek. Dactyls are strikingly present yet again in "How | *man*y goes | *is* it I | *won*der I | *wash*ed it?" and alliteration is again effectively in evidence, "I wonder I washed it" and "duddurty devil."

BECKETT: Je me demande combien de fois je l'ai déjà lavée. Je sais par coeur les endroits qu'il aime à saalir, le misérable.

JOYCE: Et combien de fois l'ai-je lavée! Je sais paroker les endroits qu'il aime à seillir, le mymyserable.

Joyce's virtuoso "How many goes is it I wonder I washed it?" is significantly flattened in French in both Beckett's version and his own. Beckett's rendering translates faithfully as "I wonder how many times I have washed it already," while partially rescuing the dactylic rhythm with "*com*bien de | *fois* je l'ai | *dé*jà la | *vée*." Joyce's own version (roughly, "And the number of times I have washed it!") simplifies rather drastically, dropping the rhetorical question of the original, but again repeating in part the original dactylic rhythm with "*com*bien de | *fois* l'ai-je la | *vée*!"

Beckett's "Je sais par coeur les endroits qu'il aime à saalir," a once again faithful "I know by heart the places he likes to saale," is humorously emended by Joyce to "Je sais paroker les endroits qu'il aime à seillir," his "paroker" conflating *par coeur* ("by heart") and *perroquet* ("parrot"), thus allowing implied access at one linguistic remove to the English river Parrett and the Australian Paroo as well as the American Rock River, while rejecting the presumably too easy conflation of the verb *salir* ("to soil") and the German Saale in favour of a combination involving the French Seille instead. Beckett's "le misérable" ("the wretch") adopts a rather flattened approach that nonetheless allows access to three new rivers, the Czech Iser, German Isar, and French Isère. Joyce's "le mymyserable" agrees with this assessment of the old cheb's character, identifies its owner with a stuttering "mymy-," and, not to be outdone, adds a further reference to the Franco-Belgian Yser.

JOYCE: Quante mai volte l'avrò ritorta! So ben io cosa quel macchiavuol. Lordo balordo!
SETTANNI: E quante mai volte l'avrò ritorta. So bene io cosa quel macchiavuol. Lordo balordo.

Rather than her Irish counterpart's "How many goes is it I wonder I washed it?" Joyce's Italian washerwoman more graphically emphasizes the number of repeated washings and rewashings by her exclamation "Quante mai volte l'avrò ritorta!," suggesting an exasperated "*How* many times have I had to wring it out!," while conflating the past participle *ritorto* ("twisted, wrung") and the Portuguese river Torto. Serenella Zanotti notes the double pentasyllable of the washerwoman's exclamation and the use of the rare form "ritorta" to translate the neutral English "washed" (2002, 284).

Plain English in the original, excepting only the final word, "I know by heart the places he likes to saale" is transformed in Joyce's Italian into an extraordinary "So ben io cosa quel macchiavuol." Since the noun *macchia* means both "stain, mess" and also "shame, disgrace," *macchia vuole* suggests that "what he really wants is just a shameful mess." But the epithet "macchiavuol" also clearly plays on the name Machiavelli (which is sometimes also spelled "Macchiavelli"), welcome grist to Joyce's onomastic mill in that it derives in distorted form from *malo* ("bad") and *chiavello* ("spike"), the latter being a euphemism for "penis" and the combination a nickname for an ancestor famous or notorious for his sexual appetite (Hanks et al. 2002, 394). In a translatorial move emphasizing that translation always involves cultural implications, sometimes quite unexpected, the Florentine Renaissance statesman Niccolò Machiavelli thus becomes an entirely unexpected model for our Dublin HCE. Since Machiavelli was notoriously (or at any rate reportedly) an advocate of ends justifying means, and since the phrase "quel macchiavuol" also suggests *che il vuole macchiare* ("that he wants to stain"), the rendering as a whole suggests, "I know very well what that ruthless character who would stop at nothing wants to stain in a shameful way." "Dudduty devil" in question, meanwhile, switching from English alliteration to Italian self-rhyme, becomes "Lordo balordo," both "dirty" (*lordo*) and, lordy lordy, just plain "stupid" (*balordo*), while evoking in passing the Canadian Lord, Russian Or, Scottish Orr, and Australian Ord.

[4] Scorching my hand and starving my famine to make his private linen public. (*ALP* 3; *FW* 196.15–16)

The language continues to be relatively simple, with a strongly Irish English flavour, and word play is correspondingly restrained. "Starving my famine" plays on "starving/famine" and "famine/family," and Patrick McCarthy suggests that the reference to famine connects HCE "with the devastation of Ireland's land and people" (2007, 165). "To make his private linen public" plays on another binary opposition – and perhaps hints also at exhibitionism (McCarthy 2007, 165). Alliteration and repetition are effectively employed, "scorching" and "starving," "private" and "public." The fluvial series continues with the Italian Orcia, English Ching, Irish Tar, English Irving, and the Austrian Inn, as well as the Irish noun *linn* ("pool, pond, lake") and the Scots noun *linn* ("waterfall").

BECKETT: Me brûlant les mains et mourant de faim afin de donner au public son linge privé.

JOYCE: Brûlant mes mains et affamant ma faim pour laver en public son propre linge.

"Scorching my hand and starving my famine" becomes Beckett's rhythmical French "Me brûlant les mains et mourant de faim" ("Burning my hands and dying of hunger"), playing on the rhyming "mains" and "faim." The Belgian Our, the Mongolian Ur, and the Basque noun *ur* ("water") may be detected in "mourant." Joyce's "Brûlant mes mains et affamant ma faim" ("Burning my hands and starving my hunger") ignores these effects, preferring the paradoxical play on "affamant" and "faim," making hunger even hungrier. The scorching and starving "to make his private linen public" in Joyce's English leads to two different solutions. Beckett's "afin de donner au public son linge privé," continuing the rhyme of "mains" and "faim" with "afin" and "linge," aims "to give the public his private linen." Joyce's "pour laver en public son propre linge," playing instead on *propre* as meaning both "clean" and "one's own," and standing on its head the notion of washing dirty linen in public, aims "to wash his own, clean, linen in public." In both renderings, "linge" visually evokes for an English-speaker – though much less so for a French reader distracted by the expected pronunciation /lɛ̃ʒ/ – the English Lin, Austrian Inn, Thai Ing, Scottish Ling, and Dutch Linge, and even the Irish noun *linn* ("pool, pond, lake") and Scots noun *linn* ("waterfall") once again.

JOYCE: Mani arroste e trippe in fumo per mandar quei panni del diavolo in demonio pubblico.

SETTANNI: Mani in bracia e trippe in fumo per mandar quei panni del diavolo in demonio publico.

Joyce's Italian is once again strikingly adventurous, suggesting at a surface level "Hands roasted (*arrostire* 'to roast') and belly (*trippa*) smoking (*in fumo*) to send those damned clothes (*panni*) into the public domain," though the play on *dominio* ("domain") and "demonio" ("devil"), echoing "diavolo" ("devil"), combined with the roasting and smoking, adds a humorously infernal overtone unsounded in the original. The Arabic *ma* ("water") is appropriately present in the washerwoman's complaint about the state of her hands (*mani*). Serenella Zanotti (2002, 285) notes the play on the colloquial phrase *tutto fumo e niente arrosto* ("all smoke and no roast"), much promised, in other words, and nothing delivered. Settanni replaces the phrase "mani arroste" by "mani in bracia," playing on *bruciare* ("to scorch") and *braccia* ("arms") to suggest "hands scorched back to the wrists" as well as an evocation of the Nigerian Acha. The Indian river Pubb ceases to flow in Settanni's correction of "pubblico" to "publico."

[5] *Wallop it well with your battle and clean it.*
(*ALP* 3; *FW* 196.16–17)

The dactylic rhythm recurs particularly strongly in "*Wall*op it | *well* with your | *batt*le and | *clean* it," while the alliteration on "wallop" and "well" is striking. The phrase plays both on "well" as adverb and as water-related noun and on "battle" as meaning both a warlike engagement and an instrument for cleaning wet laundry, namely a beater, technically known also as a beetle or battledore. Rivers cited include the English Wallop Brook, Irish Allow, Canadian Battle, and English Lean and Leen.

> BECKETT: Tape dur avec ton battoir et nettoie-la.
> JOYCE: Fous dur ton battoir et nettoie-là.

Beckett's rendering of the energetic advice plays on the near rhyme of "battoir" and "nettoie," urging "Hit hard with your beater and clean it," and approximating for the ear of an English speaker the original dactylic rhythm, "Tape | *dur* a- | *vec* ton bat- | *toir* et net- | *toie*-la." Fluvial references to the Russian Tap, Thai Tapi, English Dour, and Portuguese Ave are to varying degrees detectable. Joyce's more idiomatic version is also more concise, suggesting, roughly, "Beat hard with your beater and clean it," and likewise approximating the rhythm of the original, "Fous | *dur* ton bat- | *toir* et net- | *toie*-là." The Tap and Tapi are dispensed with, while the Laotian Ou is added.

> JOYCE: Sbatacchiali duro e falli netti.
> SETTANNI: [*without change*]

The advice is transformed in Joyce's Italian, abandoning alliteration, changing the rhythm, pluralizing the direct object, evoking the Indian Bata, Spanish Douro, and Cornish Fal, and employing the verb *sbatacchiare* ("to slam, to wallop") into "Sbatacchiali duro e falli netti" ("Wallop them hard and make them clean").

[6] *My wrists are rwusty rubbing the mouldaw stains.*
(*ALP* 3; cf. *FW* 196.17–18: "are wrusty")

The speaker's wrists are as stiff as rusty hinges from protracted rubbing and scrubbing of our hero's polluted smalls, mouldy as they are from repeated damp stains of unmentionable character. Alliteration is effectively employed with "wrists" and the implied "rusty" and "rubbing," humorously suggesting both visual ("wrists" and an implied "wrusty") and auditory ("rusty" and "rubbing") variants.[1] The German Riss and Romanian Rus are fluvially present; the Serbian Ub and Indian Uben help with the rubbing; while the Czech Vltava, known in German as the Moldau, washes the mildew and mould of "mouldaw stains."

BECKETT: Mes poignets sont rouillés à force de farotter les taches de moussisure.
JOYCE: Mes poignets sont pointus à force de farotter les taches de moldiou.

Beckett's rendering of the washerwoman's plaint evokes the African Faro, American Mouse, and Luxembourg Sûre and Syr while suggesting "My wrists are rusty (*rouillé*) from rubbing (*frotter*) the stains (*taches*) of mould (*moisissure*)." Joyce follows Beckett relatively closely but with wrists that are now alliteratively "pointus" ("worn to a point") and stains that are now of "moldiou," conflating French *mildiou* ("mildew"), English *mould*, and the Czech Moldau. Joyce's rendering, with its additional alliteration, improves considerably in stylistic terms on Beckett's (more faithful) version.

JOYCE: Ho i polsi stronchi a rimestolare la muffa.
SETTANNI: Ne ho stronchi i polsi a rimestare la muffa.

Joyce's Italian plays on the verbs *rimescolare* ("to stir") and *rimestare* ("to stir up, drag up again") as well as the Irish river Muff to suggest "My wrists are maimed (*stronco* 'maimed') from stirring and stirring up the mould (*muffa*) and the mildew (*muffa*)." Settanni, whose emendations occasionally reveal a schoolmasterly pedantry, reduces the verbal conflation to a simple "rimestare" ("to stir up") – while arguably improving the rhythm. The Chinese noun *ho* ("river") appears in both; the original alliteration disappears in both.

[7] And the dneepers of wet and the gangres of sin in it! (*ALP* 3–4; *FW* 196.18)

The dactylic rhythm recurs very overtly in a tetrameter: "the | *dneep*ers of | *wet* and the | *gan*gres of | *sin* in it!" Rivers continue to flow,

1 The 1928 Gaige edition and 1930 Faber edition of *ALP* both have "rwusty." Higginson asserts that the emendation to "wrusty" (*FW* 196.17) is "without apparent authority" (1960, 99). Rose and O'Hanlon, however, accept the reading "wrusty" (*FW2* 154).

the Russian Dnieper, South African Vet, Indian Ganges, Thai Sin, and Irish Inny, while "dneepers" simultaneously implies deep rivers of vice and "gangres" the chancres and ulcerations of venereal excess and the putrefaction of a gangrene that is at least moral if not also physical. In all of this, the washerwomen's voices are sometimes individually distinguishable, and sometimes they blend and overlap into a single voice, as if that voice were really just the voice of ALP herself, talking to herself.

BECKETT: Elle a été noyée dans la débauche et gangerenée par le vice.
JOYCE: Quelle vilainerie mouillée et quelle gangerène de vice.

The bravura formulation of "the dneepers of wet and the gangres of sin in it" is relatively blandly served in both French renderings. Beckett describes the offending shirt as "drowned in debauchery and gangrened by vice." Joyce's version prefers to co-opt the German noun *Quelle* ("spring, well"), the French Vilaine, and the New Caledonian Mou and Laotian Ou to exclaim, literally, "What damp nastiness ('vilainerie') and what gangrene of vice." While both renderings retain the reference to the Ganges, both omit the Dnieper.

JOYCE: Com'è gangerenoso di turpida tabe!
SETTANNI: Com'è gangerenoso di turpida tabe.

Joyce's Italian, once again more daring than his French, abandons the Dnieper and retains the Ganges once again, and adds the German Rhine (Italian *Reno*) and Japanese Abe to suggest, roughly, "And him putrid with tabes, the shame of it!" The medical term *tabes* denotes a chronic bodily wasting away, associated, for example, with syphilis. The dactylic rhythm of the English is replicated exactly, with appropriate alliteration: "Com'è | *gan*gere- | *no*so di | *tur*pida | *ta*be." Settanni contents himself with substituting a period for Joyce's exclamation mark.

[8] Comments and Contexts

The idiomatic Irish flavour of Joyce's English is marked in this sequence. Beckett's French provides a solid foundation for Joyce's throughout, but in every excerpt Joyce effects an improvement, whether by smoothing out a rhythm [3.1, 3.7], restoring an alliterative effect [3.2, 3.6], producing a more colloquially idiomatic French [3.2, 3.5], or introducing an additional river or two [3.1, 3.3, 3.6]. Beckett, as is normal for a translator, adheres relatively faithfully to the original throughout, whereas Joyce demonstrates his freedom from any such constraint in, for example, "Je sais paroker les endroits qu'il aime à seillir, le mymyserable" [3.3]. One of the most striking English formulations, "the dneepers of wet and the gangres of sin in it" [3.7], is disappointingly flattened in French by both Beckett and Joyce.

The most noticeable feature of the sequence, however, is certainly the degree to which Joyce's Italian asserts the degree of its growing independence from the original text. The "awful old reppe," merely a "beau saalaud" in his French, becomes an Italian "lughero malandrone," while "the shirt of him" and "the dirt of it" become a flauntedly colourful and colourfully expressive "sudiciume de camiciaccia" – where the inclusion of the Neapolitan noun *ciume* and the pejorative ending *-accia* are further indications of Joyce's delight in the possibilities of the Italian language and its various dialects and levels [3.1]. More flamboyantly still, "I know by heart the places he likes to saale," already humorously but not extravagantly rendered in his French as "Je sais paroker les endroits qu'il aime à seillir," becomes in Italian the flauntedly extravagant "So ben io cosa quel macchiavuol" [3.3], breaking entirely new ground with the introduction of Machiavelli, a humorous example of literary ends justifying extraordinary means. Specifically Italian cultural references of various kinds – and the reference to Rossini's Figaro [3.2] is another in the present sequence – frequently departing radically from the original on a semantic level, will be a recurring feature of the Italian *ALP*.

Bosinelli argues (1996, 51) with reference to this particular extravagance that while Joyce's controlling presence during the French team translation occasionally involved an at least implicit element of censorship, correcting his collaborators' misunderstandings of what he had originally intended, his much more liberated practice in the Italian rendering is to function in various instances as an author rather than a translator – "freed of the bonds that the original imposes on a translation," as Bosinelli puts it[2] – aiming not at translatorial reproduction but at authorial re-production, still continuing obsessively to extend, unrestrainedly, creatively, if via Italian rather than via English, his still continuing "work in progress."

2 Joyce's Italian is "distaccato dai vincoli che l'originale pone alla traduzione" (Bosinelli 1996, 51).

Other than mechanically replacing Joyce's exclamation marks with periods throughout this sequence [3.1, 3.4, 3.7], Settanni expands "otto giorni di bucato" by two words to "son otto giorni di bel bucato," thus handily evoking two additional rivers, the Ono and the Elbe [3.2]. He replaces the phrase "mani arroste" ("hands roasted") by "mani in bracia," suggesting "hands scorched back to the wrists," while evoking the Nigerian Acha [3.4]. He adjusts Joyce's "rimestolare," which conflates *rimescolare* ("to stir") and *rimestare* ("to stir up, drag up again"), to a simple "rimestare," thus reducing the semantic complexity while arguably improving the rhythm [3.6] – and a schoolmasterly correction deprives Joyce's text of the Indian river Pubb.

4 Animal Sendai

What was it he did a tail at all on Animal Sendai? And how long was he under loch and neagh? It was put in the newses what he did, nicies and priers, the King fierceas Humphrey, with illysus distilling, exploits and all. But toms will till. I know he well. Temp untamed will hist for no man. As you spring so shall you neap. O, the roughty old rappe! Minxing marrage and making loof. (*ALP* 4; *FW* 196.18–24)

[1] What was it he did a tail at all on Animal Sendai? (*ALP* 4; *FW* 196.18–19)

HCE, we are given to understand, behaved (or may have behaved) in a completely animal fashion (motivating in passing, since many animals have tails, a modification of the Irish English *at all at all* to "a tail at all"), but certainly not as one might expect a well-behaved animal to conduct itself on Animal Sunday – namely the closest Sunday to the annual feast of St Francis of Assisi (4 October), on which animals are traditionally blessed in various Christian denominations. How it (or he) might be expected to behave on the banks of the Japanese river Sendai, the French Seine, or the Indian Dai is left to the reader's imagination – though the fact that *tail* is a colloquialism for sexual intercourse offers the imagination some assistance. It is of course possible that HCE's behaviour, animal as he was, was due to the fact that he was not himself, was perhaps even sick: the Sendai virus, known to veterinarians and Joyce scholars, is reported to cause specific health problems in the case of some animals. The fact that Plato posited the interconnectedness of all living things, including animals (and presumably even HCE), as constituting the *anima mundi*, "the soul of the world," may afford some small degree of punning collateral comfort to HCE's friends and admirers.

BECKETT: Mais, derrière tout, qu'est-ce qu'il fit le dimanche des Ramos?
JOYCE: Mais queue fit-il comme histoire quelle histoire la fête Fauve?

Beckett renders "a tail at all" as "derrière tout," playing on *après tout* ("after all") and *derrière* ("backside, tail"), with a bow to County Wicklow's river Derry, while wondering what it was our man did "le dimanche des Ramos," a conflation of the French *le Dimanche des Rameaux* and the Spanish *el Domingo de Ramos* (both meaning "on Palm Sunday," both literally "on the Sunday of Branches"), together with the Canadian Ram, Nigerian Amo, and Mexican Ramos rivers. The Sendai and its fluvial implications disappear.

Joyce's French imports a "tail" ("queue"), not to mention a penis (*queue* "cock"), and then a doubled "tale" ("histoire") into the question, suggesting "What's the story (*histoire*) of whatever it was he did during that business (*histoire*) on Animal Day?" – with the strong implication that whatever it was was likely of a sexual nature. Both Sendai and Sunday now disappear, replaced by an invented "Fête Fauve," a celebration (*fête*) that suggests the phrase *bête fauve* ("wild beast") as well as the French Auve and Portuguese Ave rivers. The dactylic rhythm is pronounced, at least to the ear of an English-speaker, "*Mais* queue fit- | *il* comme his- | *toire* quelle his- | *toire* la fête | *Fauve*?"

JOYCE: Ma che cozzo ha fotto, per amara di donna, quel di' di Belvana?
SETTANNI: Ma che cospito ha fotto, per amara di donna, quel di' di Belvana?

Joyce's Italian rendering, immediately incorporating the Arabic *ma* ("water"), is considerably more drastic than either his English or his French. The underlying question *che cosa ha fatto?* ("What did he do?"), as Jacqueline Risset notes (1984, 18), has *cosa* ("thing") altered to "cozzo" ("cock, penis") and *fatto* ("done") changed to "fotto" ("fucked"), yielding, roughly, a very robust "What the fuck did he fucking do?" In a rapid change of exclamatory register, an incredulous *per amore di dio* ("for the love of God") becomes "per amara di donna," love (*amore*) yielding to "bitterness" (*amaro*) and the good Lord giving way to his Lady mother ("donna"), fluvially aided and abetted by the Romanian Amara and the Russian Don. Whatever the old cheb did, he did it on the "di' di Belvana," a day (*di*) named for a "wild animal" (*belva*), literally or figuratively, while simultaneously evoking, in a bravura display of hydronomous flamboyance, the Scottish, Welsh, English, Irish, and Australian Dee, English Dibb, Canadian Bell and Belle, Estonian Elva, Scottish Elvan, Romanian Vâna, American Ana, and Thai Na rivers, not to mention Anna Livia herself, a hint of the Celtic May Day festival Beltane (Irish *Bealtaine*), two nouns meaning "river" (Norwegian *elv*, Danish *elve*), and one noun meaning "water" (Norwegian *vann*).

Settanni's emendation cautiously reduces the potential for offending readers (especially the not easily amused government censors of a very right-wing Roman Catholic state) by changing "che cozzo" to "che cospito," thus conflating the offending member and the inoffensive expression *caspita* ("for heaven's sake") – but not going so far as to replace "fotto" ("fucked") by "fatto" ("done") (Risset 1984, 18). Settanni's version, evoking in passing the Philippine river Pito, would thus suggest, roughly, "What the hell did he fucking do?"

[2] *And how long was he under loch and neagh?* (*ALP* 4; *FW* 196.19–20)

At a surface level, the question "And how long was he under loch and neagh?" is clearly just how long this paragon of depravity must have spent (or should have spent) under lock and key for his criminal activities – ideally, for example, buried deep under Lough Neagh, the largest (though not the deepest) lake in Ireland. The particular location is suggestive of indefinitely extended incarceration, for Lough Neagh was once held to offer access to the Celtic underworld. The Old Irish name, *Loch nEchach* ("the lake of Eochu"), referred to one of the lords of that underworld, Eochu mac Maireda (MacKillop 1998, 187) – whose name is related to Old Irish *ech* ("horse"), thus by happy linguistic coincidence clearly anticipating ECH, alias HCE.[1] That *Neagh* and *neigh* are perfect homophones is just one more example of life imitating *Finnegans Wake*. That Lough Neagh is the specific location of the old cheb's submarine incarceration also suggests an ironic reference to Thomas Moore's romanticized vision of a glorious Irish past in his hugely popular poem

1 George Cinclair Gibson, citing R.A.S. Macalister's statement (1919, 331) that numerous ancient Irish rulers bore the name Eochu, and that that name derives from the noun *ech* ("horse"), stretches that statement considerably by asserting that the actual name of the Irish "God-King" is "ECH" (2005, 178) – the capitals, of course, immediately and conveniently evoking Joyce's HCE.

"Let Erin Remember the Days of Old," in which a nostalgic fisherman straying by the evening shore "sees the round towers of other days in the waves beneath him shining."

BECKETT: Hélac! sombien de cachot sans bourger?
JOYCE: Combien resta-t-il au bloch et sous nlefs?

As for how long the old cheb was "under loch and neagh," Beckett's rendering opens with an interjection that conflates a pseudo-sympathetic *hélas* ("alas") and, appropriately, a French *lac* ("lake"), then proceeds to conflate *combien de cachot sans bouger?* ("how much jail-time without parole?") and a series of river references to the French Somme, various North American waterways named Cache River and Cache Creek, and the Belgian Our, accompanied by the Basque *ur* ("water").

Joyce's French wonders instead how long our hero unwillingly spent "au bloch et sous nlefs," suggesting "under lock and key," playing on *rester* ("to stay") and *gonfler à bloc* ("raring to go"), and conflating French *bloc* ("prison, nick"), German *Loch* ("hole, prison, clink"), and English *loch* and *lock,* before combining *sous clé* ("locked up"), and, since the noun *clé* ("key") was formerly spelled *clef,* a complementary maritime *nef* ("ship)," the latter usually pronounced /nɛf/, but here, in a good cause, pronounced as /nɛ/, a near homophone of "Neagh." The French rivers Aube ("au b-") and Saône ("sous n-") are recruited in passing. A loose dactylic rhythm is once again in evidence, "Com- | *bien* resta- | *t-il* au | *bloch* et sous | *nlefs*?"

JOYCE: E quanto rimase dai frati Branca?
SETTANNI: E quanto rimase dai fratelli Branca?

Joyce's Italian, changing tack somewhat, and evoking the Água Branca river of Brazil rather than Ireland's Lough Neagh, wonders how long our hero remained (*rimanere* "to remain") in the custody of the police, colloquially and not particularly respectfully designated, as Risset points out (1984, 18), the *Frati Branca,* "the Brothers Grab." (Italian *branca* means "claw," whereas Portuguese *branca* means "white," as in the river name Água Branca, "white water.")

Settanni cautiously emends "frati" to "fratelli," most likely in this case in order to avoid potential offence to ecclesiastical authorities, for while *frati* unambiguously denotes brothers in a religious community, *fratelli* includes not only clerics but also, more harmlessly, siblings. Italian Joyce's humorously implied suggestion of a repressive community of belligerent friars becomes for Settanni, by implication, merely a family of truculent siblings. Carol O'Sullivan also points out the humorous reference to the Fratelli Branca distillery of Milan, which has been producing its well-known digestive liqueur Fernet Branca since 1845 (2006, 180).

***[3] It was put in the newses what he did, nicies and priers, the King fierceas Humphrey, with illysus distilling, exploits and all.* (*ALP* 4; *FW* 196.20–2)**

One of the most complex sentences so far refers, as confusedly related by the knowledgeable washerwoman, to a rumoured report that HCE was at some point involved in legal proceedings and obliged to defend himself in a court of law against a variety of charges. What he did (or did not do) was allegedly reported not just in one ("news") but in several newspapers ("newses"). Legal terminology was understandably in evidence, such as a writ of *nisi prius* to summon jurors, should the matter "not already" (Latin *nisi prius*) be settled by a judge sitting alone. While some people may be nice ("nicies"), of course, including a certain two nice girls already of our acquaintance, others are "priers," poking and prying into other people's affairs, especially, one may safely assume, in the Fiendish Park. The trial was reported as the King versus Humphrey, and one side was as fierce as the other in making their case. Our Humphrey, himself to some extent already arguably a "king" (Spanish *rey*), and thus to some extent also his own accuser, was apparently accused, presumably among other "exploits," of "illysus distilling," possibly the illicit distilling of whiskey, possibly, under another name, the illicit distilling of a novel, one *Ulysses* (Tindall 1996, 142). It may or may not have been a good sign that a Charles Humphreys, as has variously been pointed out, served as the solicitor defending another famous Irishman once famously prosecuted (and convicted) for indecency, namely Oscar Wilde. Aquatic references include Minnesota's Prior Lake, while rivers flow in torrential abundance, including the Scottish Ewse, Polish Neisse, Nepalese Nisi, Australian King, French Fier, Greek Ilissos, Austrian Ill, French Ill and Lys, English Exe, and even the Hyssus of ancient Pontus.

BECKETT: On a lu dans les jurneaux ce qu'il fit, nisi et prius, le roi contre Husparey, avec toute l'histoire du faux saônage et des exploits.

JOYCE: C'était dans les jurnaux le grabuge qu'il fit, les attendus qhuantes et les lus approuvés, le roi fiersus Onfroy avec toute l'histoire du faux saônage, les exploits illycite et le reste.

Beckett's French suggests that one could have read for oneself in the newspapers (*journaux*) what our hero did, while duly allowing for legal objections on questions of "unless" ("nisi") and "first of all" ("prius") and the like, the King against a Humphrey so full of arrogance and impudence (Hebrew *huspa* "chutzpah") as to be barely recognizable, digging up the whole story of his dirty dealings, no longer in illicit distilling as in Joyce's English but, unexpectedly, in contraband salt (*faux-saunage*), not to mention the existence of various legal "writs" (*exploits*) regarding other exploits. Rivers evoked include the Russian Ona ("on a lu"), the South Sudanese Jur, Mongolian Ur, and Scandinavian Nea (all in "jurneaux," together with the French *eaux* "waters"), the Canadian Spar Brook ("Husparey"), and the French Saône ("faux saônage").

Joyce's French gleefully gilds the linguistic lily offered by Beckett, mixing and mangling a convoluted clutter of French and Latin legal terminology. One could now have read in the same shoddy newspapers ("jurnaux" that fall one vowel short of real *journaux*) no doubt garbled accounts of the hullabaloo ("grabuge") caused by the whole affair of "le roi fiersus Onfroy," a now Frenchified accused still at least partially his own accuser (early modern French *roy* "king"). Legal matters of dispute involved in the proceedings are now reported to have included discussion of the "grounds for a decision" (*les attendus d'un jugement*) and various niceties of both *nisi* and *prius*, the former involving "whereas" (*attendu que*) and the latter the *status quo ante*, such details accompanied no doubt by impatient "booing" (*huant*) from the vulgar, not to mention multiple documents regarding "laws passed" (*les lois approuvées*) and duly stamped "read and approved" (*lu et approuvé*). Illicit dealings in contraband salt are still cited (*y cité*) among his illicit exploits and all the rest. Rivers evoked now include the South Sudanese Jur, Mongolian Ur, and Russian Urna ("jurnaux"), the Ghanaian Abu and Polish Bug ("grabuge"), the French Fier ("fiersus"), Scottish Roy ("Onfroy"), and French Saône ("saônage"), while the Greek Ilissos, Austrian Ill, and French Lys reappear discreetly ("illycite") in the watery background.

> JOYCE. Il Marco Oraglio l'ha ben strombazzato, l'attesache, laonta e tutto, la sporciaquerela e l'eccitazioni e le nevandezze di quell'entitristo.
> SETTANNI: [*without change*]

Joyce's Italian adjusts the name of an actual Roman publication that is humorously asserted to have published details of HCE's trial and tribulations. *Marco Aurelio* was one of the few Italian satirical journals of the late 1930s, named for the second-century Roman emperor Marcus Aurelius, a scholar and philosopher irreverently transformed here into a donkey: "Oraglio" includes the noun *raglio* ("bray"), while "strombazzato" is "trumpeted, brayed" (Bosinelli 1998b, 196). The journal is clearly not the only target of Joyce's wit, however, and the reference was in fact a potentially dangerous one that could certainly have led to the final suppression of *Prospettive*, which was already viewed with suspicion by the fascist authorities.

Benito Mussolini had already been dictator for the previous two decades and made no bones about his vision of himself as glorious leader of a new Roman Empire. The reference to a Roman emperor could therefore certainly be understood as a satiric reference to the authoritarian *Duce* as a would-be emperor – but one who, unlike his philosopher predecessor, merely brayed like a donkey. In a letter to Helen Joyce from Paris on 28 August 1935 Joyce had already privately mocked Mussolini, then clearly spoiling for war with Abyssinia: "May the 17 devils take Muscoloni and the Alibiscindians" (*L* 1, 381). Since *muscoloni* means "great big muscles" (*muscolo* "muscle"), Mussolini is disrespectfully transformed into a comic-book bully, Mister Muscle. Surprisingly, Settanni, a would-be censor, allowed the potentially inflammatory reference to "Marco Oraglio" (presumably not noticing the political implication) to appear unchanged in the published version.

At any rate, the news source in question allegedly trumpeted and brayed the whole affair, both the general "expectation" (*attesa*) of an appalled public and all the associated considerations (*atteso che* "considering that"), the "shame" and "disgrace" (*la onta*) and the "wherefore" (*laonde*) of it all, the legal action taken (*sporgere querela* "to take legal action") against filth (*sporcizia*), the excitement (*eccitazione*) generated by "summons" (*citazione*) and "subpoena" (*citazione*), and the general goings on (*andazzo*) of this sad (*triste*) and "wicked" (*tristo*) "being" (*ente*) who is in fact nothing short of an only lightly disguised antichrist ("entitristo").

Zanotti (2002, 283) points out the marked adherence of the sentence to the rules of Italian prosody in consisting successively of a hendecasyllable ("Il *Mar*co O*ra*glio l'ha *ben* strombaz*za*to"), a *novenario* or nonasyllable ("l'at*tesa*che, lao*n*ta e *tut*to"), another hendecasyllable ("la *spor*ciaque*re*la e *l'*eccitazi*o*ni"), and a double *senario* or hexasyllable ("e *le* nevan*dez*ze di *quell'*entit*ri*sto"). Rivers evoked include the Russian Or and Ugandan Ora ("Oraglio"), Italian Lao ("laonta"), Indian Tut ("tutto"), Italian Orcia and American Ela ("sporciaquerela"), Russian Neva ("nevandezze"), and English Ellen ("quell'entitristo").

[4] But toms will till. I know he well. Temp untamed
will hist for no man. As you spring so shall you neap.
(*ALP* 4; *FW* 196.22–3)

Readers are treated on one level to a trio of popular maxims: time will tell (as one knows it will), time and tide wait for no man, and as you sow so shall you reap. Peeping toms will also tell, as certainly appears to have happened in HCE's case. Tindall, observing that Joyce "always insisted that Eliot stole *The Waste Land* from *Ulysses*," suggests that, on another level, "toms will till" consequently also refers to "peeping Tom Eliot telling *Ulysses* over for the sake of his till in *The Waste Land*" (1996, 60, 142). And while time may very well tell, time untold and thus untamed by authorized chroniclers will never become narratively subdued history from a proper perspective, obediently posing no more awkward questions, dutifully falling silent ("hist") on demand. The underlying *tell* and *will* of "till" and "well" change places to allow a reference to a well of water, and "spring" and "neap" likewise provide obvious aquatic references, while simultaneously evoking sowing and reaping as well as the general springing and leaping one might expect in the spring of the year. Fluvial references to the Russian Tom, American Toms, and English Till are readily to hand, as the predominant rhythm temporarily becomes iambic, quickly followed by others to the Irish Tempo, English Thames ("Temp untamed"), American Spring, and Scandinavian Nea.

BECKETT: Tout sera manafeste dans l'avonir, j'en suis sura. Le temps perdu ne se retrouve jamais. On récolte ce qu'on a semé.

JOYCE: Le tems le dira. Je suis sûr de lui. Le tomps qu'on ne dompte n'attend pour personne. Tu sèmes l'avon, tu récoltes l'eaurage.

For Beckett's French, the future (*l'avenir*) will make everything "manifest" (*manifeste*), assisted in this endeavour by the English river Avon and the Russian Mana, "I am sure (*sûr*) of it," a certainty shared by the Luxembourg Sûre and Russian Sura. Time lost ("Le temps perdu") can never be regained, the humorous nod to Proust's meganovel accompanied by fluvial references to the Caribbean Perdu Temps, the English and Irish Dun ("-du n-") rivers, and the French Ouve. And, abandoning wordplay, but remembering the Russian Ona ("-on a") and English Sem, one reaps what one has sown. Oddly enough, Beckett chooses to ignore the biblical echo in the final phrase.

For Joyce's French, "time (*le temps*) will tell (*le dira*)," and so, we infer, will the Thames ("tems") and the Luxembourg Sûre. "I am sure of him," one gossip asserts of HCE. With Beckett's reference to Proust discarded, the time ("le tomps") one fails "to tame" (*dompter*) waits for no man, and the same is true of the Russian river Tom. A dactylic rhythm is once again strongly in evidence, reinforced by internal rhyme and near-rhyme: "Le | *tomps* qu'on ne | *dompte* n'at- | *tend* pour per- | *sonne*." Unlike Beckett, Joyce takes full advantage of the biblical reference, in which Hosea 8:7 admonishes us that those who have sown the wind will reap the whirlwind and Osée 8:7 in French likewise that "qui sème le vent récolte la tempète." For French Joyce, it is apparently also the case that if you sow the wind (*le vent*) or even oats (*l'avoine*) by the banks of the English river Avon ("l'avon"), you can expect to reap a whirlwind (*orage*) of raging water ("eaurage"). Ferrer and Aubert comment on the difference between Beckett's version and Joyce's, in which "the beginning is deliberately flattened, made more idiomatic, and stripped of the pun on the Avon river, to save it for the very nice culminating formula" (1998, 182).

JOYCE: Ma chi fa il rio, paga il fio. Chi se mena vanto, raccatta trambusto.
E ciò sa il suo dottore.
SETTANNI: [*without change*]

Jacqueline Risset has noted that Joyce's Italian plays on many more proverbial phrases than does his original English (1973, 49). Here he blithely ignores the semantic content of the English text while continuing (at least ostensibly) to dispense aphoristic nuggets of popular wisdom, though with a significant change of register, the focus now more on the effects of failing to observe social proprieties (Bosinelli 1998b, 195). The first such nugget, a rhyming "Ma chi fa il rio, paga il fio," asserts that he who is wicked (*rio*) or commits sin (*rio*) or more specifically plays around (*fare il rio*) "pays the price" (*fio* "penalty"). The versatile Italian noun *rio* also means "brook" and "canal," and the helpful apothegm also invokes the Asian river Ma, the Arabic noun *ma* ("water"), and the Spanish *río* ("river").

Moreover, "he who boasts (*menare vanto* 'to boast') attracts (*raccattare* 'to gather') trouble (*trambusto* 'turmoil')." The statement is also a play on "Chi semina vento raccoglie tempestà" (Lobner 1986, 87), "He who sows the wind reaps the whirlwind," a proverbial version of the Italian biblical wisdom of Osea 8:7. Older and wiser heads already know these things, of course, as a humorously deployed tag from Dante has it, "E ciò sa il suo dottore" ("and this his teacher knows"). The context is the fifth canto of the *Inferno*, where Dante, led by his mentor Virgil, meets the doomed lovers Paolo and Francesca and is dolefully assured by the latter that there is "nessun maggior dolore / che ricordarsi del tempo felice / nella miseria; e ciò sa 'l tuo dottore" (*Inferno* 5.121–3), "There is no greater sorrow / than thinking back upon a happy time / in misery – and this your teacher knows" (Mandelbaum 1982, 47), the teacher in question being Virgil.

Zanotti (2002, 283) once again points out Joyce's marked adherence to the rules of Italian prosody in constructing a *novenario* or nonasyllable ("Ma *chi* fa il *rio*, *pa*ga il *fio*"), followed by a double *senario* or hexasyllable ("Chi *se* mena *van*to, rac*cat*ta tram*bus*to"). The dactylic rhythm immediately strikes the anglophone reader.

[5] O, the roughty old rappe! Minxing marrage and making loof. **(*ALP* 4; *FW* 196.24)**

The "awful old reppe" has graduated to "roughty old rappe." Colloquially, a *rep* is a reprobate; a *rip* is a worthless, dissolute fellow (*OED*), though more usually applied in Ireland to a woman rather than a man; and a *rap*, as used by Swift in the *Drapier's Letters*, is a bad or counterfeit coin (*OED*). None of these epithets redounds to the credit of the egregious HCE, who, for his part, rep, rip, or rap, may or may not care a rap. "Roughty" includes "right" – HCE as a "right old rep" – and "raughty" (rhyming with "naughty" and defined by the *OED* as "fine, splendid, jolly, etc.") as well as "rough," while evoking in passing the Rough River of Kentucky, the Roughty River of County Kerry, the French Reppe again, the German Rappach (*Ach* "river"), and by fluvial extension even the Scottish Rappach Water.

The old reprobate adds to his long list of reported failures and derelictions, as enthusiastically calculated by our delightedly scandalized washerwomen, the fact that he is "minxing marrage and making loof," offering as a surface meaning the fact that he is "mixing marriage and making love," the former apparently excluding the latter. Marriage, of course, or, at any rate, "marrage," can be a complicated affair. One need only turn to French for confirmation: it can clearly offer one a good time (*se marrer* "to have a good time"), it can even make a person laugh (*faire marrer quelqu'un* "to make somebody laugh"), but one can also, in the long run, become fed up with it (*en avoir marre* "to be fed up with"). The fact that a modern "minx" is a pertly impudent girl, meanwhile, while in earlier days a minx was nothing less than a wanton woman, might well offer some distraction, especially for a person fascinated (in a Dublin park, for example) by female micturition (Latin *minxi* "I made water"). Scarcely any wonder if such a person might decide, possibly while himself urinating in a convenient loo, to luff his sail and steer his ship closer to the wind. The Russian Loo and Canadian Loof are in sympathetic fluvial attendance.

BECKETT: Ô le vieux polisson! Mari mixte et amant acharné.
JOYCE: O ce vieux rot de canail. Maréage mixte ou amour en thémise.

For Beckett, the roughty old rappe is a "vieux polisson," a "dirty old scoundrel," a husband (*mari*) whose performance in a decidedly mixed marriage (*mariage mixte*) is indeed mixed at best, while he can otherwise and elsewhere play the role of a passionate lover (*amant acharné*). His activities are disapprovingly attended by the Italian Po, Chinese Li, French Isson, and English Char. The introductory "Ô" repeats the first word of *ALP* and recaptures its resonances.

For Joyce's own French, he is a "vieux rot de canail" ("rot de" suggested by "roughty"), a less than complimentary compilation of *rot* ("belch") and *canaille* ("scoundrel"), navigating between the less than exciting tidal (*marée* "tide") pools (*mare* "pool") of a mixed "maréage" and the anticipated delights of fondling an alternative object of desire, ideally clad for example in a baby doll nightdress (*chemise d'amour*), and possibly even on the romantic banks of the English Thames (French *Tamise*), a river preceded in this scenario by the German Rot, Indonesian Anai, Egyptian Nile, Belgian Our, and Mongolian Ur, the latter accompanied as usual by the Basque noun *ur* ("water"). The opening "O" once again recalls the first word of *ALP* – and thus ALP herself, partner in this "maréage mixte."

JOYCE: Forcadea, che carogna! Bene gli stanno, le postribolazioni.
SETTANNI: [*without change*]

Joyce's Italian begins with a colourful oath, "forcadea," conflating an already adequately colourful, not to mention blasphemous *porco dio* (literally, "pig of a god"), with *forca* ("gallows") and *dea* ("goddess"), and continues with "che carogna," giving us CHE as well as *che carogna* ("what a swine"), while hinting at the Scottish Carron and the Venezuelan Caroní. Any subsequent (*pos-*) trials and tribulations (*tribolazioni*) experienced after visits to the brothel (*postribolo*) just serve the old scoundrel right (*bene gli stanno*). The brothel itself is fluvially associated with the English Rib, Swiss Ribo, and Japanese Ibo.

[6] Comments and Contexts

Joyce's French is less dependent on Beckett's rendering in this sequence, though still adopting a number of the translational solutions offered. The English "a tail at all" [4.1] leads in Beckett's French, "derrière tout," to no more than a glimpse of a backside, mildly sexualized in its turn by Joyce's "queue fit-il," substituting a French penis for a French backside [4.1]. The predatory implications of "Animal Sendai" disappear in Beckett's version, reappearing in Joyce's French as "la Fête Fauve" [4.1], and Beckett's "Hélac! sombien de cachot sans bourger?" is significantly improved by Joyce's much bolder "Combien resta-t-il au bloch et sous nlefs?" [4.2]. Joyce happily accepts Beckett's unexpected suggestion that HCE was also trafficking in contraband salt (*faux-saunage*), while otherwise developing that rendering with some extravagance [4.3]. Beckett's humorous invocation of Proust ("Le temps perdu ne se retrouve jamais") is discarded by Joyce, who for once prefers to stay closer to the original text [4.4]. "The roughty old rappe" is given a quite different treatment in the two French versions, Beckett opting for a "vieux polisson," Joyce for a "vieux rot de canail" [4.5].

Joyce's Italian "che cozzo ha fotto" [4.1] is an example of the fact that overtly sexual references are frequently much more drastic in his Italian than in either his English or his French. His "E quanto rimase dai frati Branca?" for "And how long was he under loch and neagh?" [4.2] is another indication of his entire willingness to deviate from his own original text. The same is true of the introduction of "Il Marco Oraglio" [4.3], which also continues to demonstrate his very evident intention to construct a specifically *Italian* version of *ALP*, with a whole gamut of specifically Italian references in different registers, from popular sayings and proverbs (or quasi-proverbs) [4.4] to Dante [4.4], from colourfully blasphemous oaths [4.5] to overt political barbs aimed, none too cautiously, at Mussolini's fascist regime and even the *Duce* himself [4.3]. Fluvially, meanwhile, the "di' di Belvana" [4.1] generates more than a dozen rivers, including the Scottish, Welsh, English, Irish, and Australian Dee, English Dibb, Canadian Bell and Belle, Estonian Elva, Scottish Elvan, Romanian Vâna, American Ana, and Thai Na.

Joyce's provocatively overt sexual references are regularly toned down by Settanni, who begins in this sequence by cautiously reducing the potential for offence by changing the robust "che cozzo" to a more discreet "che cospito" [4.1]. He also tones down potential offence to the very right-wing Italian ecclesiastical authorities, such as in this case the reference to the "Frati Branca," changed by him to the "fratelli Branca" [4.2]. Despite an apparent intention also to avoid possible political offence to the Italian fascist party and their leader, he occasionally surprises, as in the potentially dangerous reference to Mussolini as "Marco Oraglio" [4.3], by leaving the reference unchanged.

5 Duke Alien

Reeve Gootch was right and Reeve Drughad was wrong! And the cut of him! And the strut of him! How he used to hold his head as high as a howeth, the famous eld duke alien, with a hump of grandeur on him like a walking rat. And his derry's own drawl and his corks-own blather and his doubling stutter and his gull-away swank. Ask Lictor Hackett or Lector Reade or Garda Growley or the Boy with the Billyclub. How elster is he a called at all? Huges Caput Early-fouler? (*ALP* 4; cf. *FW* 197.01–8).

[1] Reeve Gootch was right and Reeve Drughad was wrong! (*ALP* 4; cf. *FW* 197.01: "was sinistrous!")

Yet another of HCE's multifarious failings, as unsparingly identified by the rigorous washerwomen, appears to be that he is incapable of telling right from wrong, or indeed, if it comes to that, right from left. This particular failing is once again expressed in fluvial terms.

The 1928 text of *ALP* asserts in relatively simple terms that "Reeve Gootch was right and Reeve Drughad was wrong." Higginson notes (1960, 109) that the uncomplicated adjective "wrong" was emended in the 1930 Faber text (and in *FW*) to "sinistrous." The original assertion, as read, may be understood either as personal (one person was right and another was not) or as complicatedly fluvial (a left bank was right and a right bank, for whatever reason, presented a problem of some sort) or, of course, both. "Reeve," while evoking the Irish Lough Ree, combines a French *rive* ("riverbank") and the English title of a local official, a reeve. "Gootch" ostensibly provides this official with a surname, while simultaneously suggesting French *gauche* ("left") and offering faint hints of the Kenyan Gucha and Canadian Goose rivers. "Reeve Drughad" is both a second named official and suggests a combination of French *droit* ("right"), Irish *droichead* /'drɪhəd/ ("bridge") – Higginson notes that "Drughad" was originally "Droched" (1960, 109) – and the waters of the Irish Drogheda Bay and the Canadian Drogheda Lake, as well as hints of the English Uck and Indian Gad. At double and triple removes, the Esperanto *rugha* /'rudʒa/ ("red") adds the American Red River orthographically and the Romanian Ruja /'ruʒa/ phonetically. The rightness of the left bank is left undistorted, but the eventual progress of the right bank from merely "wrong" to the much more interesting "sinistrous" introduces an archaic English term suggesting "inauspicious" as well as playing the literal meaning of Latin *sinister* ("left") against its standard modern English meaning. For an Irish ear, meanwhile, remembering accounts of Oliver Cromwell's Irish campaign of the 1600s, any suggestion of Drogheda evokes the butchery of war, while hooch and drugs appear to be contributory factors of the hostilities hinted at here.

The situation of the two "reeves" on opposite banks suggests the relevance of the archaic verb *to reave* (to rob, to despoil), reminiscent of medieval robber barons on opposite banks of, for example, the German Rhine, reaving left and right, regardless of right or wrong. The rival "reeves" may also be taken as referring to HCE's warring sons, the rival twins Shem and Shaun. Specifically, Reeve Gootch and Reeve Drughad refer to Shem and Shaun respectively if we think we are talking about the *rive gauche* and *rive droite* of the Seine – but to Shaun and Shem respectively if we think we are talking about the left and right banks of the Liffey, for, as Louis Mink has pointed out, Shem is associated in the larger context of *Finnegans Wake* as a whole with the south side of both the Liffey (right bank) and the Seine (left bank, *rive gauche*) and Shaun correspondingly with the north side of both the Liffey (left bank) and the Seine (right bank, *rive droite*), while the two together, Reeve Gootch and Reeve Drughad combined, add up to HCE, "who as the city itself combines the often opposite characteristics of his twin sons" (Mink 1978, xxiv).

BECKETT: Rive gauche était droite et rive druite était sinistre.
JOYCE: Sbire Kauche était droit mais Sbire Troyt senestre.

For Beckett's "Rive gauche était droite et rive druite était sinistre," the context is primarily fluvial, with the *rive gauche* right but the *rive droite*, though allowing a passing reference to the Vietnamese Rui river, no longer just "wrong" but unambiguously "sinister," already anticipating the development to "sinistrous" in *Finnegans Wake.*

For Joyce, in a play on linguistic rather than martial opposition, namely that of voiced and unvoiced stops, Reeve Gootch and Reeve Drughad become "Sbire Kauche" and "Sbire Troyt." "Sbire" combines the colloquial French *sbire* ("thuggish policeman") and its hostile implications, the standard French *spire* ("swirl"), as of water, and the Rhodesian river Biri, while "Kauche" combines French *gauche* and, appropriately for the nocturnal world of the *Wake*, the suggested beginning of a *cauchemar* ("nightmare"). "Troyt" is not only *droit* but evokes in passing the "strait" (*détroit*) and narrow Detroit River of North America, while gesturing towards ancient wars between Greeks and Trojans. As in the original, "droit" is undistorted, but Beckett's modern French *sinistre* becomes Joyce's Old French *senestre*, emphasizing the rivalry theme by the use of the technical heraldic term for features on the left of a shield – the shield bearer's left, that is to say, while for an opponent the same features are on the right (O'Shea 1986, 130). The Irish river Shannon, which appeared on the Greek geographer Ptolemy's second-century map of Ireland as *Senos*, puts in a discreet appearance, accompanied by the French Seine and Scottish Ness.

> JOYCE: Ha regiona Ciulli, e Piesse pure, che le prove dirotte non mancano mica.
> SETTANNI: [*without change*]

Joyce's Italian appears to ignore the riverbanks altogether, opting instead for a completely and extravagantly rewritten version. In it, Reeve Gootch and Reeve Drughad give place to (or are perhaps renamed as) Ciulli and Piesse, the former name not uncommon in Italy as a family name, the latter a somewhat less common English surname. (The name Chully also exists as an English-language surname, apparently of Indian origin. The combination carries a faint suggestion of an invented comic duo – as in Chully and Pease, à la Mutt and Jute.) As to who may be in the right (or the right place) and who not, Ciulli's name seems to suggest that whether one or the other is "here or there" (*ci o li*) is in fact not of any great importance. Joyce's cryptic formulation is readable as implying "Ciulli is right (*ha ragione*), and Piesse too (*pure*), that direct proofs (*prove dirette*) are not at all lacking (*non mancano mica*)."

Alternatively, and undermining any such assumed certainty, it is readable as "Ciulli is right, and Piesse too, even if (*se pure*) direct proofs are not at all lacking," implying, that is to say, "even if direct proofs *to the contrary* are not at all lacking." The nouns *ragione* ("reason") and *regione* ("region") are conflated, meanwhile, as are the adjectives *diretto* ("direct") and *dirotto* ("copious"), the latter commonly occurring in the idiom *piovere a dirotto* ("raining cats and dogs"), while the English name Piesse is clearly readable in the same context as punningly suggesting English *pee* and *piss*.[1] Water, that is to say, whether as rain or as urine, is appropriately present, and evocations of a whole spate of rivers are duly detectable, including the Afghan Hari, Swiss Giona, Thai Chi, Indian Ull, Scottish Ullie, Thai Pi, German Esse, and English Ure, as well as the medieval Spanish Ove (the modern Eo), the Dutch Rotte, and the Mica Dam of British Columbia.

[2] And the cut of him! And the strut of him! How he used to hold his head as high as a howeth, the famous eld duke alien, with a hump of grandeur on him like a walking rat. **(*ALP* 4; cf. *FW* 197.01–4: "a walking wiesel rat")**

Yet another of HCE's shortcomings is his ridiculous conviction of his own importance in the scheme of things, preening and strutting, alliteratively (and trochaically) holding his head not just as high as a house, but as high as Howth Head itself, watered here by the Nigerian river Owe. Readers of *ALP* in 1928 would not necessarily have been aware that Howth Head was to figure in *Finnegans Wake* as the huge head of the sleeping giant Finn MacCool, a mythological avatar of HCE.

The "eld duke" suggests a faint hint of *eldritch* ("weird, unnatural") as well as *old*, while coopting the German river Elde – and an alien is one who, like HCE in many people's estimation, belongs elsewhere. His "hump of grandeur" is onomastically reflected in his given name, Humphrey, and in *Finnegans Wake* it will also be revealed that he is in fact a hunchback. The Canadian and English Rat and the Romanian Rât rivers put in appropriately rodent-flavoured appearances, accompanied

1 The obvious urinary pun notwithstanding, the English name Piesse or Pisse appears in fact to be a variant of *Peace* or *Pearce* (Hanks et al. 2002, 481, 487). A possible corruption of *Pius* has also been suggested (Lower 1988, 267).

by the North American Río Grande. A splendidly alliterative "wiesel," combining a hump-backed weasel and the Polish Vistula (*Wisła* in Polish) in "a walking wiesel rat," was added only in *Finnegans Wake* and does not appear in either the 1928 or 1930 text of *ALP*.

The "duke alien" is also the Deucalion of Greek mythology, the Hellenic counterpart of the biblical Noah: Deucalion and his wife Pyrrha, having built an ark on the advice of Deucalion's father Prometheus, were the sole survivors of a flood unleashed upon the pre-Greek Pelasgians, found impious by an angry Zeus. Landing on the shores of Thessaly, Deucalion and Pyrrha eventually, following the gods' instructions, produced a new and purer race, the Greeks. The name Deucalion (Greek *Deukaliôn*) appears, according to Liddell and Scott, to combine the elements "new wine" and "sailor" – from *deukos*, a variant of *gleukos* ("sweet new wine") and *halieus* ("sailor"). Deucalion thus also shares with the biblical Noah the combination of wine and water, since the sailor Noah is also held to be the first cultivator (and over-enthusiastic consumer) of wine (Genesis 9:20–1). The combination (with an appropriate Irish substitution for wine) is also an appropriate one for HCE, a publican by trade (as will emerge in *Finnegans Wake*) and an imputed arrival from overseas by origin.

A secondary competitor for the title of "duke alien" is Napoleon's nemesis, the Duke of Wellington, Arthur Wellesley (1769–1852), who though born in Dublin is famously reported to have rejected the notion that he was Irish – thus declaring himself from an Irish point of view an alien – on the grounds that being born in a stable does not necessarily make one a horse. Whether or not the real Wellington ever actually said this (and he appears in fact not to have done so), the Wellington of popular imagination certainly did – and the distinction is entirely irrelevant for Joyce's literary purposes.

Deucalion's wife, Pyrrha, meanwhile, is onomastically described as sharing with both Nora Joyce and Italo Svevo's wife Livia Schmitz the colour of her hair (Greek *pyrrhos* "red, red-haired"). Joyce wrote to Svevo on 20 February 1924 that his wife's name would also be that of "the Pyrrha of Dublin," Anna Livia (*L* 1, 211–12). In this scenario, HCE and ALP figure as bringers of civilization to Irish and other shores and thus as initiators of a new Viconian circle (Reichert and Senn 1970, 28). Joyce further observed to Harriet Weaver on 13 January 1925 that the figure of Noah's wife in the medieval mystery plays "is one of the models for Anna Livia" (*L* 1, 224). Six months later, in July 1925, writing from Fécamp in Normandy, he asked Sylvia Beach if she had succeeded yet in finding "a copy of the York, Towneley and Chester Mystery Plays" for him, adding that he "cannot remember the absurd names given to Mrs Noah (who is as quaint as Δ) in them" (*L* 1, 230).

> BECKETT: Et son chic! Et ses tics! Sa crête couronne le bec de l'aigle, le vieux deuc alien célèbre, avec sa bosse de mégalamanic en véritable vieux marcheur.
>
> JOYCE: Et son chic! Et ses tics! Et son bec haut en pic de crête de monts, le vieux deuc alien célèbre, avec sa bosse de follyo grandeur tel sieur rat qui sort de sa tourte.

The rhyming cut of him and strut of him become his likewise rhyming "chic" and "tics," his flaunted airs and graces, for Beckett's French, allowing for a double reference to the Russian river Ik. So elevated is our man in his own estimation that his headpiece, his martial crest (*crête*) inflated like a strutting barnyard rooster's comb (*crête*), rises like a crown (*couronne*) over the Bec de l'Aigle ("Eagle's Beak"), a 5,500-foot peak in the French Massif Centrale. The inflation is even more ludicrously exaggerated in translation, the Howth Head of Joyce's English tag, "as high as a howeth," ridiculously inflated already, is less than 600 feet high. HCE as "le vieux deuc alien" is an old and alien *duc* ("duke") who is also, appropriately for his mythological stature, a French Deucalion. His hump of grandeur is now a "bosse de mégalamanic," a hump (*bosse*) of megalomania (*mégalomanie*), a condition that allows for fluvial reference to the French Osse, the Scottish Gala Water, and the Manic of far-away Quebec. Thus equipped, and accompanied by the Australian river Archer, the old cheb is in a position to enjoy life's pleasures as a real old reveller (*vieux marcheur*).

Joyce's French retains Beckett's rhyming "chic" and "tics" and adds a "pic" ("peak") and a third Russian Ik for good measure. It is our hero's beaky nose (*bec* "beak") held high in the air, higher even than Howth ("haut"), that now evokes a high peak ("haut en pic") on the ridge (*crête*) of a mountain range. The celebrated "deuc alien" now carries a hump ("bosse") of "follyo grandeur," indicative of his delusions of grandeur (*folie de grandeur*), as he grandly emerges ("sort"), for example, twisted (Latin *tortus*) like Mister Rat, from his tower (*tour*) for a stroll (*tour*), idiot (*tourte*) that he is. Fluvial references include the French Osse ("bosse"), the various Rat and Rât rivers once again, the Portuguese Rio Torto ("tourte"), and the Belgian Our ("tourte" again), while "follyo grandeur" hospitably accommodates the Río Grande as well as the Hungarian noun *folyó* ("river").

> JOYCE: E l'incesso di quel desso capeggiando da gradasso di gransasso, qual il degno duca Lione, con quella gobba boriosa come ser topo ch'esce a zonzo!
>
> SETTANNI: Oh! che incesso di quel desso che capeggia da gradasso di gransasso, qual il degno duca lione, con sua gobba boriosa a sacco come ser topo che esce a zonzo.

Joyce's Italian once again goes its own flamboyant way, playing extravagantly with rhyme and a succession of Italian octosyllables. The cut and strut of our hero have now become the "stately stride" (*incesso*) of the rhyming "very same person" (*desso*), his head (*capo*) held as high as if his name were Gradasso di Gransasso – or as if he were the leading (*capegggiare* "to be head of") braggart (*gradasso*) of Gran Sasso. His inflated sense of his own importance has attained to new heights: the Gran Sasso ("Big Rock") mountain boasts the highest peak, at more than 9,500 feet, of the Italian Apennines. Corinna del Greco Lobner suggests that since Gradasso is in fact the name of a braggart in Ludovico Ariosto's mock epic *Orlando Furioso* (1516–32), while the Gran Sasso is located in Abruzzo, the phrase "gradasso di gransasso" constitutes a humorous reference not only to Ariosto but also to Gabriele D'Annunzio (1863–1938), who was a native of Abruzzo (Lobner 1989, 82). Since D'Annunzio was one of Joyce's major early literary heroes, she reads the phrase as also "a posturing parody of Joyce's former self" (45).

This "degno duca Lione" is an Italian Deucalione masquerading as a worthy (*degno*) duke (*duca*) alternatively named Lione, in this case onomastically suggesting also the martial valour of a very lion (*leone*). Even his hump (*gobba*) is arrogant (*borioso*), conceited (*borioso*), and swaggering (*borioso*) as he emerges (*esce*) for a casual saunter (*zonzo*) like Mister (*ser*) Rat (*topo*). He is fluvially accompanied by the Ando of the Solomon Islands, the French Asse, South American Ucali, Chinese Li, Russian Ob, Nigerian Oba, Indian Bori, German Oos, Norwegian Opo, and Angolan Onzo.

Settanni simplifies the syntax of Joyce's opening phrase by substituting the relative phrase "che capeggia" for the present participle "capeggiando," but loses the river Ando in the process. He compensates by specifying that our hero's hump is "a sacco" ("on his back"), *sacco* meaning a "rucksack" as well as evoking the Italian river Sacco. Two separate references to HCE as CHE are included, in the phrases "che capeggia" and "che esce" respectively.

[3] And his derry's own drawl and his corks-own blather and his doubling stutter and his gull-away swank.
(*ALP* 4; cf. *FW* 197.04–6: "corksown," "gullaway")

HCE's general arrogance finds expression also in his egregious speaking manner as public figure, described here in terms of high disapproval involving the four corners of Ireland, north, south, east, and west, and the four provinces, Ulster, Munster, Leinster, and Connacht, as represented respectively by the cities of Derry, Cork, Dublin, and Galway. All four, as cities, refer primarily to HCE as master builder, while the names of all four also provide complementary fluvial reference to ALP, for County Wicklow has a river Derry, and the other three place names derive respectively from the Irish *Corcaigh* ("swampy place"), *Duibhlinn* ("black pool"), and *Gaillimh* ("stony river"). The repeated "own" once again evokes the common anglicized element in Irish river names, *owen* (Irish *abhainn* /'auɪn/ "river"). HCE's devil's own drawl becomes a "derry's own drawl," and since opposites attract, a devil's own drawl evokes a god's own blather, and blather, apparently, is nowhere more at home than in Cork (near neighbour to Blarney Castle). The man's stuttering duplicity is already well known in Dublin, and his fraudulent airs and swanking graces would no doubt equip him to gull Galway too if he so chose. The term "gullaway" also reminds us once again not only of his status as suspected foreigner (Irish *gall*) and interloper from far away, but also of the universally shared desire that this particular *gall* should indeed just "go away."

> BECKETT: Et sa voix qu'il traîne derryère chaque phrase de sa bouche onflée de mots corquets et tous ses bégaiements à dublintente, le farceur qu'il est sans égalouégaux.
> JOYCE: [*without change*]

For both Beckett and (adopted word for word) Joyce, HCE's voice drawls and drags (*traîne*) in French after every phrase, with "derryère" doing double duty for *derrière* ("behind") and the city of Derry. Each phrase falls from a "bouche onflée de mots corquets," from a "mouth crammed (*enflée*) with cajoling (*coquet*) words," where the city of Cork can be found lurking not only in "mots corquets" but also in the phrase "bouche onflée," since a French *bouchon* is literally a "cork" for a bottle.

HCE's "bégaiements" ("stutterings") are both literally "double meaning" (*à double entente*) and associated ("à double en-") with Dublin, this evidence of his duplicity confirming him as the matchless joker (*farceur*) he is universally agreed to be. The phrase "sans égalouégaux" (*sans égal ou égaux* "without equal or equals") conveniently incorporates an approximate French pronunciation ("-galoué-") of *Galway* as well as ("-gaux") of an English *go*, as in the devout wish, in French as in English, that he should, once and for all, just go away, back to where he came from and should ideally have stayed.

> JOYCE: Un ghigno derriso del corcontento, ma chiazze galve dal cervel debolino.
>
> SETTANNI: E la voce che ogni frase si trascina, gonfiabocca, ma chiazze galve dal cervel debolino.

In Italian, Joyce completely ignores the deficiencies of HCE's oral delivery, choosing to focus instead on his equally unprepossessing facial appearance. We thus hear of his irritating sneer (*ghigno*), where "derriso" does duty for both *derisivo* ("derisive") and Derry, a sneer presumably the product of a "corcontento," a perversely contented Cork ("corc-") heart (*core*), but accompanied by unsightly blotches (*chiazza* "stain") resulting from drunken (*albo* "drunk") misbehaviour in some riverbed (*alveo*) in Galway ("galve") and which are caused ultimately by a "cervel debolino," a brain (*cervello*) made feeble (*debole*) by the rigours and excesses of life in a feeble-minded Dublin.

Settanni once again helpfully simplifies Joyce's convoluted Italian, even rewriting the entire first clause, though this time only at the relatively high contextual cost of deleting Derry and Cork altogether. HCE's voice becomes the focus of attention once again, a voice (*voce*) that drags out (*trascinare* "to drag") and drawls every phrase, from a mouth (*bocca*) that inflates (*gonfiare* "to inflate") and exaggerates and stutteringly doubles.

[1] Ask Lictor Hackett or Lector Reade or Garda Growley or the Boy with the Billyclub. **(*ALP* 4; cf. *FW* 197.06–7: "Lector Reade of Garda Growley")**

Like all respectable critics, our pair of critical commentators quote their sources and authorities. Inadvertently or otherwise, however, some doubt seems to have crept in. It is uncertain, for example, whether

Garda Growley and the Boy with the Billyclub are one and the same or a matching pair of surly constabulary stalwarts.The 1928 Gaige edition and the 1930 Faber *ALP* both have "Ask Lictor Hackett or Lector Reade *or* Garda Growley [my emphasis] or the Boy with the Billyclub," which may be taken either as implying "ask anyone at all" or, alternatively, as a more specific but more oblique reference to the four old men who will later reappear from time to time in *Finnegans Wake*.[2]

All four (assuming four) of the proposed referees appear to be in positions of authority of some sort. In ancient Rome a lictor (a title possibly derived from the Latin *ligare* "to bind") was an official who served as bodyguard to a magistrate and was authorized to carry out certain sentences – in token of which he carried the fasces, a badge of office consisting of an axe in a bundle of wooden rods; a lector (whose title is derived from the Latin *legere* "to read") reads lessons in a church service. A lector (like Lector Reade) reads, a lictor (like Lictor Hackett) leads, and potentially hacks with his conveniently available ceremonial hatchet. Garda Growley's name, for his part, suggests a short-tempered Irish policeman possibly named Crowley or Rowley, whose disposition is surly ("growly"), possibly since – as Gilbert and Sullivan's *Pirates of Penzance* (1879) has it – a policeman's lot is not a happy one. As a member of the *Garda Síochána*, the Irish police force founded in 1922, his official title in Irish is *Garda* ("guard," the equivalent of "officer" or "constable"). Growley may very well carry a billyclub or truncheon to assist him in indulging his unhappy disposition, as does the Boy with the Billyclub, who may or may not be a similarly armed constabulary colleague.The Russian Ik, Dutch Lek, French Gard, Italian Lago di Garda, Scottish Loch Ard, Italian Arda, American Rowley, English Lea, Irish Lee, Chinese Li, American Boy, Chinese Ili, and Austrian Ill add a richly varied aquatic dimension, supported by fainter hints of the American Licking and English Lickle.

BECKETT: Tu n'as qu'à le demander à Lictor Hackett ou à Lector Reade ou a Carda Crowley ou à Victoire de Massue.

JOYCE: Demande à Lictor Huckett ou à Lector Noiret ou à Gardar de Norval ou au Boy dit Browning.

---

2 Higginson notes that the change from "or Garda Growley" to "of Garda Growley" in *Finnegans Wake* (*FW* 197.07) is "without apparent authority" (1960, 99). Rose and O'Hanlon restore the reading "or Garda Growley" (*FW2* 154).

One of Beckett's French washerwomen advises the other that she only has to ask Lictor Hackett or Lector Reade, both names left unchanged from the original, or else "Carda Crowley" or "Victoire de Massue." The change from "Growley" to "Crowley" substitutes an actual (Irish) name for an obviously invented one, improves the temper of the individual in question, and allows for a reference to the American Crow River. The change from "Garda" to "Carda" – substituting the Italian river Carda for the French Gard and Italian Lago di Garda of Joyce's original – appears to be the result of an alliterative impulse rather than otherwise, removes the reference to the Irish police force, and leaves it up to the reader to decide whether Crowley, who may well be something of a card, is also a policeman. The Boy with the Billyclub, meanwhile, is rather surprisingly replaced by a strapping female personage, one Victoire de Massue, whose (invented) family is named for their original skill as wielders of a club (*massue*). It seems likely, given the context, that Victoire shares her invented family's martial taste for *coups de massue*, "crushing blows" leading without any nonsense to an equally crushing victory (*victoire*). The Javanese Mas, European Maas or Meuse, and Brazilian Assu all flow quietly.

Joyce's French transforms the lictor and lector of his English into humorous representatives of a rather odd couple of French Victors – possibly prompted by Beckett's Victoire de Massue. The original Lictor Hackett is transformed into "Lictor Huckett," which allows for a reference to the English river Uck while playing on the name of the French Romantic poet Victor Hugo (1802–1885). The original Lector Reade becomes "Lector Noiret," evoking the Rivière Noire of Quebec while playing on the name of Victor Noir, the pseudonym of the French journalist Yvan Salmon (1848–1870), who was fatally shot in the course of a roadside scuffle by Prince Pierre Bonaparte, Napoleon's great-nephew. As a result Salmon was in due course acclaimed as a revolutionary hero – but was later to become rather better known because the recumbent bronze statue on his grave in Père Lachaise cemetery has a prominent bump in the trousers that looks very much like an erection and has consequently served since the 1870s as a much admired and much polished fertility symbol.

The original Garda Growley, meanwhile, becomes "Gardar de Norval," allowing for a supplementary reference to the Irish river Nore while playing on the name of a second French Romantic poet, Gérard de Nerval (1808–55), who, as it happens, was much admired by Victor Hugo. The Boy with the Billyclub, finally, assumes his original gender as the "Boy dit Browning," the "Boy called Browning," here evoking the

Brown River of New Zealand while playing on the name of Lieutenant-General Sir Frederick Browning (1886–1965), known as "Boy" Browning, a high-ranking and much decorated British officer during the Great War. Browning's unexpected inclusion in the otherwise French company here was doubly suggested, both by his nickname Boy and by a family name that suggested much more effective weapons than a mere billyclub, namely the wide range of shotguns, pistols, rifles, and eventually machine guns manufactured from its beginnings in the 1880s by the (otherwise unrelated) American Browning Arms Company.

> JOYCE: Chiedi a Manganelli, o al Randelloni, o al Mazzaferrata, o al Fracco la Frombola.
> SETTANNI: Chiedi al Manganelli, o al Randelloni, o al Mazzaferrata, o al Fracco la Frombola.

Joyce's already extravagant French rendering of the quartet is more than matched for extravagance by his Italian, in which the weaponry of the Boy with the Billyclub acquires a more threateningly central prominence. The four potential referees are now renamed (and completely italianized) as Manganelli, Randelloni, Mazzaferrata, and Fracco la Frombola. Their invented names derive respectively from the Italian nouns *manganello* ("cudgel, club, blackjack"), *randello* ("cudgel, club"), *mazza ferrata* ("mace, sledgehammer"), *frombola* ("sling") and, just to make things quite clear, the Latin verb *frangere* ("to smash"). Jacqueline Risset aptly observes that Italian readers will recognize these names immediately as "designations of the phallus transformed into characters of popular comedy" (1984, 9). On the one hand, we thus have a comic Punch-and-Judy group of Masher and Smasher and Crusher and Thump; on the other, as Rosa Maria Bosinelli has observed, there is also a very perceptible satiric reference to the overt brutality of Italian fascism (1996, 62). The reference to the *manganello* immediately makes the point, evoking as it does an iconic product of Italian fascist art, namely the so-called *Madonna del Manganello*, a quasi-religious statue created in the 1930s out of an excess of fascist enthusiasm by the Italian sculptor Giuseppe Malecore (1876–1967), depicting the Virgin with the Christ child on her left arm – and, incongruously, a threateningly raised (and decidedly phallic) club in her right hand. Intended to symbolize the perennial strength of the indefeasible union of fascist Church and fascist State, the statue was multiply replicated in miniature form in Mussolini's Italy.

Oddly enough, Settanni, who ostensibly wished to avoid giving political offence to the fascist regime, also left this particular taunt once again untouched, limiting himself to making a very slight grammatical improvement to Joyce's phrasing.

[5] How elster is he a called at all? Huges Caput Earlyfouler? (*ALP4*; cf. *FW* 197.07–8: "Qu'appelle? Huges Caput Earlyfouler.")[3]

"How else is he called at all?" asks Joyce's English, playing on assonance and on two German rivers both called the Elster. The "he" in question is doubly identified by the word initials *ehc* and *HCE*, and HCE, it is now suggested, can boast of noble and indeed royal bloodlines, as the legitimate descendant if not indeed the bodily reincarnation of two famous tenth-century monarchs, French and German respectively. Hugues (or Hugh) Capet was king of France and ancestor of a long line of French monarchs; Henry the Fowler (Heinrich der Vogler), so named for his passion for falconry, was king of Germany and ancestor of a long line of German emperors. As Campbell and Robinson observe, the two together, France and Germany, "as representatives of the brother pair, are united in the father, HCE" (1961, 133), the head (Latin *caput*) of this archetypally warring family. And the "Huges Caput" is also the huge head (otherwise Howth) of the sleeping giant and legendary champion Finn MacCool, whose name in Irish, Finn mac Cumhaill, literally means "Fairhaired (*finn*), son (*mac*) of Champion (*cumhall*, genitive case *cumhaill*)."

HCE's illustrious forebears, however, cannot disguise the embarrassing fact that the appellation *Huges Caput Earlyfouler* is also suggestive of a huge but all too enthusiastic erection (Latin *caput* "head") followed by a no doubt likewise huge but all too premature ejaculation (German *kaputt* "finished, over and done with"). The Canadian Hughes River, American Lake Earl, and Australian Fowlers Bay bear silent witness. Serendipitously, Chinese *hù* means "lake."

> BECKETT: Comment s'preenomme-t-il encore? Huges Caput Earlyfowler.
> JOYCE: Comment le préenomme-t-on encore? Hughes Caput Earlyfowler.

---

3 The question "Qu'appelle?" first appears in the 1930 Faber text. Both the 1928 Gaige text and the 1930 Faber text have a question mark after "Huges Caput Earlyfouler," changed to a period in *FW* 197.08.

"What does he call himself again?" (*se prénommer* "to call oneself"), asks Beckett's French, switching to a reflexive verb in order to evoke a sextet of rivers, the German Spree, American Eno, Alaskan Nome, Russian Om, Danish Omme, and English Till, as well as the Irish Lough Ree and the arcane term *reen*, meaning an open ditch or drain – and which for added fluvial value is also, according to the *OED*, sometimes written *rhine*. "What do they call him again?" asks Joyce's French, changing person presumably for idiomatic reasons, but abandoning in the process Beckett's mention of the German Spree and English Till. Beckett's "Earlyfowler," meanwhile, adopted by Joyce, gives greater prominence to Henry the Fowler, less to HCE's emissions, and simultaneously introduces the Canadian Owl River.

> JOYCE: Che saarebbe il suo superanome? Hugo Capeto L'Eccellatore.
> SETTANNI: [*without change*]

"What would his surname be?" asks Joyce's Italian, which Settanni leaves unchanged, first conflating *sarebbe* ("would be"), the German river Saar, the Swiss Aar, and an English ebb tide, before going on to conflate *soprannome* ("surname") and *superare* ("to surpass"), while hinting at *superbia* ("pride, haughtiness"), the Turkish noun *su* ("water"), and the South American Paraná River. The errant chief is here translingually elevated to "Hugo Capeto L'Eccellatore," thus both restoring an Italianized Hugo to his Capetian origins (*Capeto*) and recognizing him as one who, apart perhaps from an occasional uncontrolled fart (*peto*), excels (*eccellere*), whether as fowler (*uccellatore*), as trickster (*uccellatore*) – or, by heavy implication, as fucker without compare, since *uccello*, literally "bird," is colloquially "cock, penis."

[6] Comments and Contexts

Joyce improves on Beckett's French solutions in two excerpts [5.1, 5.2], but adopts his version of one complex sentence ("His derry's own drawl ...") word for word [5.3]. The names of Lictor Hackett and his friends are already adjusted by Beckett in two of the four cases, but are completely restructured in Joyce's French [5.4]. The change from Beckett's "Comment s'preenomme-t-il encore?" to the more pedestrian "Comment le préenomme-t-on encore?" [5.5] is arguably a disimprovement, however, if only to the extent that it loses two river references.

Joyce's original passages relating to Reeve Gootch and Reeve Drughad [5.1] and to the "eld duke alien" [5.2], already significantly rewritten in his French, are in each case completely and extravagantly rewritten in Italian. The names of Lictor Hackett and his colleagues, already completely restructured in his French, are once again restructured, and this time even more extravagantly, in his Italian [5.4]. The name of Huges Caput Earlyfouler in his English, meanwhile, is adjusted only minimally ("Huges" becoming "Hughes") in his French, but heavily sexualized in his Italian [5.5].

Settanni simplifies particularly convoluted passages of Joyce's Italian on two occasions in this sequence, adding a phrase ("a sacco") and a river in one case [5.2] and rewriting an entire clause in another, adding two references to HCE in the process [5.3]. Oddly once again, considering his ostensible aim to soften references deemed too outspoken, Settanni leaves unchanged a reference to the fascist Madonna del Manganello, and thus by implication to fascist brutality, that could easily have led to very unpleasant political repercussions for *Prospettive* and its already suspect editorial staff [5.4].

6 Phenician Rover

In a gabbard he barqued it, the boat of life, from the harbourless Ivernikan Okean, till he spied the loom of his landfall and he loosed two croakers from under his tilt, the gran Phenician rover. ... That marchantman he suivied their scutties right over the wash, his cameleer's burnous breezing up on him, till with his runagate bowmpriss he roade and borst her bar. ... When they saw him shoot swift up her sheba sheath, like any gay lord salomon, her bulls they were ruhring, surfed with spree. Boyarka buah! Boyana bueh! (*ALP* 5; *FW* 197.28–31, 33–5, 198.03–5)

***[1] In a gabbard he barqued it, the boat of life, from the harbourless Ivernikan Okean, till he spied the loom of his landfall and he loosed two croakers from under his tilt, the gran Phenician rover.* (*ALP* 5; *FW* 197.28–31)**

The marital union of the parental protagonists HCE and ALP is a turbulent one, as Margot Norris writes, "conjuring sailors on troubled waters, the mythical flood of Deucalion, the biblical deluge of Noah, the journey of a proto-Odyssean Phenician rover" (2015, 137). The biblical version of Deucalion is indeed Noah, hero of the deluge, whose ark saved all human and animal life from extinction. HCE as culture hero embarques like Noah in a "boat of life," a gabbard or "sailing barge" (*OED*), his progress fluvially attended by the Australian Abba, the French Arc and Arques, and the Irish *Life* or Liffey. The Greek geographer Ptolemy's second-century map of Ireland shows the Irish Sea as *Iouernikos ôkeanos*, HCE's "Ivernikan Okean," "harbourless" because of the worldwide Flood of Genesis. The English Ver and Irish Erne join Homer's world-encircling river Okeanos. Having spied the distant outline of his proposed landfall, HCE as Noah loosed two "croakers" from under his "tilt," accompanied by the Russian Loo, German Oos, American Oak, English Till, and Scottish Tilt. Noah reportedly sent forth a raven and a dove, but since doves coo rather than croak, HCE seems to favour two ravens, perhaps in fluvial deference to the Canadian Raven River.

A "tilt," meanwhile, cognate with German *Zelt* ("tent"), is a canopy or canvas covering, but in a more martial context a tilt is a place of jousting combat, one tilts with a lance, and the sexual overtones are evident. A favourable wind is important for any sailor, and the two croakers from under HCE's tilt are simultaneously two resounding farts from under his kilt, parodically recalling the martial trumpet call of Dante's demon Barbariccia: "ed elli avea del cul fatto trombetta" (*Inferno* 21.139), "and he had made a trumpet of his arse" (cf. Mandelbaum 1982, 109). The doubled *-bar-* of "gabbard" and "barqued" may be read as already anticipating the appearance of Barbariccia – whose name, however, surprisingly inoffensive for a demon, merely suggests that he has a beard (*barba*) that is curly (*riccio*). The doubled *-bar-* also, however, obliquely suggests HCE not only as a stutterer (Sanskrit *barbaras* "stammering") (Onions 1966, 74) but also as a barbarian (Greek *barbaros*) and as the leader of a barbarian incursion rather than as a biblical saviour of humankind.

This "gran Phenician rover," this conquering hero of epic proportions whose linguistic association with both Finn ("Phen-") MacCool and the Phoenix Park is evident, is not just a Phoenician explorer of the Mediterranean. Given the "Ivernikan Okean" as his theatre of operations, he is by implication also a Scandinavian marauder with pillage and rapine in mind, a Viking "embarqued," in Grace Eckley's felicitous phrase, "on a sea voyage with fornication aforethought" (1975, 136). He is also the father of the city of Dublin (founded by Scandinavian settlers in the ninth century).

Complicating matters still further, in Old Irish usage *Féni* was another name for the Goídels or Gaels, designating them specifically as the "true" Irish, as opposed to members of other groups of inhabitants who were, by implication, foreign (MacKillop 1998, 209–10). The name *Goídel*, on the other hand, is more appropriate for our hero as maritime raider, despite his own foreign origins: it derives from the marauding activities of early Irish raiders harassing the coast of Wales, whom the beleagured Welsh called *gwyddel*, a term that eventually came to mean "Irishman" but is directly related to modern Welsh *gwyllt* ("wild") and modern Irish *gealt* ("mad"). Further fluvial echoes evoke in passing the Slovak Gran, Chinese Fen, Indian Feni, Cornish Enni, Japanese Nishi, the Rove River of the Solomon Islands, the Zimbabwean Ove, and the English Ver.

> BECKETT: Il l'embarqua dans une gabarre, canot de sauvietage, de la côte sans havres de l'Okéan Hivernique, jusqu'au jour où il vit enfin de haut la promasse de son atterritoire et lâcha deux croassiers de dessous sa proue, le grand loup de mer Phénicien!

Beckett retains the doubled *-bar-* of Joyce's English in having HCE embarque in a "gabarre," a *gabare* or sailing barge – extended to accommodate the Swiss river Arre as well as the French Bar – that is a "canot de sauvietage," a lifeboat (*canot de sauvetage*) as well as a boat (*canot*) of life (*vie*). HCE sailed from the coast (*côte*) without harbour or haven (*havre*) of the "Okéan Hivernique," at once Joyce's "Ivernikan Okean" and a Franco-Greek ocean (*océan*) of winter (*hiver*), into which the French Avre, English Ver, Irish Erne, and New Caledonian Ni may be seen to flow. He continued on his voyage until the day (*jour*) when he saw from on high (*de haut*), from the masthead, first the promise (*promesse*) and then the physical mass (*masse*) of his "atterritoire," the territory (*territoire*) at which he intended to make a landfall (*atterrir*). The evocation of Moses' vision from on high of the Promised Land (Deuteronomy 34:1–4) is clear. HCE's voyage is further watered by the South Sudanese Jur ("jour"), Javanese Mas, Dutch Maas, and Belgian Attert.

HCE's Barbariccian trumpet call becomes a military signal for action, for at this sight he let loose (*lâcha*) two "croassiers," a term evoking the American Crow, French Asse, and Lebanese Assi while conflating Joyce's "two croakers" (*croasser* "to caw, to croak") à la Noah and a pair of cuirassiers, armoured soldiery as an advance guard of a full-scale attack. The play on flatulation is thus replaced by the overt threat of both military and sexual assault, launched from under the phallic prow (*proue*) of the grand old sea dog (*loup de mer*) whose predatory appetites are evidently more literally those of a wolf (*loup*). Since HCE is now unambiguously Phoenician (*Phénicien*), the possible play on Finn MacCool and the Phoenix Park, while not excluded, is less obvious than in Joyce's overtly punning "Phenician." The Chinese Fen, Indian Feni, and Cornish Enni continue to be evoked.

> JOYCE: Il navigua en gabarre, archecanot, de la côte sans hâvres de l'Okéan Hivernike, jusqu'au jour où il vit de longue la promasse de son atterritoire et lança deux croasseurs de dessous ses dessous, le raabe rouleur phéniedcien!

Joyce's rendering remains close to Beckett's, retaining several of its best translational effects. The play on the doubled *-bar-* disappears, however, HCE now having simply "sailed" (*navigua*) rather than "embarqued," a choice allowing for the substitution of the Russian river Viga for the French Arc and Arques. The "boat of life" becomes an "archecanot," conflating *arche* ("ark") and *canot* ("boat"), allowing for a doubled appearance of HCE, as both CHE and HEC, comfortably sitting on his sea-faring arse (German *Arsch*). Beckett's "Okéan Hivernique" is adjusted to a slightly more quasi-Greek "Okéan Hivernike," otherwise retaining the same resonances. Beckett's rendering of "the loom of his landfall" is retained, though viewed from afar off ("de longue") rather than from a height ("de haut"). While Beckett's mariner "lâcha" ("loosed") two "croassiers," Joyce's rover "lança" ("launched") two "croasseurs" ("croakers"), introducing the aquatic term *anse* ("cove") and retaining the American Crow and French Asse, while presumably considering Beckett's cuirassiers a step too far. The fart joke of the original is reinstated instead and even enhanced, the croakers now launched "de dessous ses dessous" ("from underneath his underwear") by the "phéniedcien" HCE, who is not only a Phoenician "rolling stone" (*rouleur*) but, interlingually, a positively or potentially rabid "ruler" as well (*en rab* "in addition"). Rivers evoked include the Canadian Soo ("dessous"), Austrian Raab, Chinese Fen, Indian Feni, Cornish Enni, and German Nied.

> JOYCE: Salpò in maona, l'Arca di Barca, sull'inapprodabile Satantrionale, finché avvistò la sua sponsa promessa, e mollò due gracchi di sotto il saio, il gran fenicio lope de mara.

Joyce's Italian mariner "weighed anchor" (*salpò*) in a "barge" (*maona*) heavily freighted with hypertextual resonances, including Arabic *ma* ("water") and Maori *moana* ("sea") (Epstein 2009, 302) as well as Triestine *andar in mona* ("to go to the devil") and, coarsely suggestive of his marauding ambitions, Venetian *mona* ("cunt") (Zanotti 2002, 295). The "boat of life" is now, combining *arca* ("ark") and *barca* ("barque"), "l'Arca di Barca," literally the "barque-ark," evoking Noah's Ark (*l'arca di Noè*) as well as the English Lark, Siberian Arka, Sudanese Barca, and the French Arc, Arques, and Bar. Since *orco* ("ogre") and *porco* ("pig") are both common colloquial terms of insult, "arca di barca" also suggests a piece of (invented) rhyming invective proleptically descriptive of our Phenician rover, namely *orco di porco* ("filthy brute").

HCE, Noah redivivus, is underway "sull'inapprodabile Satantrionale," a sea where land is *inapprodabile* ("unapproachable"), offering no shore (*proda*) on which to land (*approdare*). This harbourless sea is no longer just the "Ivernikan Okean," but rather the "Satantrionale," a name combining *settentrionale* ("northern") and Satan (Hebrew *sātān* "adversary"), simultaneously characterizing HCE as a diabolical enemy and a Scandinavian Viking from the northern seas – into which flow the Polish Ina, German Roda, Romanian Aţa, Kenyan Tana, Russian Ona, the Nali of Bangladesh, and no doubt many a Spanish river (*río*). He proceeds undaunted until (*finché*), as CHE, he "sighted" (*avvistò*) his "sponsa promessa" ("promised spouse"), a designation that combines Latin *sponsa* ("spouse") and *pons* ("bridge") as well as Italian *sposa* ("spouse") and *sponda* ("riverbank"), while humorously playing for Joyce's Italian readership on the title of a venerable Italian literary classic, Alessandro Manzoni's novel *I promessi sposi* (*The Betrothed*) of 1827. Clearly, Joyce's acrobatic intertextual leap here is not at all suggested by his original English phrase "the loom of his landfall," but rather by Beckett's French version, adopted by him, "la promasse de son atterritoire," with its hint of the Mosaic vision of the Promised Land.

At this point, ancient mariner HCE "let go" (*mollò*) "due gracchi," two choughs, small crows chosen for the textual purpose here, first, because their name (*gracchio*) is related to the verb *gracchiare* ("to caw, to croak"), and, second, because of the opportunity afforded for Italian cultural play on the two Gracchi brothers, Roman politicians of the second century BC whose attempted and well-intentioned land reforms were so unpopular with the wealthy as to cause their assassination. HCE as Scandinavian invader of Ireland has of course his own long-term plans for thorough-going land reforms. The fart joke, evidently a Joycean favourite, is faithfully recycled once again, the two croakers being loosed "di sotto il saio," from under his "habit" (*saio*), by "il gran fenicio lope de mara."

The latter designation is undoubtedly prompted less by Joyce's own original phrase "the gran Phenician rover" than by Beckett's French rendering "le grand loup de mer Phénicien," which, oddly enough, Joyce had chosen *not* to adopt in his own French rendering. HCE is again a Phoenician – which happens to be translated as *fenicio* in both Italian and Spanish. This happy linguistic coincidence, together with the grammatical fact that the Spanish adjective *grande* ("great") is regularly truncated to *gran* before a masculine noun, prompts the irrepressible Italian Joyce to convert the Italian *lupo di mare* ("old sea dog") into a quasi-Spanish personal name, as if HCE's name were really Lope de Mara. The reference plays in this case on the name of the Spanish Golden Age dramatist Lope de Vega, whose astonishingly prolific output earned him the nickname, entirely appropriate for Joyce's purposes here, of "the Phoenix of Spain," and whose name, since *Lope* derives from Latin *lupus* ("wolf"), might humorously be taken to mean "wolf of the plain (Spanish *vega*)" rather than "wolf of the sea" (cf. Hanks et al. 2002, 637, 811). The onomastic joke is accompanied by a quartet of rivers from near and far, the Slovak Gran, Chinese Fen, Indian Feni, Cornish Enni, Nigerian Mayo Lope, Russian Dëma, and Tanzanian Mara.

The complicating presence of Old Irish *Féni*, designating the marauding raider as in fact a true Irishman, more Irish than the Irish themselves, is even clearer in the Italian "fenicio" than in the original "Phenician." As it happens, meanwhile, the anglicized Irish names Meara /'ma:rə/ and O'Mara derive from *Ó Meadhra* /o'ma:rə/, celebrating an ancestor characterized by *meadhar* ("mirth, joy") (Hanks et al. 2002, 464). Joyce believed (erroneously) that his own family name similarly derived from the Latin *jocosus* ("joyous").[1]

> SETTANNI: Salpò in maona, l'Arca di Barca, sull'inapprodabile Ibernicano, fin ch'avvistò lungi la sponsa promessa, e mollò' due gracchi di sotto vento, il gran fenicio lope de mara.

Settanni, in one of his more sustained interventions, makes four relatively significant adjustments to Joyce's version. First, reverting to the original "Ivernikan Okean," he changes "Satantrionale" to "Ibernicano," playing on the similarity of "Hibernia" and "Iberia," and thus converting the northern sea into a southern one and HCE from a marauding Scandinavian into a heroic Milesian, one of the mythical race of Irish pseudo-history who colonized Ireland from Spain, defeated the semi-divine Tuatha Dé Danann, became the revered ancestors of the Gael, and were entirely innocent of any satanic taint. Joyce's "finché avvistò" ("until he sighted") is adjusted to "fin ch'avvistò," which loses the reference to HCE as CHE, but compensates by foregrounding the hero (and avatar) Finn MacCool instead. The promised land is sighted "lungi"

1 Modern scholarship derives the name Joyce from the Breton personal name Iodoc, a diminutive of *iudh* ("lord"), introduced into English by the Normans in the form *Josse* (Hanks et al. 2002, 329).

("from afar off"), allowing reference to both the Irish river Lung and the Indonesian Lungi – and perhaps reminding readers that in Irish legend the Milesians invaded Ireland only after having, like Moses, sighted that Promised Land from afar, namely from the north coast of Spain (a mere 1,000 kilometres away). The two sonorous farts, finally, are punningly relocated from "di sotto il saio" ("from under his habit") to "di sotto vento" ("from downwind"), replacing heroic flatulation by maritime concern for sailing conditions.

***[2] That marchantman he suivied their scutties right over the wash, his cameleer's burnous breezing up on him, till with his runagate bowmpriss he roade and borst her bar.* (*ALP* 5; *FW* 197.33–5)**

HCE as "marchantman" is a merchant in a merchant vessel who "suivied their scutties right over the wash," followed (French *suivre* "to follow") the scut tails of the croakers (avian) across the surging waves, while fluvially evoking the Spanish Marchan, Scottish Archan, the Sui of Papua New Guinea, the Ugandan Ivi, the English Ash, and the Wash on England's eastern coast. He clearly comes from very far foreign shores, with "his cameleer's burnous," the hooded cloak worn by Arab camel drivers, "breezing up on him." Rivers flow in abundance, evoked by the thirsty desert sands: the Vietnamese Cam and Cornish Camel, the Irish Lee, English Lea, and Chinese Li, an unnamed Scottish burn, the Russian Urna, the English Ouse, and the South African Breë. Since the river Camel owes its name to its crooked course, Cornish *kammel* meaning "crooked," HCE as predatory conqueror of ALP has an unpleasant crooked leer on his cameleer's face as "with his runagate bowmpriss he roade and borst her bar." This wandering renegade's phallic bowsprit, an Italian *bompresso,* was like a boom made from a whole tree (German *Baum*) as he burst through the shoreline sandbank, ravaging ALP's maiden breast (Dutch *borst*). Rivers pullulate excitedly, the English Till, Spanish Runa, Brazilian Una, Russian Aga, Canadian Bow, German Riss, and French Bar, together with the American Borst Lake.

> BECKETT: Ce marchechand, il a circonsuivi leurs bouts de qul par-dessus la grande tasse, son burnous de chamelier retroussé par les vents, jusq'à tant qu'avec son boutpré rutnégat il a enchaussé sa barre et l'a porfendue.

Beckett's marchantman is a stuttering ("-checha-") merchant (*marchand*), clearly identified (CHE, ECH) as HCE, who followed (*suivre*) and even did circles around (*circonscrire* "to circumscribe") the tails (*queue* "scut") and the tail ends (*cul* "arse") of his two "croassiers." A maritime flavour is enhanced by the fact that *bout* means "anchor" as well as "end" and "bottom." The pursuit "over the wash" becomes "pardessus la grande tasse," literally, "over the big cupful," playing on the colloquial *boire la tasse,* "to swallow a mouthful" while swimming. The English Tas and French Asse are added to the Sui of Papua New Guniea and the Ivi of Uganda. HCE's burnous, like that of a camel driver (*chamelier*), is hitched up (*retroussé*) by the wind, facilitating the use of his "boutpré," a "bowsprit" (*beaupré*) in search of any available bottom (*bout*), "rutnégat" as he is, both renegade (*renégat*) and in rut (*en rut*). With this phallic maritime instrument he drove (*enchâsser* "to embed") a causeway (*chaussée*) through ALP's sandbar (*barre*) and cleft it in two (*pourfendre* "to cleave in two").

The term "enchaussé" provides another cryptic reference to Finn MacCool: "la Chaussée des Géants" is the standard French name for the Giant's Causeway of County Antrim, constructed according to legend by none other than Finn as mythical giant. In a proleptic historical irony, the village of Roussillon in Provence – where Beckett, more than a decade later, would spend the war years as a member of the French Resistance – also has a "Chaussée des Géants" in its extensive ochre quarries.

> JOYCE: Ce digne marchant ensuivit leurs bouts sur la grande lessive, son burnous de chamelier balloné par la brise jusqu'à ce qu'avec son Baumpresse rutnégat il monte et pourfend sa barre.

For Joyce, once again retaining some of Beckett's best translational solutions, this worthy (*digne*) merchant (*marchand*) on the march (*marchant*), but no longer stuttering, accompanied by the Scottish Dee, Spanish Marchan, and Scottish Archan, follows the bottoms of his "croasseurs" over the grand wash that is at once the ocean aforementioned and a load of domestic washing (*lessive*). His camel driver's burnous is helpfully ballooned (*balloné*) by the wind, while the Belgian Lesse, Irish Allow, and German Riss and Ise flow. Thus unencumbered, he mounts (*monte*) and cleaves (*pourfend*) ALP's sandbar (*barre*) with his renegade (*renégat*) bowsprit in rut (*en rut*), an Italian *bompresso* that also conflates German *Baum* ("tree") and *pressen* ("to force").

JOYCE: Seguì brigantone gli scodinzolini in sui marosi difilato, rigonfio il manto di burracano, e col suo bravo bompresso prese il rincorso e le ruppe la barra.

In Joyce's Italian, HCE, a great brigand (*brigantone*) in a brigantine (*brigantino*), followed (*seguì*) the little tails of the little tail-waggers (*scodinzolare* "to wag a tail") through the surging billows (*maroso* "billow, surge") right away (*difilato*). The Sui of Papua New Guinea continues to flow, accompanied by the Romanian Maros and the Italian Lato. His cloak (*manto*), a burnous (*barracano*), is "swollen" (*rigonfio*), though this is no longer attributed to the wind, and with his trusty (*bravo*) assassin's (*bravo* "hired assassin") bowsprit (*bompresso*) he took a run (*prendere la rincorsa* "to take a running start") and broke (*rompere* "to break") her sandbar (*barra*). Fluvial references include the Australian Burra ("burracano"), the Mexican Río Bravo, and, in "rincorso," the Italian noun *corso* ("stream"). "Rincorso" also evokes in passing Vico's crucial term *ricorso*.

SETTANNI: Seguì' brigantone gli scodinzolini in sui marosi difilato, rigonfio il manto di buracano, e col suo bravo bompresso filò in rincorsa e ne schiantò la barra.

Settanni, in a mood to restrain linguistic excesses, alters HCE's "manto di burracano" to a "manto di buracano," protection against a hurricane (*uracano*) rather than against sun and desert sand. The English Bure, Mongolian Ur, and Russian Ura, as well as the Basque noun *ura* ("the water"), are in evidence, though the Australian Burra no longer flows. HCE now set off (*filare* "to run") "at a sprint" (*rincorsa*) and rather than just breaking ALP's sandbar, he more violently, as in the original, "burst" it (*schiantare* "to burst").

[3] When they saw him shoot swift up her sheba sheath,
like any gay lord salomon, her bulls they were ruhring,
surfed with spree. Boyarka buah! Boyana bueh!
(*ALP* 5; *FW* 198.03–5)

In the biblical account (1 Kings 10), the Queen of Sheba, bearing rich gifts, comes to Jerusalem to pay a state visit to King Solomon, renowned for his wisdom, and in due course returns to her own country. HCE's arrival combines narratives of the biblical Solomon, the golden days of old when lords were gay and damsels fair, and the migratory return of salmon to their natal river. HCE is a strapping fellow (French *gaillard*), and "like any gay lord salomon," he shoots swift and alliteratively up ALP's "sheba sheath" and clearly has no intention of returning to his own country. The North and South Bulls, as two major sandbanks on either side of the mouth of the Liffey, are so called from the roaring of the surf breaking on them; as powerful male animals, they roar boisterous approval – "Boyarka buah! Boyana bueh!" – of HCE's sexual conquest of ALP while simultaneously celebrating, as guardians of the river mouth, the perennially necessary union of HCE and ALP, sea and river, male and female. Rivers in celebratory attendance include the American Swift, Nigerian Eba, Peruvian Heath, Russian Ay, Peruvian Ylo, Vietnamese Lô, Canadian Lord, American Salmon and Solomon, German Ruhr and Spree, Colombian Boyacá, American Boy, African Oya (otherwise the Niger), English Yar, French Arc and Arques, Siberian Arka, Ukrainian Buh, African Bua, Bulgarian Boyana, Irish Boyne, American Boy and African Oya again, Chinese Yan, Russian Yana, American Ana, and the Ukrainian Buh again.

"Boyarka buah!" celebrates HCE, first as wild colonial boy, then, marking his arrival from the mysterious east, as a boyar or high-ranking Russian aristocrat, then, reprising the ark, as the culture hero Noah, saviour of humankind, and finally, with the Irish battle cry *abú!* ("to victory!") as victorious conqueror. Ptolemy's second-century map of Ireland, meanwhile, shows the river Boyne as *Bouvinda*, from a proto-Celtic **Bou vindā* ("white cow"), the fertility goddess later called Bóann (O'Rahilly 1946, 3; MacKillop 1998, 45). "Boyana bueh!" celebrates Anna as Bóann, creator of the Boyne, site of innumerable battles through history; the Czech female name Bojana is derived from a Slavic *boi* ("battle") (Hanks et al. 2002, 716), while Romanian *boi* means "oxen"; and Italian *bue* ("ox") is cognate with modern Irish *bó* ("cow").

Battle is indeed joined here, the battle of invader and invaded, of male and female, of impregnator and impregnated, but the "ruhring" of the bulls arguably celebrates primarily sexual union rather than sexual assault. For Grace Eckley, it even represents "the sound of Anna's eagerness for Earwicker's love during their courting" (1975, 191). The ruhring celebrates that bull needs cow, that boy needs girl and girl boy, celebrates the incoming tide in the mouth of the river, the incoming invader who in due course will become settler and solid citizen, the return of the salmon ("salomon") to its spawning place. It is appropriate that Finn MacCool's legendary salmon of knowledge came from the Boyne – and that the name of Solomon, who was famed for his wisdom, derives ultimately from Hebrew *shalom* ("peace") (Hanks et al. 2002, 543).[2]

> BECKETT: Quand ils le virent remonter – prrout! – son canal de chas bas, tout comme un gaillard sire saulomon, il y avait ses brisons qui meuseglaient asseillis sans mersey. Boyarka buah! Boyana bueh!

For Beckett, ALP's "sheba sheath" becomes her "canal de chas bas," where /ʃabɑ/ plays on the possible identity of the biblical realm of Sheba and the ancient Arabian kingdom of Saba. HCE navigates (*remonter* "to go up") his prow (*proue*), with a fart (*prout*) of effort, up the channel (*canal*) of her nether (*bas*) orifice (*chas* "eye of a needle") – and simultaneously up the Romanian river Prut, whose name in French, Prout, is homonymous with a discreet Bloomian fart. His performance, fluvially evoking the Austrian Gail, Luxembourg Syr, and Indian Sau, is that of a "gaillard sire saulomon," a combination of a strapping (*gaillard*) lord (*sire*) Solomon and the likewise biblical "Saul of Rehoboth by the river" (Genesis 36:37). Witnessing the performance were breakwater shoals (*brisants*), like the Cornish reefs (*brisants*) called the Brisons, which were bellowing (*meugler* "to moo"), attacked (*assaillis*) as they were without mercy (*sans merci*). The French Isson, Meuse, and Seille, together with the English Mersey, are all in evidence.

While the "ruhring" of Joyce's bulls allows for a celebratory reading, Beckett's anonymous breakwaters, sprayed with surf but hardly surfed with spree, are unambiguously under attack, just as ALP is under attack. "Boyarka buah! Boyana bueh!" appears to be just the sound of their mournful bellowing – recalling the folk tradition of three great waves that allegorically harass the shores of Ireland from time to time (MacKillop 1998, 410). One of these was "the Wave of Clíona," and Beckett may well have been acquainted with James Stephens's poem of that name in the latter's collection *Reincarnations* (1918), lamenting the collapse of the old Gaelic order at the hands of foreign invaders: "O Wave of Clíona, cease they bellowing! / And let mine ears forget a while

2 In Old Irish onomastic lore, meanwhile, the Boyne as mother of rivers is known "as the Severn in England, as the Tiber in Rome, as the Jordan and the Euphrates in the East, and as the Tigris 'in enduring paradise'" (Rees and Rees 1989, 53).

to ring / At thy long, lamentable misery: / The great are dead indeed. The great are dead."

> JOYCE: Il enfila – ffuit – son fourreau de chas bas, tout comme un saulomon verge galant et ses brisons rhurlaient repus à coeurjoie. Boyarka buah! Boyana bueh!

For Joyce's French, playing on the fact that *chas* means the eye of a needle, HCE "threaded" (*enfila*) the "sheath" (*fourreau*) of her nether orifice (*chas bas*). Colloquially, however, the verb *enfiler* also means "to fuck," and this activity is accompanied not by Beckett's flatulatory "prrout!" but by the interjection "ffuit," suggesting rather an alliterative *fuite en avant*, a "headlong rush," carried out fortissimo (*ff.*). The performance is fully that of a Beckettean "saulomon," now characterized more specifically as a "verge galant," a combination of *vert galant* ("old charmer") and *verge* ("penis"). The breakwaters, adopting and adapting Beckett's "brisons," now "howled" (*hurlaient*) and howled again (*r-*), aided by the French Isson and, as in the original, the German Ruhr. Unlike Beckett's bellowing "brisons," however, here the "brisons" are "repus à coeurjoie," "satiated (*repu*) to their hearts' content." Their roar of "Boyarka buah! Boyana bueh!" is overtly celebratory.

> JOYCE: A vederlo guizzar in quella sua guaina, come Salomon reo e Saboletta, le sue dune rhurlavano di foia satolle. Bayorka buah! Boyana bueh!

In Italian, HCE is like a Solomon (*Salomone*) who is not only a king (*re*) but also wicked (*reo*) and ALP his "Saboletta," like a queen of Sheba (*regina di Saba*), whose alliterating name, a not unusual Italian family name, evokes the Romanian Sabo and the Corsican Oletta and hints at the rape of the Sabine women (*il ratto delle Sabine*). On seeing him "dart" (*guizzare*) into her "sheath" (an alliterative *guaina*), her "dunes" (*dune*) were "howling" (*urlare* "to howl"), "satiated" (*satolle*) with "lust" (*foia*). The Irish and English rivers Dun, the Danube (Hungarian *Duna*), the German Ruhr, and the Cornish Fowey /'fɔɪ/ are all in evidence. Zanotti notes the archaizing effect of "di foia satolle," reminiscent of Dante's formal linguistic register (2002, 284). The roar of "Boyarka buah!" is adjusted (possibly inadvertently) to "Bayorka buah!" – eliminating the original resonances of boy, boyar, and ark, though substituting evocations of an American bayou or marshy estuary, the Russian Ay and American York, and, reintroducing the salmon motif of the original, the Norwegian Orkla (Old Norse *Orka*), noted for the abundance of salmon (Italian *salmone*) in its waters. The concluding roar of "Bayorka buah! Boyana bueh!" now seems to imply primarily applause for HCE's sexual performance rather than celebration of procreative union.

SETTANNI: A vederlo guizzar in quella sua guaina, come Salomon reo e Saboletta, le sue dune riurlavan di foia satolle. Bayorka buah. Boyana bueh.

Settanni contents himself with altering the overtly non-Italian "rhurlavano" to "riurlavan," combining *ri-* and *urlavan* to suggest "howled and howled again." The two concluding roars are deprived of their exclamatory status, and the German Ruhr disappears.

[4] Comments and Contexts

In this sequence we find two clear examples of Beckett's influence not only on Joyce's French but also, and more unexpectedly, on his Italian almost a decade later. "The loom of his landfall" [6.1] is translated by Beckett, and taken over unchanged by Joyce in French, as "la promasse de son atterritoire," the "promasse" later serendipitously inspiring Joyce's Italian "la sua sponsa promessa," an overtly playful reference to Manzoni's classic early-nineteenth-century novel *I promessi sposi*. "The gran Phenician rover" of the same excerpt is rendered by Beckett as "le grand loup de mer Phénicien," while Joyce himself opts instead for "le raabe rouleur phéniedcien" [6.1]. In Italian, however, Joyce's "il gran fenicio lope de mara" is clearly prompted by Beckett's French rather than by either his own English or his own French, while additionally incorporating a once again overtly playful reference, this time to the Spanish Golden Age dramatist Lope de Vega. As to the immediate relevance of both of these embellishments, it is entirely clear that in both cases Joyce did so simply because Joyce *could* do so.

French Joyce once again retains a number of Beckett's key translational decisions, though with some significant reservations. While the original "ruhring" of Joyce's bulls allows for a reading that celebrates sexual and procreative union [6.3], Beckett's anonymous breakwaters are unambiguously under attack, their mournful bellowing recalling the tradition of three great waves that allegorically assault the shores of Ireland. On this occasion Joyce's French prefers to revert to the original note of celebration. His Italian rendering, however, goes on to imply applause for HCE's masterful sexual performance rather than celebration of procreative union.

Settanni, in one of his more sustained interventions, makes four relatively significant adjustments to Joyce's Italian version of the first excerpt in this sequence [6.1], converting the northern sea into a southern one, and the "Phenician rover" thus from a marauding Scandinavian invader into a heroic Milesian invader, while also foregrounding the hero Finn MacCool and relocating the heroic double flatulation from "di sotto il saio" to "di sotto vento," with sailing conditions replacing any associated endeavours. We later find him soberly restraining Joycean linguistic excess (though losing a river) by altering HCE's "manto di burracano" to a "manto di buracano," while emphasizing the violence of HCE's "bursting" rather than merely "breaking" ALP's virginal bar [6.2].

7 Nearly as Badher

Shyr she's nearly as badher as him herself ... Do you know she was calling backwater sals from all around to go in till him, her erring cheef, and tickle the pontiff aisy-oisy? ... Letting on she didn't care, the proxenete! Proxenete and phwat is phthat? Tell us in franca langua. And call a spate a spate. Did they never sharee you ebro at skol, you antiabecedarian? ... For coxyt sake and is that what she is? Botlettle I thought she'd act that loa. Didn't you spot her in her windaug, wubbling up on an osiery chair, with a meusic before her all cunniform letters, pretending to ribble a reedy derg on a fiddle she bogans without a band on? Sure she can't fiddan a dee, with bow or abandon! ... And then she'd esk to vistule a hymn. *The Heart Bowed Down* or *The Rakes of Mallow* or Chelli Michele's *La Calumnia è un Vermicelli* or a balfy bit ov *old Jo Robidson*. Sucho fuffing a fifeing 'twould cut you in two! She'd bate the hen that crowed on the turrace of Babbel. (*ALP* 6, 8; cf. *FW* 198.09–12, 16–20, 23–7, 199.30–1)

[1] Shyr she's nearly as badher as him herself ... Do you know she was calling backwater sals from all around to go in till him, her erring cheef, and tickle the pontiff aisy-oisy? **(*ALP* 6; cf. *FW* 198.09, 10–12: "calling bakvandets sals from all around, nyumba noo, chamba choo")**

Even Phenician rovers, once they have founded their cities and given up roving and settled down to an all too sedate bourgeois existence, can grow despondent and sluggish and no longer interested in conjugal joys that have become just boringly routine. On a broader canvas, Grace Eckley sees the matter in terms of a springtime vegetation ritual, HCE, dejected and comatose, "wears the face of a land destitute in archetypal winter, a land physically and spiritually dead" (1975, 137), while ALP's role is one of "lamenting the dead winter, awakening spirits to new life, stimulating productivity" (1975, 139). ALP, at any rate, undertakes various activities to jolt her man out of his torpor, leading to a disapproving washerwoman's opinion that sure she's nearly as bad as he is, if not badder.

The assertion is supported by the Irish Suir and Luxembourg Syr as well as the American Bad River and the Indian Badhra, and by the reported fact that at one point ALP was calling salty Sallys (Latin *sal* "salt, salt water") of no doubt dirty habits (French *sale* "dirty") from all around and from every backwater, not to mention the three Irish Blackwaters, the Indian Sal, and the Ugandan Alla. The backwater sals are all to some extent aspects of ALP herself, encompassing a plurality of Plurabelles. Their assignment was to go in to her erring "cheef," identified as HCE alias CHE, and "tickle the pontiff aisy-oisy" to reignite his *joie de vivre*, "to restore HCE's potency," as Margot Norris writes, "in an effort to reverse HCE's downfall" (1976, 66). His pontifical qualifications are of course less ecclesiastical than fluvial, namely as a builder of bridges (Latin *pontifex* "bridge-builder") over rivers. For the moment at least, he is also an avatar of the fallen Irish hero Charles Stewart Parnell, a would-be political bridge-builder, whom John Morley, in his 1903 *Life of William Ewart Gladstone*, had referred to as Ireland's "erring chief" (McHugh). Further rivers evoked include the English Till, Pont, and Tiffey, the Lebanese Assi, and the French Oise.

> BECKETT: Pour shire elle-même n'est pas moins trompeuse que lui. ... Sais-tu qu'elle appelait de tous les coins de l'intérieur des salaudines pour lui allier audevant (lui, son maître égaré) et chatouiller ce pontife en taptinoise?

For Beckett's French, ALP is no less a deceiver (*tromper* "to deceive") than he is, and that is for sure (*pour sûr*), with "pour shire" adding the Chinese Shi and Indian Shir to the Suir and Syr. She has, for example, been calling dirty (*salaud*) little tramps (*salaudines*) from all backwood corners of the interior to meet with (*aller au-devant*) her erring master HCE and tickle (*chatouiller*) that pontiff in all secrecy (*en tapinois*), the secrecy enhanced by the Russian Tap and the French Tinée and Oise. Other fluvial references include the French Elle, Brazilian Trombetas ("trompeuse"), French Aude ("salaudines," "audevant") and Allier, the

American Chato, the Touille Bridge on the French Salat, and the Laotian Ou ("chatouiller").

> JOYCE: Pour shire qu'elle en a comme lui elle-même.... Elle embauchait deci delà des salaudines de margottons pour entrer chez lui, Herr aarand chief, et chatouiller ce pontife en taptinoise.

"Pour shire," Joyce's French concurs, likewise invoking the French river Elle, she is indeed much the same as he is (*elle en a comme lui*). ALP was taking on (*embaucher* "to recruit") the little tramps (*salaudines*) aforesaid, salty little Maggies (*Margotton* is a diminutive of *Margot*) from here, there, and everywhere (*deci delà*) to go in to "Herr aarand chief," and tickle that pontiff just as Beckett suggested. Other than the rivers already evoked by Beckett, Joyce's "margottons" conflates, in a bravura performance, references to the Austrian Mahr, German Ahr, American Argo Pond, the Otto of New Zealand, and the Indian Tons, while "aarand" even more succinctly evokes the French Aa, Swiss Aar, Irish Ara, French Aran, and Nigerian Randa as well as three aquatic nouns, Sumerian *a* ("water"), Icelandic *á* ("river"), and Swedish *å* ("river").

> JOYCE: Già, ed ella allora, c'è poca schelda. ... E non racimolò a dritta e a manca putte fiumane che non furo al corrente per far da ganze al capo reone, e solleticarlo lemme lemme?
>
> SETTANNI: [*without change*]

And indeed (*già*), says Joyce's Italian washerwoman, ALP herself now (*allora*) is no paragon, no chosen one (*scelta*), a statement that fluvially includes the Irish Allow, Vietnamese Lô, Norwegian Lora, Russian Or, Ugandan Ora ("allora"); the Italian Po and Spanish Oca ("poca"); and the Dutch Schelde ("schelda"). And didn't she pick out (*racimolare* "to glean grapes") right (*a dritta*) and left (*a manca*) floods (*fiumane*) of riverside (*fiumane*) strumpets (*putte*) who were not the brightest (*al corrente* "au courant") to act like lovers (*ganze*) towards the wicked (*reo*) chief (*capo*), the accused (*reo*) ringleader (*caporione*), and tickle him (*solleticarlo*) nice and easy (*lemme lemme*)? Further rivers include the Kenyan Molo ("racimolò") and Australian Lett ("solleticarlo"), followed by the Italian Lemme and Swiss Emme; while the *corrente* of "al corrente" also means both "current" and "stream."

***[2] Letting on she didn't care, the proxenete! Proxenete and phwat is phthat? Tell us in franca langua. And call a spate a spate. Did they never sharee you ebro at skol, you antiabecedarian?* (*ALP* 6; cf. *FW* 198.16–20: "and phwat is phthat? Emme for your reussischer Honddu jarkon!")**

ALP, as the narrating washerwoman triumphantly asserts, drawing in passing on her store of ancient Greek, was in fact no more than a "proxenete," a bawd, a procuress. "And phwat is phthat?" splutters her evidently less learned colleague in linguistic disbelief, scattering Greek phis and thetas while demanding – and echoing in the process Molly Bloom's "Tell us in plain words" (*U* 4.343) – to be addressed in "franca langua," the phrase a Wakeanized example of the principle of a lingua franca. The latter term literally means "Frankish language," and refers to a jargon consisting of Italian mixed with French, Spanish, Greek, and Arabic and originally used in Mediterranean ports in early modern times as a common language in intercourse with peoples of the Levant (Onions 1966, 530). In plain language, urges the listener, one should call a spade a spade and a spate a spate.

The listener is evidently just an "antiabecedarian," sneers the teller, who, clearly under the impression that the Greek word *proxenêtês* is Hebrew, wonders superciliously if they ever taught her unlettered colleague any Hebrew at all at school (Danish *skol*). More specifically, "Did they never sharee you ebro at skol?" where "sharee" conflates showing and sharing the fruits of knowledge and the Hebrew verb *hôrāh* ("to show, to teach") (McKenzie 1965, 869) – with a perceptible hint of the Russian noun *šarý* ("balls") thrown in for good measure – as well as the Chinese river Sha, the African river Shari, and the Irish Lough Ree, while "ebro" reminds us that the word *Hebrew* itself (Middle English *ebreu*) derives from the Hebrew noun *'ibrî* ("from the other side of the river") (Onions 1966, 434). And since an abecedarian is a person learning their *ABC* from a primer, an "antiabecedarian" is clearly one either opposed to this practice (*anti-*) or at an altogether earlier stage of their journey of learning (*ante-*) or both. Other rivers evoked include the Australian Lang Lang ("langua") and English Cole ("skol"), as well as the Japanese Abe and the American Darien, supported by the Old English noun *bece* ("beck, brook") ("antiabecedarian").

BECKETT: Faisant celle de ne s'en pas soucier, la proxénète! Proxénète, kèsque çedonkça? Traduis en franca lingua. Et appelle une crue une crue. Est-ce qu'on t'a jamais anseigné l'ébreu à l'eskole, espèce d'analphabête?

JOYCE: Faisant celle qui s'en fiche pas mal, la proxénète! Proxénète, mais kesxécé kesxeçà? Pousse le en franca lingua. Et appelle une crue une crue. Ne t'a-t-on pas instruit l'ébreu à l'escaule, espèce d'antibabébibobu?

"Kèsque çedonkça?" enquires Beckett's flummoxed listener, "*Qu'est-ce que c'est donc ça?*" demanding a translation in "franca lingua" and that a spate (*crue*) be called a flood (*crue*). *Appeler un chat un chat* (literally, "to call a cat a cat") is the normal French equivalent of the English *to call a spade a spade*. While Joyce's "spate" is closer to "spade" than Beckett's "crue" is to "chat," an aquatic bridge is provided for Beckett's rendering by the Danish Kattegat, a sea strait so narrow that medieval Dutch mariners considered it a passage (Dutch *gat*) that even a cat (Dutch *kat*) would be hard pressed to squeeze through. Nobody, meanwhile, seems to have taught (*enseigné*) the unlettered listener any Hebrew (*hébreu*) at school (*école*), as her more learned colleague observes, unkindly classifying her on this account as a stupid (*bête*) illiterate (*analphabète*). A generous selection of aquatic features evoked includes the Scottish Ling ("lingua"), the Anse Cochon ("anseigné") of Santa Lucia, the Spanish Ebro and Brazilian Breu ("l'ébreu"), the English Esk and Cole and Belgian Escaut ("l'eskole"), the American Peace ("espèce"), and the Irish Lough Dan as well as the Israeli Dan, American Ana, Pakistani Nal and Hab, the Japanese Abe, and Alph, the sacred river of Coleridge's Xanadu ("d'analphabête").

"Kesxécé kesxeçà?" Joyce's listener splutters more graphically and even more confusedly, though otherwise with the same demand for linguistic simplicity as Beckett's. The complicated play on "sharee" is once again abandoned, giving way to an uncomplicated "instruit" ("taught") and an evocation of the Vietnamese Rui. The presence of the Belgian Escaut (otherwise the Dutch Scheldt) is made clearer by altering Beckett's "eskole" to "escaule," which also allows reference to the English Caul, and the listener is now not just a "babébibobu," a stuttering simpleton, but worse than one (*anti-*), with her infantile babble (French *babil*) reminiscent of the Babelian confusion of languages. The stuttering motif also evokes in passing the stuttering of HCE, revealed as something of a "babébibobu" himself.

Joyce is also learnedly indulging in an arcane French historical reference here. François-Antoine de Boissy d'Anglas (1756–1826) served as president of the National Convention of the first French Republic in the early 1790s. Since the policies his government espoused were denounced as simple-minded by his political adversaries, and since his own speeches were impaired by an unfortunate stutter, wits of the day unkindly dubbed him "l'orateur Babébibobu" (Clark 1980, 174). The Japanese Abe, Ebi, and Ibo, meanwhile, accompanied by the Russian Ob, put in discreet appearances in the epithet, while, as Dirk Van Hulle has observed (2004, 77), the final syllable, "-bu," as the past participle of the verb *boire* ("to drink"), provides a supplementary liquid reference.

JOYCE: Facendo finta che non se ne caleva, la prosseneta. Prosseneta, che mai vuol dire? Dillo in lingua franca. E chiama piena piena. T'hanno mai imparato l'ebro all'iscuola, antabecedariana che sei?
SETTANNI: [*without change*]

Pretending (*facendo finta*) she didn't care (*calere*), indeed, sneers the righteous one. Closing a linguistic circle, Joyce's English "franca langua" and French "franca lingua" become an Italian "lingua franca," the standard phrase in English. In Italian, the phrase "to call a spade a spade" is *chiamare pane al pane* ("to call bread bread"), and as *spade* became "spate," so *pane* becomes "piena" ("flood"). The Ebro reappears, standing in for *ebreo* ("Hebrew") in a possibly inebriated (*ebro*) state. Never having been taught (*imparato*) any Hebrew at school (*scuola*), the disadvantaged listener, clearly an "antabecedariana," has clearly not even reached the preliminary stage (*ante-*) of learning her basic *abbecedario* or *ABC*. New rivers evoked include the Nigerian Inta ("finta"), Italian Cale ("caleva"), French Osse and Welsh Senni ("prosseneta"), and the Corsican Liscu ("all'iscuola").

Experimenting less with direct than with possible implied resonances and distant echoes, Lobner detects in "antabecedariana" additional hints of Tuscan *becera* ("woman of the people") and *ciana* ("vulgar in speech and manners"); sees *-ariana* as implying both an "Indo-European woman," an Aryan, and also Ariadne (Italian *Arianna*), "who guides the reader through *FW*"; and finds Anna herself signalled as the object of the commentary by the opening *an-* and closing *-na* (1989, 12). While no other reader might necessarily detect even a single one of these suggested resonances, it is appropriate to remember Clive Hart's dictum that "we must not dismiss too lightly Joyce's delight in the chance meanings of words, the peculiar interaction often caused by their juxtaposition, and the power of verbal circumstance" (1985, 114). Hart, famously, even goes so far as to claim that ultimately there is no such thing as an incorrect reading of *Finnegans Wake* (112).

[3] For coxyt sake and is that what she is? Botlettle I thought she'd act that loa. Didn't you spot her in her windaug, wubbling up on an osiery chair, with a meusic before her all cunniform letters, pretending to ribble a reedy derg on a fiddle she bogans without a band on? Sure she can't fiddan a dee, with bow or abandon! **(*ALP* 6; *FW* 198.23–7)**

So the well-informed teller condescends to explain what a proxenete is: "It's just the same as if I was to go for examplum now out of telekinesis and proxenete you" (*ALP* 6; *FW* 198.10–12). The "explanation," using bigger words and more complicated terms than the one to be explained, is parodically reminiscent of Samuel Johnson's dictionary, as Grace Eckley notes (1975, 203) – and may be regarded as a humorous reference to it in passing. Unsurprisingly, the listener is no wiser, but is pleasantly horrified anyway. "For God' sake," Joyce initially had her exclaim, before modifying this to "for cox' sake" (Higginson 1960, 37, 48) and finally to "for coxyt sake," invoking the Australian Cox River, the homonymous *cocks*, and, appropriately in the context of classical learning, Cocytus, the underworld river of "lamentation" (*kôkutos*) in Greek mythology. But little the listener had thought that ALP would act that low, invoking for fluvial emphasis the Botletle of Botswana and the Chilean Loa. The more hard-boiled teller is unsurprised, having herself spotted ALP at her window (Old Norse *vindauga*), perched wobbling on a wickerwork chair with sheets of music before her covered in indecipherable signs, pretending to scrape out a wavering dirge on a fiddle she bows with a bow that has lost all its hairs – though in actual fact she can't play a note anyway, bow or no bow. Margot Norris suggests that ALP's fiddling on a wobbling chair in her window may in fact be for soliciting donations, as an ageing, idle, and depressed HCE loses any ambition to support the family (2015, 138).

A generous selection of fluvial references includes the South African Pot ("spot"), Latvian Windau and Daugava ("windaug"), Chinese Wu, Serbian Ub, Chinese Li, English Lin, and Scottish Ling ("wubbling"), French Oise ("osiery") and Meuse ("meusic"), Australian Lett ("letters"), English Ribble, American Reedy and Irish Lough Ree, Irish Derg and Lough Derg, Australian Bogan, Irish Bandon, Suir, and Fiddaun, Scottish Dee, and Canadian Bow. The "cunniform letters" might as well be Egyptian cuneiform as far as the narrator is concerned, though allowing for some significant interplay between Latin *cuneus* ("wedge") and Latin *cunnus* ("cunt") (Ayto 1991, 150).

BECKETT: Par le coccyte, voilà donc ce qu'elle vaut? Je n'audrais jamais crû ça d'elle. Ne l'avais-tu pas repérée à sa fennyêtre, se dandelinant

> sur une chaise en osier, et devant elle une meusique toute en caractères ruséiformes, affectant de faire suérinter une lémantation lugubre d'un violon qu'elle frobichait avec un archet sans crin d'atout? Sûrement qu'elle ne peut pas juer un faa, que l'archet soit ou non à tous crins.

Beckett's "par le coccyte" adroitly captures the Cox, the cocks, and the Cocytus (French *Cocyte*). Never, says the listener, would I have (*je n'aurais jamais*) believed (*crû*) that of her, adding the French river Aude and the French noun *crue* ("flood") for emphasis. The narrator, however, has noticed (*repéré*) ALP at her window (*fenêtre*), swaying to and fro (*se dandelinant*) on a wickerwork chair (*chaise en osier*), with a sheet of music covered in cunning (*rusé*) signs in front of her, pretending to be sweating away ("suerinter") at grinding out a mournful (*lugubre*) lament ("lémantation") on a violin that she was scraping (*frotter* "to rub") with a bow without a single hair – though in fact she can't play (*jouer*) a single note ("un faa") anyway, whether the bow has all its hairs or not. An extraordinarily generous selection of aquatic references includes not only the Indian Feni ("fennyêtre") but also no fewer than thirteen rivers, two lakes, and four water-related nouns generated by the single word "dandelinant," thus including all of the Israeli Dan, Angolan Dande, Russian Delin, French Elle, Chinese Li, Irish Lee, English Lea, Lean, Leen, and Lin, Polish Ina, Thai Nan, and Scottish Nant as well as the Irish Lough Dan and Scottish Loch Nant and a collection of four water-related nouns: Irish *linn* ("lake"), Scots *linn* ("waterfall"), Cornish *lyn* ("lake"), and Welsh *nant* ("stream"). The more than generous flow continues with the French Oise ("osier") and Meuse ("meusique"), Romanian Rus ("ruséiformes"), Lake Geneva (French *Lac Léman*) ("lémantation"), Canadian Frobisher Bay ("frobichait"), the Luxembourg Syr and Sûre ("sûrement"), Chinese Jue ("juer"), and French Aa ("faa"). The coinage "suérinter" conflates two different types of sweating, *suer* ("to sweat, to labour") and *suinter* ("to sweat, to ooze"), while "un faa" conflates the river Aa and the musical note fa or F.

> JOYCE: Nom de flieuve, voilà ce qu'elle est? Je n'aurais jamais pensé qu'elle eure fait ça. Ne l'avais-tu pas répérée à sa fennyètre se dandelinant sur une chaise en osier, et devant elle une meusique en tricroches conéiformes, affectant de faire suérinter une lémantation en saule d'un pleureur qu'elle frobichait avec un archet sans crins du touch? Sûrement elle ne peut pas juer un faa, que l'archet soit ou non à tous crins.

"Nom de flieuve," exclaims Joyce's French listener, abandoning Cox, cocks, and Cocytus alike, while conflating *nom de Dieu* ("in God's name") and *fleuve* ("river"), she would never have thought that ALP would do that, further conflating the subjunctive *eût* ("would have") and the French river Eure. The narrator echoes Beckett's narrator in having seen ALP swaying to and fro on her wickerwork chair, but the music in front of her is now "en tricroches," in demisemiquavers (*triplecroches*), and might as well be in cuneiform, conflated with *con* ("cunt"). As in Beckett's rendering, she is pretending to be labouring to produce a lament, scraping away with a hairless bow, even though she is in fact unable to play a single note – but the lament she pretends to produce is now specified as being like a weeping willow (*saule pleureur*) in the key of G major (*en sol majeur*). In addition to the many rivers conjured up by Beckett, we find the English Roch ("tricroches"), eastern European Sau ("saule"), and French Touch (the English "touch" substituted for the French *tout*).

JOYCE: Ostrigotta, ora capesco! Mairavrei credutala cosí bassenta. Non l'hai scorta al suo varone, a dondolarsi su un vacillavimine, con un foglio spartito in samassi di sigle, come chi suonasse chissà quale anienia, su un villanacello senza groppa né corda? Ma costei non sa paganeniare cordevolmente.

SETTANNI: Ostrigotta, ora capisco! Mairavrei credutala cosí bassenta. Non l'hai scorta al suo verone, a dondolarsi su un vacillavimine, con un foglio spartito in samassi di sigle, come chi suonasse chissà quale nienia, su un villanacello senza groppa né corda? Ma costei non sa paganeniare cordevolmente.

"Good God, now I understand!" exclaims Joyce's Italian listener, though the implied semantic meaning is tightly wrapped in a bravura word play. "Ostrigotta" conflates the Triestine exclamation *ostregheta* (roughly, "by gosh") and the standard Italian *ostrogota* ("Ostrogoth") (Zanotti 2001, 424), the reference to the Ostrogoths invoking, appropriately for many readers, the idiomatic phrase *Questo per me è ostrogoto* ("That's all Greek to me"). Umberto Eco further observes that while *ostregheta* literally means "little oyster" (Italian *ostrica* "oyster"), it is also, in the context, a euphemism for the blasphemous oath *ostia!* ("by the host!"), leading to the further inclusion of a German *Gott* ("God") in "ostrigotta" (2001, 116). The exclamation also evokes the Romanian Gota, American Oyster, and English Otter rivers, while "ora capesco" conflates *ora capisco* ("now I understand") and the Russian Or, Ugandan

Ora, and English Esk as well as the Romanian noun *ape* ("waters"). Never (*mai*) would I have (*avrei*) believed her (*credutala*) so low (*basso*), she adds, evoking in the process the Italian Maira ("mairavrei"), Indonesian Tala ("credutala"), and South American Senta ("bassenta"), as well as the Arabic *ma* and Kikuyu *mai*, both meaning "water."

Her companion, however, confirms that she has seen (*scorta*) ALP on her balcony (*verone*), rocking herself (*dondolarsi* "to rock") on a wickerwork rocking chair (*vacillare* "to rock," *vimine* "osier"), with a musical score (*spartito*) spread out (*sparto*) on a sheet (*foglio*), with great masses (*masse*) and blocks (*masso* "boulder, block") of signs (*sigle*). ALP was like someone playing (*come chi suonasse*) some dirge (*nenia*), a theme song (*sigla musicale*), perhaps (*chissà*), on a rustic (*villano*) cello without either a back (*groppa*) or a string (*corda*) to it. But that same ALP (*costei*) is no Paganini (*non sa paganeniare*) and certainly does not know how (*non sa*) to play a dirge (*nenia*) with as much feeling (*cordialmente*) as him. Rivers evoked include the French Var ("varone"), Russian Don, French Onde, Kenyan Ndo, Swiss Aar, German Ahr, and Croatian Arsa ("dondolarsi"), South American Sama and Lebanese Assi ("samassi"), French Asse ("suonasse"), Belarussian Isa ("chissà"), Togolese Anie and Italian Aniene ("anienia"), Albanian Lana and Indonesian Ello ("villanacello"), Czech Oppa ("groppa"), Australian Ord ("corda"), American Pagan, Chinese Nen, New Caledonian Ni, Papua New Guinean Niar, and Congolese Niari ("paganeniare"), and the Australian Ord and Albanian Devoll ("cordevolmente").

Settanni feels it incumbent upon himself to correct "capesco" to "capisco"; "varone" to "verone"; and "anienia" to "nienia," thus achieving impeccably normal Italian vocabulary, but losing in the process the English Esk, French Var, Togolese Anie, and Italian Aniene.

***[4] And then she'd esk to vistule a hymn.* The Heart Bowed Down *or* The Rakes of Mallow *or Chelli Michele's* La Calumnia è un Vermicelli *or a balfy bit ov* old Jo Robidson. *Sucho fuffing a fifeing 'twould cut you in two! She'd bate the hen that crowed on the turrace of Babbel.* (*ALP* 8; *FW* 199.30–1)**

In order to cheer up (and sexually reinvigorate) her depressed husband, ALP would sometimes ask if she could whistle an occasional "hymn" (for him, Hum), celebrating in the process three musical Dubliners, Michael Kelly (1762–1826), Michael Balfe (1808–1870), and Joseph Robinson (1815–1898). *The Heart Bowed Down* is an aria from Balfe's

The Bohemian Girl (1843), according to which "the heart bowed down by weight of woe to weakest hopes will cling," but all to no avail, for "memory is the only friend that grief can call its own." The traditional and very jaunty Irish song "The Rakes of Mallow," on the other hand, not at all bowed down, cheerfully celebrates instead the carefree joys of "kissing the girls against their will."

La calunnia è un venticello ("calumny is like a little breeze"), cynically advocating the uses of calumny as a strategic political tool, is the hypocritical Don Basilio's aria in Rossini's *The Barber of Seville*, with the "breeze" adjusted here, demonstrating a fine disregard for grammatical nicety, to a dish of pasta – whose name, *vermicelli*, appropriately for the potentially insidious effects of calumny, literally means "little worms." Authorship of the aria is transferred from the Italian Rossini to the celebrated Irish tenor Michael Kelly, correspondingly adjusted for the sake of the rhyme to "Chelli Michele," and who played the role of Don Basilio in the world premiere of Mozart's *The Marriage of Figaro* (Ewen 1963, 238), while Michael Balfe, a likewise celebrated baritone, appeared in 1829 in the French premiere of *The Barber of Seville*.

Joseph Robinson, for his part, arranged Thomas Moore's *Irish Melodies* as well as several other volumes of Irish songs for voice and piano. "Poor Old Joe," meanwhile, changed from an original "Old Black Joe" (1853), is an American parlour song by Stephen Foster, but applied here to poor old Joe Robinson. The phrase "a balfy bit or *old Jo Robidson*," introduced in the 1927 *transition* text, suggesting two separate musical items, was changed to "a balfy bit ov *old Jo Robidson*" on galley proofs of the 1928 Gaige *ALP* (Higginson 1960, 63, 81). The change may conceivably have been due to advance news reports that the Czech village of Bítov, surrounding iconic Bítov Castle near the confluence of two rivers, was to be drowned in 1934 after one of them was dammed. Rose and O'Hanlon, however, ignoring the rising waters of Bítov, have ALP persist in whistling either "a balfy bit or *Old Joe Robidson*" (*FW2* 156.37–8).

Margot Norris sees ALP's musical efforts as also "the water music made by the bubbling Liffey," used by ALP "to soothe and encourage the fallen HCE, reviving him, like the unconscious Lear, with melody" (1982, 208), her "reedy derg" like the mournful sound of the wind in the reeds, her whistling like the eerie sound of the wind in the trees on her banks. Rivers evoked in this musical interlude include the English Esk, Polish Vistula ("vistule"), American Heart, Canadian Bow, Irish Allow, Vietnamese Lô ("Mallow"), American Lumni ("calumnia"), English Ver ("vermicelli"), Alph the sacred river ("balfy"), and the American Obids

("Robidson"). Such puffing and piping there was, reports the narrator, that she'd bate the hen that crowed on the turrace (Latin *turris* "tower") of Babbel – while perhaps also not above "biting the hand" that feeds. The Babelian confusion of languages ensures that the crowing, a cock's prerogative, is attributed instead to the hen – who otherwise shares some affinity with the Capitoline geese whose cackling in ancient times allegedly saved Rome from Gaulish invaders. Further rivers include the Costa Rican Sucio ("sucho"), Nigerian Ife ("fifeing"), American Crow, Romanian Tur ("turrace"), and Australian Abba ("Babbel").

> BECKETT: Alors elle demandait à sievfler un hymne. *Je n'ai gardé dans mon malheur* ou *J'ai fait trois fois le tour du monde* ou *La calunnia è un vermicelli* de Chelli Michele, ou un morceau bien charbentié du *Gouronnement de la Buse*. Un tel boucquan de bordel, ça te fendrait les oreilles. Elle en remontrerait à la poule qui chantait sur la tourrasse de Babil!

Beckett's ALP would also sometimes ask to whistle (*siffler*) a hymn. Her selection now included *Je n'ai gardé dans mon malheur*, properly *L'amitié d'une hirondelle*, a popular French song of the 1860s, in which a mournful captive's sole recollected pleasure was the song of a swallow, now no longer to be heard, at the window of his prison cell, "Je n'ai gardé dans mon malheur / Que l'amitié d'une hirondelle" ("All I kept in my misfortune / was the friendship of a swallow"). *J'ai fait trois fois le tour du monde* ("Three times I've been around the world") is a tenor aria from the once very popular French operetta *Les cloches de Corneville* (*The Bells of Corneville*) by Robert Planquette. *La calunnia è un vermicelli*, still rhymingly attributed to Chelli Michele, remains an item in ALP's repertoire, though now without any reference to the river Lumni.

Her *pièce de résistance*, however, is a well-polished piece (*bien charpenté* "well built") from an otherwise unrecorded work entitled *Le Gouronnement de la Buse*. The phrase *couronnement de buse* refers in an engineering context (and hence the term *charpenté*, literally, "carpentered") to the capping (*couronner* "to crown") of a conduit or tube (*buse*) such as a well-shaft. Changing the context radically, Beckett combines *couronnement* ("coronation") and the very colloquial terms *gourer* ("to make a mistake, to blow it") and *buse* ("idiot") to suggest as a song title something like "The idiot's crowning blunder." There is also a humorous reference – appropriately after the account of the Phenician rover HCE – to the notorious French pirate, Olivier Levasseur (1690–1730), the original "Captain Blood," who accumulated enormous amounts of treasure trove before being hanged for piracy, and who was known, because of his rapacity, as La Buse (The Buzzard). Beckett's invented musical offering might thus be taken to celebrate also both the crowning achievement (*couronnement*) and crowning mistake (allowing himself to be captured) of the redoubtable La Buse.

The racket (*boucan*) the whistling ALP made, a veritable whorehouse (*bordel*) racket (*bordel*), would split (*fendre*) your ears. She could teach a thing or two (*en remontrer*) to the hen (*poule*) that sang (*chantait*) and squawked (*chantait*) and crowed (*chantait*) on the terrace (*terrasse*) of the Tower (*tour*) of Babel, already noted for babbling (*babil*) of all sorts. Rivers evoked in all of this include the Italian Sieve ("sievfler"), French Gard ("gardé") and Eure ("malheur"), English Char and Indian Benti ("charbentié"), Chinese Quan ("boucquan"), Australian Ord ("bordel"), American Poule, and finally the Belgian Our, Mongolian Ur, Russian Ura, and French Asse ("tourrasse"), a more than adequate collective contribution to the waters of Babylon (Arabic *Bābil*).

> JOYCE: Aleure elle demandait à sièvler un hymne, *Je n'ai gardé dans mon malheur*, ou *Cadet Roussel a trois cheveux* ou *La calunnia e un vermicelli* de Chelli Michele ou un morceau bien charpenté du *Gouronnement de la Buse*. Fifrant et foufrant à vous fendre en douix. Elle en montrerait à la mère poularde qui faisait cocurico sur la tourasse de Babil!

And then (*alors*), says Joyce's French teller of the tale, she would ask to whistle a hymn, just as Beckett's ALP had done, and had shared with the latter three of her four pieces. Beckett's *J'ai fait trois fois le tour du monde* gives way to the cheerier *Cadet Roussel a trois cheveux*, three trips around the world supplanted by Cadet Roussel's three scant remaining hairs. *Cadet Rousselle* (the original spelling) is a French song of the 1790s, initially mildly satirical of a local official of that name and subsequently widely popular as a folksong. Cadet Rousselle has three of everything, distinctly oddly in many cases, and one verse runs "Cadet Rousselle a trois cheveux, / Deux pour la face, un pour la queue, / Et quand il va voir sa maîtresse, / Il les met tous les trois en tresse" ("Cadet Rousselle has just three hairs, / two in front and one behind, / and when he goes to see his mistress, / he puts all three of them in a braid"). Joyce clearly liked the song: he has Jimmy Doyle and his foreign friends sing it as they march along with linked arms in "After the Race" (*D* 40). ALP's fuffing and fifeing ("fifrant et foufrant") would cut you in two (*en deux*), and she could certainly teach a thing or two to the fat mother hen ("la mère poularde") that went cockadoodledoo (*cocorico*), possibly celebrating the fact that her cock was a cuckold (*cocu*), on the terrace of the babbling tower of Babel. Rivers added to Beckett's fluvial collection include the French Eure ("aleure") and Elle ("Roussel"), French Doux and Russian Ik ("douix"), and the Nicaraguan Coco and Argentine Rico ("cocurico").

JOYCE: E poi con permesso vistolava un inno, *Fenesta ca' lucive*, o *Evviva Noei*, o *La calunnia è un vermicello* di Michele Chellini, o una cabvaletta del mastro Pulcini. Uno zufolamento da rompere i timpani. Peggio che le cento galline del Checco!

SETTANNI: E poi con permesso vistolava un inno, *Fenesta ca' lucive*, o *Evviva Noei*, o *La calunnia è un vermicello* di Michele Chellini, o una cavaletta del mastro Pulcini. Uno zufolamento da rompere i timpani. Peggio che le cento galline del Checco!

Joyce's Italian ALP would also, with permission, venture to whistle a hymn (*inno*). *Fenesta ca lucive*, for example, is a Neapolitan song recycled in Bellini's opera *La sonnambula* (1831): the hero, returned after a long absence, and seeing that the window (*fenesta*) that used to be lighted (*ca lucive*) is lighted no more, learns to his sorrow that his beloved is dead. *Evviva noi* ("Here's to us"), on the other hand, is a popular Italian children's song happily celebrating the joys of life and family; "*Noei*" combines *noi* ("us") and Noè, bibulous father Noah, who notoriously celebrated the joys of wine, not wisely but too well. Joyce himself zealously followed Noah's example in this, and Ellmann (1982, 215) reports his boisterously inebriated late-night singing in Trieste of a popular drinking song, *Viva Noè, il gran patriarca* ("Long live Noah, the great patriarch"). Another of ALP's choices would be *La calunnia è un vermicello*, with the *vermicelli* now singularized and the alleged author no longer Chelli Michele but Michele Chellini, conflating the Irish Kelly and the Italian Bellini.

Puccini also comes in for some serious onomastic readjustment. Puccini was in fact a favourite of Joyce's, who attended no fewer than eight consecutive performances of *La Bohème* in Trieste in 1908 (Bowker 2011, 175). ALP's final musical selection was a "cabvaletta" that was partly a *cavaletta* (an aria), rendered as if by a chirping locust (*cabaletta*), and in any case just a piece of trickery (*cavalletta*). It was the work of one "mastro Pulcini," celebrating a Puccini who may indeed be a master (*mastro*) but whose name is here combined with *pulcino* ("chick") to suggest a buffoon, a *Pulcinella* ("Punch"). In the Italian *commedia dell'arte* Pulcinella was characterized *inter alia* by a squeaky nasal voice, a characteristic apparently echoed here by the chirping locust.

At any rate, ALP's performance was a display of whistling ("zufolamento") deafening enough to burst (*rompere*) one's eardrums (*timpani*). It was worse even than Checco's hundred hens, we are assured. Lobner observes (1986, 87; 1989, 40) that the cryptic phrase "Peggio che le cento galline del Checco!" is a playful subversion of the by now proverbial Tuscan phrase *Egli è il gallo della Checca / tutte segue tutte becca* ("He's Checca's cock, he follows them all, he pecks them all," in other words, "he pecks just as many as he wants to"). The phrase in question derives originally from a humorous sixteenth-century Italian poem, *Il gallo di Madonna Checca*, by Giulio Cesare Croce (1550–1609), blacksmith and self-taught poet, recounting the amatory vicissitudes of one Madonna Checca and her lover or *gallo* (literally, "cock, rooster"), who has a very roving eye when it comes to other ladies. The expression acquired new life (and musical resonance) in Donizetti's *L'elisir d'amore* (1832), in which the quack doctor Dulcamara sings of a competitor that "Egli è il gallo della Checca, / tutte vede, tutte becca" ("He's Checca's cock, he sees them all, he pecks them all").

Joyce's subversion implies that his Checco, a comic would-be Don Juan, is the pursued rather than the pursuer, turned on by his hundred unamused and highly vocal "hens." Joyce may also have recalled a *cause célèbre* in Renaissance Florence involving an assassin named Checco Orsi murdering a prominent patrician of that city and being subsequently almost lynched himself by the murdered man's outraged family and supporters, clamouring for vengeance. Joyce's Checco, moreover, hints at the delinquencies, amatory and otherwise, of HCE, onomastically present in the name as both CHE and HEC – a presence further underlined by the exclamation *ecco* ("there he is"). It may or may not be entirely coincidental, finally, that the Italian poet, essayist, and journalist Emilio Cecchi (1884–1966) was one of the first writers in Italy to discover *Ulysses*. His work appeared in various Italian journals, as well as in *transition*, whose pages he occasionally shared with Joyce. Fluvial references are provided to the Polish Vistula ("vistolava"), Austrian Inn ("inno"), Indonesian Ello ("vermicello"), Australian Lett ("cabvaletta"), and Dutch Maas ("mastro").

Settanni, meanwhile, evidently considering an aria (*cavaletta*) no fit place for a locust (*cabaletta*), sternly removes the latter, but leaves Joyce's Italian otherwise unmolested.

[5] Comments and Contexts

The present sequence focuses inter alia on self-reflexive play on language and languages, including Greek ("proxenete"), Hebrew ("sharee"), and "cunniform letters." Joyce's English "franca langua" and French "franca lingua" become an Italian "lingua franca," the standard phrase in English. In his Italian, the exclamation "ostrigotta" conflates the Triestine *ostregheta* and the standard Italian *ostrogota*, the latter invoking the idiomatic phrase *Questo per me è ostrogoto* ("That's all Greek to me"). Even "the hen that crowed on the turrace of Babbel" expresses herself, appropriately confused, in a language not her own, namely the language of cocks rather than hens.

Beckett, whose French is in this sequence largely taken over unchanged or only minimally changed by Joyce, achieves a considerable feat of hydronymy in combining no fewer than an impressive nineteen fluvial and aquatic references in the single word "dandelinant" [7.3], adopted unchanged by Joyce. His invention of *Le Gouronnement de la Buse* for ALP to whistle, meanwhile, is a jocularly ingenious stroke, and is likewise adopted without alteration by Joyce [7.4].

This sequence is also particularly rich in cultural references on Joyce's part, especially but not exclusively musical. His English thus refers to Parnell and Samuel Johnson as well as to Michael Kelly, Michael Balfe, Joseph Robinson, and Rossini; his French to Boissy d'Anglas as well as Cadet Rouselle; and his Italian, particularly strikingly, to all of Paganini, Bellini, Puccini, Pulcinella, Giulio Cesare Croce, and Donizetti.

Settanni pedantically converts three of Joyce's punning coinages, individual words in each case, into standard Italian, the three would-be improvements costing the evocation of four rivers [7.3]. He likewise manages to undo a rather more complicated pun in humourlessly removing a Joycean locust (*cabaletta*) from a Joycean aria (*cavaletta*) [7.4].

8 Simps and Signs

And didn't she up in sorgues and go and trot doon and stand in her douro, puffing her old dudheen, and every shirvant siligirl or wensum farmerette walking the pilend roads, Sawy, Fundally, Daery or Maery, Milucre, Awny or Graw, usedn't she make her a simp or sign to slip inside by the sullyport? ... And legging a jig or so on the sihl to show them how to shake their benders and the dainty how to bring to mind the gladdest garments out of sight and all the way of a maid with a man and making a sort of a cackling noise like two and a penny or half a crown and holding up a silliver shiner. Throwing all the neiss little whores in the world at him!To inny captured wench you wish of no matter what sex of pleissful ways two adda tammar a lizzy a lossie to hug and hab haven in Humpy's apron! (*ALP* 9–10; *FW* 200.17–21, 23–8, 29–32)

***[1] And didn't she up in sorgues and go and trot doon and stand in her douro, puffing her old dudheen, and every shirvant siligirl or wensum farmerette walking the pilend roads, Sawy, Fundally, Daery or Maery, Milucre, Awny or Graw, usedn't she make her a simp or sign to slip inside by the sullyport?* (ALP 9; FW 200.17–21)**

Former marauding Phenician rover and duke alien, HCE, as we have seen, eventually falls into a deep depression as the excitement of pillage and plunder give way to the boredom of domestic life. ALP intensifies her activities as procuress in hopes of jolting him out of his inertia. So exchanging her unproductive sorrow (German *Sorge*) for practical socks, she ups and trots down to stand in her door, accompanied by the French Sorgue and Sorgues, Scottish Doon, and Spanish Douro (reinforced by the Breton *dour*, Welsh *dŵr*, and Basque *ur*, all meaning "water"), and puffing away for comfort on her stump (Irish *dúid*) of an old clay pipe (Irish *dúidín*), an activity perhaps unexpected but permitting reference to the French Doubs, Indian Dudhi, English Duddon, Scottish Dee, and English Dean. "Joyce's ambivalent, complex portrait of Anna Livia Plurabelle requires simultaneous characterization on a number of levels," Norris reminds us. ALP, "puffing her old dudheen," for example, is simultaneously a woman going to extraordinary lengths to reanimate her depressed and impotent husband, recruiting young whores for the purpose, and "a polluted, industrial Liffey feeding the smokestacks on her bank" (1982, 201).

Arrived at her douro, we are told, she made simpering signs and signals to various of the passing backwater sals, to sally in to her unresponsive man through the sallyport that was in this case also a sullyport. Some of them were silly servant girls, some of them winsome country lasses, professionally engaged in walking the roads of the island of Ireland – more specifically, for example, Dublin's South Bull Wall, the end of which was originally called the Pile Ends, referring to the piles on which the wall was originally constructed (McHugh). Joyce, "the most daring of innovators, has decided to be as local as a hedge poet," Padraic Colum wrote, adding that this localness in fact "belongs to James Joyce's innovations" (1928a, 320–1). Rivers so far evoked in the account include the Chinese Shi and Indian Shir ("shirvant"), Siberian Siligir and Swiss Sihl ("siligirl"), English Wensum, and the Indian Pili and Mexican Pilon ("pilend").

Seven of the winsome siligirls are mentioned by name, anticipating the seven dams that HCE will later [9.4] be said to have had to wive him and constituting one set of variations on the many names of the seven rainbow girls who will later appear at various points in *Finnegans Wake*. All seven of the present set have their roots in Irish mythology, Joyce very likely having been familiar with all of these names from such sources as the *Transactions of the Irish Ossianic Society*, published in Dublin in the 1850s, and later reworkings of the legends they contained.[1]

Sawy is thus a transformed Sadhbh /saɪv/ ("sweet"), previously transformed by enchantment into a deer and subsequently mother of Finn mac Cumhaill's son Oisín ("fawn"). Fundally, doubtless fun

1 On Joyce's considerable knowledge of early Irish legend and pseudo-history, see Maria Tymoczko (1994). See also, with reservations, Gibson (2005).

to dally with, is a metamorphosed Finnuala /fɪn'uələ/ ("fair-shouldered"), daughter of the sea god Manannán mac Lir, transformed by enchantment into a swan. Daery, no doubt a dairymaid when not otherwise engaged, takes her name from Dáire /'dɑɪrə/ ("virile"), any one of several legendary male figures, but transgendered here in order to provide a rhyming Daery for Maery – whose name derives from Máire /'mɑɪrə/ the English *Mary*, but also recalls a legendary virago named Máir, who unsuccessfully attempted to seduce Finn. Milucre, no doubt also a milkmaid, is Milúachra /mɪ'luəxrə/ (a name of uncertain meaning), and Awny is Áine /'ɑɪnjə/ ("radiance"), the two of whom were sisters who vied with great determination for the love of Finn. Graw, finally, is Gráinne /'grɑɪnjə/ (another name of uncertain meaning), who was betrothed to the ageing Finn but eloped with his virile young lieutenant Diarmaid instead, leading to the tragic death of the latter in one of the best known of the Fenian stories, *The Pursuit of Diarmaid and Gráinne*. "Graw" accordingly also recalls the Irish noun *grá* ("love")

The septet are accompanied by numerous rivers and one large bay, the Indian Sai and Croatian Sava ("Sawy"); the Canadian Bay of Fundy, the Swedish Dal, and the Russian Alei ("Fundally"); the Indian Dai and the Scottish Daer Water ("Daery"); the American May and Austrian Mahr ("Maery"); the Canadian Milk and Welsh Lugg ("Milucre"); the Scottish Awe and Indonesian Anai ("Awny"); and the Scottish Awe again, with the Polish Grawe ("Graw"). The Russian Sim and a foreshortened Canadian Simpson also appear ("simp").

> BECKETT: Et ne s'est elle pas insorgnée et mise à descendre au golo, puis à se tenir sur sa portenza tirant sur sa vieille bouffarde, et toutes les serbantes à tête de linotte, toutes les garcieuses fermierettes qui cheminaient sur les raderoutes de l'île, Sawy, Frindally, Daery ou Maery, Milucre, Awney ou Graw, voilà t'il pas qu'elle leur faisait des grimaces en signe qu'il fallait entrer en douce par la porte dissimulée.

And didn't she go and dress herself up (*s'orner* "to adorn oneself"), asks Beckett's French washerwoman, and set off down, clowning around (*au golo*), at a gallop (*au galop*) and then stand at her door (*porte*) pulling (*tirant*) on her old pipe (*bouffarde*). Rivers accompany her: the Austrian Inn and French Sorgue ("insorgnée"), the Corsican Golo ("au golo"), and the Italian Potenza. And it was all the servant girls with brains like birds (*tête de linotte* "bird-brained") and all the graceful (*gracieuses*) farmgirl tarts (*garces*) walking (*cheminaient*) the roadstead (*rade*) roads of the island (*île*), at whom ALP pulled faces (*faisait des grimaces*) as a sign that they should go in, on the sly (*en douce*), through the hidden door (*la porte dissimulée*). The cast of the septet has two minor name changes: Fundally, no longer so much fun to dally with, has become Frindally to accommodate the Scottish river Fruin and the German Inde, while Awny has for similar reasons become Awney in order to evoke the Canadian Ney. Other rivers evoked include the Irish Bann ("serbantes"), German Notte ("linotte"), German Ahr and Swiss Aar ("garcieuses"), English Erme and Romanian Ier ("fermierettes"), Dutch Maas ("grimaces"), Thai Sin ("signe"), Caribbean Douce ("en douce"), and Russian Sim ("dissimulée").

JOYCE: Et ne s'est-elle pas insorguée et mise à descendre à golo, puis à se tenir sur sa portenza tirant sur sa vieille bouflarde, et toutes les servantes à têtes de linottes, toutes les garcieuses fermierrettes qui cheminaient sur les raderoutes de l'île, Sawy, Fundally, Daery ou Maery, Milucre, Awny ou Graw, voilà-t-il pas qu'elle leur faisait des moues et des signes qu'il fallait entrer en douce par la porte étroite.

Joyce's French remains very close to Beckett's, though altering "ne s'est elle pas insorgnée" to "ne s'est elle pas insorguée," dispensing with ALP's adornment of herself and playing on the Italian verb *insorgere* ("to appear, to rise up") as if it were a French verb in order to refer to the river Sorgue again. And didn't she rise up (Italian *insorge* "rises up"), says his speaker, and and set off down at a gallop (*au galop*), still clowning around (*à golo*), and then stand at her door (*porte*) pulling (*tirant*) on her old pipe ("bouflarde"), which has now been adjusted to accommodate the eastern European river Ufla. Unlike Beckett, Joyce avoids any alteration to the original names of the seven backwater sals. Rather than pulling faces, ALP now employs more ladylike pouts (*moue* "pout") as signs that these ladies should enter by the door that is now not concealed but just narrow (*étroit*). The two changes permit mention of the New Caledonian river Mou and the American Detroit River.

JOYCE: Ed ecco che insorgue e giú a galoppo alla porta piantona, sbuffando di pipastrello, e ad ogni sciocca d'inserverniente, ad ogni ganziosa fattorelletta che cercava la sua in corso Belline, Sawy, Fundally, Daely e Maery, Milucre, Awny e Graw, non le faceva segno di smorfia d'insinuarsi per l'usciolino?

SETTANNI: Ed ecco che insorgue e giú a galoppo alla porta piantona, sbuffando di pipastrello, e ad ogni sciocca d'inseverniente, ad ogni

> ganziosa fattorelletta che cercava la sua in corso Belline, Sawy, Fundally, Daely e Maery, Milucre, Awny e Graw, faceva sí o no segno di smorfia d'insinuarsi per l'usciolino?

In Italian, lo and behold (*ecco*), she rises up (*insorge*) and heads down (*giú*) at a gallop (*a galoppo*) to the door (*porta*), where she waits (*di piantone*), mounting guard (*piantona*) like a sentry (*piantone*), puffing (*sbuffando*) on a pipe (*pipa*), lurking in the shadows like a bat (*pipistrello*). The river Sorgue is pressed into service once again ("insorgue") as are the Scottish Gala and Norwegian Opo ("a galoppo"), followed by the Indonesian Ello ("pipastrello"). And to every silly goose (*sciocca*) of a servant girl (*inserviente*) and every farm girl ("fattorelletta") offering love (*ganza* "lover") and on the look-out for love herself ("che cercava la sua") on the Corso Belline, including the seven we already know, ALP gave a sign (*segno*) by pulling faces (*smorfia* "grimace") to slip inside (*insuarsi*) by a door that is now neither concealed nor just narrow, but is certainly very small, a tiny little door (*usciolino*) in fact, smaller even than an *usciolo* ("little door"), which itself is smaller than any ordinary *uscio* ("door"). Lobner sees, by heavy implication, a complementary reference also to the Tuscan *uccellino* ("cock, penis") (1989, 38). The seven names remain unchanged from the original with just one exception: Daery is altered to Daely, now a reflex of Della, one of the first women to migrate to Ireland in a legendary pre-Deluge invasion (Ó Corráin and Maguire 1990, 71). The change also permits a reference to the Australian river Daly.

As for the "corso Belline" on which the ladies were looking for and offering love, there are streets called Corso Bellini in various Italian cities and towns, named for the revered composer of *La sonnambula*, *Norma*, and other well-loved Italian operas. The mononymous and unrelated Belline was a self-professed French seer of the 1850s who devised a special pack of Tarot-like cards for use in fortune telling. The ladies in question may thus have been either walking up and down the Corso or just considering taking a course (*corso*) in Belline's system of foretelling the future and its associated amatory possibilities. Rivers evoked include the English Severn and Ver ("inserverniente"), French Elle and Australian Lett ("fattorelletta"), Indian Mor ("smorfia"), Thai Sin ("insuarsi"), and the Nigerian Oli and English Lin ("usciolino").

Settanni simplifies Joyce's "inserverniente" to "inseverniente" without either semantic or fluvial loss, and alters "non le faceva segno" ("didn't she give them a sign") to a more colloquial "faceva sí o no segno" ("she gave, yes or no, a sign"), thus economically achieving fluvial reference to both the Kenyan Sio and the Japanese Ono.

[2] ***And legging a jig or so on the sihl to show them how to shake their benders and the dainty how to bring to mind the gladdest garments out of sight and all the way of a maid with a man and making a sort of a cackling noise like two and a penny or half a crown and holding up a silliver shiner.*** **(*ALP* 9–10; *FW* 200.23–8)**

ALP took pains to train her recruits personally, kicking her legs in something like a jig on her doorsill to show them how to show their own legs to best advantage and the most alluring way to reveal a hint to the eye or the mind's eye of "the gladdest garments out of sight," and, in general, reversing the biblical reference to "the way of a man with a maid" (Proverbs 30:19), how to maximize the way of a maid with a man. Cackling like a fairytale witch, she quotes the going rates for various services, ranging from an amusingly precise two and a penny (just one penny more than two shillings) through half a crown (two shillings and sixpence) to even the possibility of a full crown (five shillings), a shining silver coin in the latter amount held up invitingly to encourage amatory initiative. The relatively restrained nature of the language still allows for a number of fluvial references, including the Dutch Lek and American Egg ("legging"), Swiss Sihl, French Ain ("dainty"), English Adde ("gladdest"), and the American Silver and Chinese Ili ("silliver").

BECKETT: Et elle leur gigotait quelques gignes sur le sihleuil afin de leur montrer comment s'agiter les courbières et la façon chic de suggérer les parures cachées les plus affriolantes, et toutes les manières de la jeune fille devant l'homme, en émettant un bruit claquetant comme pour dire "c'est douze francs" ou "c'est quinze francs" et en brandissant un écul doré.

Beckett's French *ALP* wriggled and jiggled (*gigoter* "to wriggle") a few jigs (*gigue* "jig") for them on the threshold (*seuil*) by way of a sign (*signe*) as to how they should shake their own benders (*courber* "to bend") and to demonstrate the smartly sophisticated (*chic*) way for suggesting the most alluring (*affriolant*) hidden treasures (*parure* "finery, jewels") and all the ways of a young girl with a man. All of this while making a sort of cackling noise (*caqueter* "to cackle like a hen") like a hen in a whorehouse (*claque*), as if to say "that's twelve francs" or "that's fifteen francs" and temptingly holding up (*brandir* "to brandish") a golden ecu that in the context was oddly evocative of holding up a bare bottom (*cul*). The fact that gold ecus had long ceased to be legal tender in France was probably regarded as irrelevant by all parties concerned. Rivers evoked include the Swiss Sihl ("sihleuil"), Belgian Our and Mongolian Ur ("courbières"), Nigerian Eme ("émettant"), and English Ouse ("douze").

> JOYCE: Gigotant des gigues sur le sioul de la porte pour montrer comment on agitait les courbières et le chic sousgestif des parures cachées et les toutes manières des puelles devant homme, huitant un cliqueticlaque comme pour dire "c'est cent sous" ou "c'est six francs trente" et en brandissant un écul doré.

Joyce's French ALP once again stays very close to Beckett's, jigging her jig on the threshold (*seuil*) to very like effect, showing the ladies how to shake their benders, showing how to exploit the suggestive (*suggestif*) nature of the hidden treasures underneath ("sousgestif"), encouraging all the behaviours of girls (Latin *puellae*) who are not quite virgins (*pucelle* "virgin, maid") when it comes to men, and all of this while sort of hooting (*huer* "to hoot") and going clickety-clack ("cliqueticlaque"), evoking the jingle (*cliquetis*) of coins associated with a whorehouse (*claque*), as if to say "it's a hundred sous" – if only for the pleasure of saying /sɛsãsu/ – or "it's six francs thirty," while likewise brandishing an "écul doré." Rivers evoked include the Kenyan Sio ("sioul"), Belgian Our and Mongolian Ur ("courbières"), French Elle ("puelles"), and Chinese Hui in "huitant" – the latter term humorously arrived at by deleting the Nigerian Eme in Beckett's "émettant" and replacing it (and why not?) with the Chinese Hui and a hint of the verb *huer* ("to hoot").

> JOYCE: Sgambettando sulla sillarosoglia a mostrar loro le genuiflesse e come si deve fare presente ciò che si suole a non dimandare e tutta l'arte del tiramoglie garrendo una specie d'ecquiquacquecco come cinque baiocche e un paollo e mezzo, e lasciando veder un chiaro scudo.
>
> SETTANNI: Sgambettando sulla sillarosoglia per mostrar loro le genuiflesse e come si deve fare presente ciò che si suole a non dimandare e tutta l'arte del tiramoglie, garrendo una specie d'ecquiquacquocco come cinque baiocche o un paollo e mezzo, e veder lasciava un chiaro scudo.

The Italian ALP is described as "scampering" (*sgambettando*) on the doorsill (*soglia*) to show them the art of going on bended knee (*genuiflesso*) and how to display (*fare presente*) that which one does not normally ask to see (*ciò che si suole a non dimandare*), and, indeed, all the arts of feminine seduction (*tira* "attraction"; *moglie* "woman"). All of this while twittering away (*garrire* "to chirp, twitter") with a sort of distorted quack-quacking sound (*qua qua qua* "quack-quack") like five *baiocchi* and a *paolo* and a half, and letting them see (*lasciando veder*) a bright (*chiaro*) *scudo*. A *baiocco* was a low-value copper coin of central Italy; a *paolo* was a Tuscan coin worth about ten times as much; and a *scudo*, usually translated as a "crown," was a coin of much higher value still. The five *baiocchi* are feminized as *baiocche* in order to evoke CHE, alias HCE. Rivers evoked include the Swiss Sihl and Italian Sillaro ("sillarosoglia"), Nigerian Amo ("a mostrar"), German Esse ("genuiflesse"), and central Asian Ollo ("paollo").

Jacqueline Risset (1973, 57) points out the humorously irreverent redeployment of Dante's line "ciò che si vuole, e più non dimandare" in the *Inferno*. Here Virgil instructs the demon Charon to let them pass without further question or hindrance, for "our passage has been willed above, where One / can do what He has willed; and ask no more" (Mandelbaum 1982, 25), "vuolsi così colà dove si puote / ciò che si vuole, e più non dimandare" (*Inferno* 3.95–6).

Other than two minor stylistic changes, one of which ("per mostrar" for "a mostrar") loses the Nigerian Amo, Settanni tidies ALP's "specie d'ecquiquacquecco" to a "specie d'ecquiquacquocco," still a sort of quacking sound, but now intertextually reminiscent of a Latin declensional paradigm such as *hic, haec, hoc*. Almost 300 pages later in *Finnegans Wake*, we find "*Qui quae quot at Quinnigan's Quake*" (*FW* 496.36–497.01).

***[3] Throwing all the neiss little whores in the world at him! To inny captured wench you wish of no matter what sex of pleissful ways two adda tammar a lizzy a lossie to hug and hab haven in Humpy's apron!* (*ALP* 10; *FW* 200.29–32)**

ALP, the pleasantly scandalized teller relates, was throwing every nice little whore she managed to catch, whether of one sex or another, at HCE, just as long as they were of a pleasant manner, and paying every one of them the sum of two shillings and sixpence each, every Lizzy and every lassie of any sort, to hug and to snuggle in HCE's lap. A good dozen rivers are evoked in the process, including the Polish Neisse,

American Little, English Hore, Austrian Inn, Irish Inny, German Pleisse, Italian Adda, English Tamar, Portuguese Liz, Scottish Lossie, Pakistani Hab, Indian Habb. The phrase "two adda tammar" carries a relatively weighty load of implied meaning. First of all, "two and a tanner" was a colloquialism for two shillings and sixpence or half a crown. Second, "tammar" evokes not only the English river Tamar but also the etymologically unrelated name of the biblical Tamar, who disguised herself as a prostitute in order to have sexual congress with her father-in-law (Genesis 38:6–30). Third, this biblical reference is followed by another, the phrase "haven in Humpy's apron" serving as a playful variation on the story of the righteous man of Saint Luke's gospel who after death awaits the Day of Judgment in the bosom of Abraham (Luke 16:22), the prophet's name humorously suggested by the combination of "Humpy" and "apron" producing an "Aprahum" with a hump.

> BECKETT: Lui jeter au coul totutes les doubces filles d'amour de la terre? A n'importe laquelle de ses captures, quel que fût son sexe, pourvu qu'elle fût pleissante à voir, elle donnait deux douros d'argens, deux thunes chacune, pour travoir hembrassé Humpy et hormi dans son Gironde.

For Beckett's French teller, ALP was throwing every sweet (*douce*) young "daughter of love" (*fille d'amour*) in the country (*terre*) at HCE's head (*cou* "neck") – not to mention HCE's other end (*cul*). To any one of those she had caught (*captures*), whatever their sex, as long as they were pleasant to look at (*plaisante à voir*), she gave two silver duros of money (*d'argent*), two smackers each, for having (*avoir*) hugged (*embrassé*) and kissed (*embrassé*) Humpy and slept (*dormi*) in his bosom (*giron* "lap, bosom"). The actions of having hugged, kissed, and slept are delicately disguised as "hembrassé" and "hormi" rather than *embrassé* and *dormi*. Rivers evoked include the Indian Tut ("totutes"), French Doubs and Caribbean Douce ("doubces"), German Pleisse ("pleissante"), Spanish Douro (reinforced by the Welsh *dŵr* again), French Argens ("d'argens"), German Trave ("travoir"), French Hem and Asse ("hembrassé"), French Orme ("hormi") and the French Gironde estuary, confluence of the Garonne and Dordogne.

The slang term *thune*, originally *tune*, referred during the 1600s to alms given to a beggar, the chief of whom was jocularly known as the Roi de Tunes ("King of Tunis"). About 1800 it came to mean a five-franc piece (Dauzat et al. 1971, 772). Some recipients of ALP's beneficence seem to have done rather better than others financially, two Spanish *duros* was worth 10 pesetas, while ten French francs has typically been worth about 50 pesetas. A *thune*, however, has in fact come colloquially to mean just money in general ("dosh, smackers"), so the comparison is irrelevant.

> JOYCE: Lui jetant au cou toutes les putes de la terre. A n'importe quelle de ses captures de doubs sexes de minette pleissante deux douros d'argent, deux thunes chacune, prix de pelottage pour faire l'amarre dans le gironde de Pantalon cruel.

Joyce's French ALP, keeping relatively close to Beckett's, but not without some interesting variations, was throwing all the prostitutes (*putes*) of the land at HCE's head – and was thus rather more restrained in this respect than in Beckett's scenario. To any one of those she had caught (*captures*) of either (*deux* "two") sex whose performance (*faire minette* "to indulge in oral sex") was pleasing (*plaisant*), she gave two silver duros, two smackers each, the piloting (*pilotage*) rate for mooring (*amarrer*) and making love (*amour*) in the estuary ("gironde") and lap (*giron*) respectively of cruel Pantaloon – or perhaps it was Pantagruel. Pantaloon (Italian *Pantalone*), a character in the Italian *commedia dell'arte*, is a foolish bespectacled old dotard in carpet slippers and too-tight pants; Pantagruel is an outlandish giant with outlandish appetites in François Rabelais's sixteenth-century classic *The Life of Gargantua and Pantagruel*. Rivers evoked other than in Beckett's rendering include the Indonesian Elo, Japanese Ota, and English Otter ("pelottage") and the Philippine Talon and Canadian Lake Talon ("Pantalon"). The French adjective *cruel* harbours the French noun *crue* ("flood").

> JOYCE: Scaraventavagli tutte putte. E a qualsivoglia accattivata d'un sessiallaltra se lescivina, a Nure o Nore, due litri a tagliamento per fare lamone nel grembo di Brembo.
>
> SETTANNI: Scaraventavagli tutte putte. E a qualsivoglia accattivata d'un sessiallaltra se lescivina, a Nure o Nore, due liri e tagliamento per fare lamone nel grembo di Bembo.

Italian ALP was hurling (*scaraventare* "to hurl") all the whores (*putte*) at him. And to every one of those she had begged (*accattare* "to beg") or caught (*cattivare* "to take prisoner"), of one sex (*sesso*) or another (*all'altra*), she doles out (*lesinare* "to dole out grudgingly"), to every Nura or Nora, two lire – or perhaps the promise of two litres of some unspecified beverage – as a reward (*taglia*) for making if not love (*l'amore*) then at least something close to it ("lamone") in the bosom (*grembo*) of Brembo – in whose name are conflated not only Abraham (Italian *Abramo*) and his bosom but also the scholarly Venetian cardinal and poet Pietro Bembo (1470–1547), who as editor of Petrarch's and Dante's works was influential in the development of Tuscan as a literary language. Rivers evoked include the Siberian Kara, Irish Ara, Portuguese Ave, Lithuanian Venta, and Indian Tava ("scaraventavagli"), the Uganda Alla ("sessiallaltra"), Chinese Shi and Ugandan Ivi ("lescivina"), Belgian Our and Mongolian Ur ("Nure"), Irish Nore ("Nore"), the Italian Liri and Philippine Iti ("litri"), and the Italian Lamone and Brembo, as well as the Canadian Brem and the Mbou of the Solomon Islands.

Settanni simplifies "litri" to "liri," presumably to avoid confusion with *litro* ("litre"), but sacrifices in the process the Philippine Iti, though retaining the Italian Liri. His ALP shows herself more generous than Joyce's in offering two lire "and" (*e*) a reward (*taglia*) rather than two lire "as" (*a*) a reward. The "grembo di Brembo" becomes for Settanni the "grembo di Bembo," abandoning Abraham, evoking the Australian river Bemm rather than the Italian Brembo, and more overtly evoking the memory of the scholarly Cardinal Bembo.

[4] Comments and Contexts

The English *ALP*, with its reference in this sequence to Finn MacCool and his various lovers, would-be lovers, and other amatory associates, here summarized as Sawy, Fundally, Daery and Maery, Milucre, Awny and Graw [8.1], shows some considerable familiarity on Joyce's part with Fenian legend. The seven legendary ladies survive in French and Italian with only minor adjustments. Joyce's French once again remains very close to Beckett's in this sequence, though not without several interesting variations.

Settanni on two occasions [8.1, 8.2] feels impelled once again to make Joyce's highly convoluted Italian more accessible for Italian readers. On one of these occasions, however, adding a simple "sí o no" economically allows him to add two new rivers, the Sio and the Ono [8.1], while he loses a river in each of two other emendations [8.2, 8.3]. He oversimplifies Joyce's "nel grembo di Brembo" to "nel grembo di Bembo" [8.3], making the reference to the sixteenth-century Italian scholar more obvious for challenged Italian readers but at the relatively high cost of losing the biblical Abraham and reducing both the humour and the complexity of Joyce's onomastic pun.

9 Gammer and Gaffer

Ah, but she was the queer old skeowsha anyhow, Anna Livia, trinkettoes! And sure he was the quare old buntz too, Dear Dirty Dumpling, foostherfather of fingalls and dotthergills. Gammer and gaffer we're all their gangsters. Hadn't he seven dams to wive him? And every dam had her seven crutches. And every crutch had its seven hues. And each hue had a differing cry. ... But at milkidmass who was the spouse? Then all that was was fair. Tys Elvenland! Teems of times and happy returns. The seim anew. Ordovico or viricordo. Anna was, Livia is, Plurabelle's to be. Northmen's thing made southfolk's place but howmulty plurators made eachone in person? Latin me that, my trinity scholard, out of eure sanscreed into oure eryan! (*ALP* 34; *FW* 215.12–27)

Our final two chapters no longer have any French version by Beckett, who, together with Péron, translated only the opening pages. Instead, we have access to Ogden's Basic English, Ogden for his part having translated only the closing pages (*ALP* 30–5; *FW* 213.11–216.05).

[1] *Ah, but she was the queer old skeowsha anyhow, Anna Livia, trinkettoes!* (*ALP* 34; *FW* 215.12–13)

OGDEN: Ah, but she was a strange little old woman, anyhow, Anna Livia, with drops from her toes.

Our washerwomen, weary after much washing and much discussion, offer the backhanded summary that Anna Livia, all things considered, "was the queer old skeowsha anyhow," the adjective *old* indicative of affection rather than advanced age, though Ogden takes the literal meaning. "Skeowsha" is a metathesized variant of the colloquial and humorously affectionate Irish English *segocia* ("comrade, friend"), a term of unexplained origin (and conventionally preceded by "old"). The rearranged spelling here allows for similarly rearranged references to various Esk rivers (the name related to Irish *uisce* "water") in Britain and elsewhere as well as the Ow River of County Wicklow, the Sha River of China, and two Shaw Rivers of Australia. Even the opening "ah, but" manages to refer to the French Aa and Ghanaian Abu. The epithet "trinkettoes" suggests dancing twinkletoes, trinkets, rings on her fingers, bells on her toes, and refers in passing to the Gambian river Ketto. Ogden glosses the term as meaning "with drops from her toes," the trinkling drops perhaps twinkling in sunshine. The *Navire d'Argent* text of 1925 had "twinkletoes," the 1928 Gaige text and subsequent texts "trinkettoes" (Higginson 1960, 95, 109). The *Restored Finnegans Wake* of Danis Rose and John O'Hanlon has "trinklytoes" (*FW2* 168.37) instead, abandoning the Ketto.

JOYCE: Tu parles, mais quelle drôle de drôlesse quand même qu'Anna Livie petontintamahr.

In Joyce's French, "you can talk" ("tu parles"), but when all is said and done the "queer old skeowsha" really was a "drôle de drôlesse" (roughly, "a really funny old biddy") "quand même" ("all the same") – evoking in passing the Croatian Drau and Belgian Lesse – while "Anna Livia, trinkettoes" leads to a linguistic fireworks display with "Anna Livie petontintamahr," combining her *peton* ("tiny little foot") and the resulting publicity *tintamarre* ("racket, hullabaloo") it allegedly evokes as well as nodding to the Austrian Mahr, German Ahr, and Swiss Aar, supported by the Arabic *ma* ("water") and the Spanish *mar* ("sea").

JOYCE: Ma lascia, era una stramba duenna, quell'Anna Livia, zampolona.
SETTANNI: Ma lascia, era una stramba duenna, quell'Anna Livia, zampilina.

But enough said, "just leave off" (*lasciare* "to leave"), says Joyce's Italian, adroitly evoking the Arabic *ma* ("water") once again as well as the Romanian river Mala. Anna Livia is here, with unusual restraint for Joyce's Italian, merely a "strange (*stramba*) lady (*donna*)." Her "trinkettoes," however, oddly enough, are transformed into a much less ladylike "zampolona," an augmentative of *zampa* ("foot, paw"), thus literally a "great big foot" – further evoking the Russian river Amba, two other rivers of the same name in India and Nigeria, the Romanian Badu, the Italian Enna and Olona, and the Russian Ona. Settanni, with less humour but greater fidelity to the delicacy of Anna's trinkettoes, arranges for a fluvial changing of the guard by altering the augmentative "zampolona" to the diminutive "zampilina" ("tiny little foot"), simultaneously dismissing the Italian Olona and Russian Ona in favour of the Indian Pili and English Lin.

[2] And sure he was the quare old buntz too,
Dear Dirty Dumpling, foostherfather of fingalls
***and dotthergills.* (*ALP* 34; *FW* 215.13–14)**

OGDEN: And Dear Dirty Dublin, he, on my word, was a strange fat old father to his Danes light and dark, the female and the male.

In darker mood, dear dirty Dublin, despite Lady Morgan, is here just a dirty (and expensive) dump – and HCE, "Dear Dirty Dumpling," is now both stupid (German *Dümmling* "fool") and an unprepossessingly dumpy little dumpling of a fellow (German *Däumling* "Tom Thumb") who belongs in a refuse dump. "And sure he was the quare old buntz too," a peculiar, tubby little old so-and-so, the epithet supported by the Alemannic *bunz* or *buntz*, denoting a little barrel (Bahlow 1980, 86), and by the fluvial presence of the Irish river Suir, the Quare River of Trinidad and Tobago, and the African river Bunce. HCE's reported qualifications include being "foostherfather of fingalls and dotthergills," fosterfather and foostering fumblefather of fine girls and girl daughters, but mythical father also of foreign Galls and native Gaels, indeed of all kinds of guys and gals, including fluvial gills (or brooks) with a hard *g* and cuddlesome gills (or jills) with a soft *g*.

His Scandinavian origins are adumbrated by "fingalls," evoking not only the *Fionnghaill* or Norwegian "fair foreigners" of medieval Ireland but also the area of north County Dublin known as Fingal, from the Irish *Fine Gall* ("territory of foreigners"), once the abode of Scandinavian raiders turned settlers. Swedish *dotter* ("daughter") is at home in the linguistic context, while hospitably offering a home to the English river Otter. Finn MacCool is evoked in passing as Macpherson's Fingal, while the German Oos and Congolese Inga flow in "foosther" and "fingalls" respectively. The quare old buntz retains his fatness in Ogden's rendering – which tactfully ignores his foostering activities, however, while transforming the Norwegian "fingalls" more inclusively into "Danes light and dark."

JOYCE: Et lui comme andouille fut azay rideaucul, Cher Crasseux Compère, papa lait en chef des titifils et de tétéfilles.

In Joyce's French, the old buntz, a great fat fool (*andouille*) stuffed like a great sausage (*andouille*), was ridiculous (*ridicule*) enough (*assez*) himself – the phrasing "azay rideaucul" referring (and why not?) to the château of Azay-le-Rideau, built on an island in the French river Indre, as well as to the Canadian Rideau, and (why not again?) to the wrinkles (*rides*) on our man's aged bum (*cul*). The Ando of the Solomon Islands is also in evidence – as also the Austrian Ill, if only visually ("andouille"). "Dear Dirty Dumpling," with its alliterative echo of "Dear Dirty Dublin," is now "Cher Crasseux Compère" ("Dear Filthy Fellow"), casually shifted to a set of initials more evocative of Cork than of Dublin. (That Joyce's father was a native of Cork is no doubt completely coincidental.) The French rivers Cher and Asse and the Russian Om appear briefly. The "foostherfather of fingalls and dotthergills" metamorphoses into a "papa lait en chef des titifils et de tétéfilles." A foster brother in French is a *frère de lait*, literally a "milk brother," having shared a wet nurse. Whether a foster father should share this facility is questionable. Meanwhile, "papa lait" is also a colloquial German *Papale*, Milly Bloom's *Papli* ("daddy"), daddy in chief of "titifils" and "tétéfilles," little (*'tits*) urchin (*titi*) sons (*fils*) and little suckling (*téter* "to suckle") daughters (*filles*). Serendipitously, *papa* also includes the Romanian *apă* ("water").

JOYCE: E lui po', che norciume, Sugna Purca Qua Ramengo, padre saturno di quinti e quante!
SETTANNI: [*without change*]

In Joyce's Italian, left unchanged by Settanni, the "quare old buntz" receives unsympathetic treatment: "E lui po', che norciume" suggests *che marciume* ("what rottenness"), conflated with the Irish river Nore (to accompany the Italian Po) and the Neapolitan noun *ciume* ("river, stream"). The "Dear Dirty Dumpling" loses his Dublin *DDD* in favour of the ancient acronym *SPQR*, which once signified *Senatus populusque romanus* ("The senate and people of Rome") and is still an emblem of the city of Rome, but is here adjusted, in an octosyllabic exercise in trochaic schoolboy humour, to "Sugna Purca Qua Ramengo," suggesting "fat (*sugna* 'lard, fat') pig (*porca* 'sow') that I am, I go wandering about (*andare ramingo* 'to go wandering') here (*qua*)." Zanotti (2002, 300) notes a double play on the Triestine *andar a remengo* ("to go to rack and ruin") and the related imprecation *andè a remengo* ("go to the devil"). The Mongolian Ur and Belgian Our, the Mengo of the Solomon Islands, and the Quare of Trinidad and Tobago as well as the Basque *ur* ("water") put in appearances as the Dublin Dumpling changes gender from hog (*porco*) to sow (*porca*).

Recalling Joyce's lasting dislike for the city of Rome – which he had described to his brother Stanislaus in 1906 as reminding him of "a man who lives by exhibiting to travellers his grandmother's corpse" (*L* 2, 165) – Zanotti understandably sees the phrase as also a potentially dangerous commentary on the fascist movement, of which Rome was of course both the actual and the symbolic capital (2002, 299). But Italian readers of early 1940 might well have been forgiven for wondering if the reference to a fat pig wandering the streets of Rome might not also be intended to apply very directly to the *Duce* himself. Joyce, who was "viscerally anti-authoritarian," as Gordon Bowker puts it (2011, 447), had no high regard for Mussolini, who as leader of the fascist party had set up a legal dictatorship in 1925 – and subsequently ordered the acronym *SPQR* inscribed on a number of civic buildings and manhole covers in Rome as propaganda for his imperial ambitions. When Joyce was asked in 1936 if he still liked Italy with Mussolini in power, he carefully dissociated the two, replying that not to like Italy because of Mussolini "would be just as absurd as to hate England because of Henry the Eighth" (Ellmann 1982, 694). The *Duce*, who would very shortly, in June 1940, throw in his lot with Hitler, was fond of appearing in public striking a heroic pose as an ideal specimen of imperial Roman manhood. That heroic pose required sustained effort, however, for he was reportedly self-conscious about his weight and was forced to adhere to a strict diet as a result. Settanni, inexplicably, was content to leave unchanged what was potentially a highly offensive personal reference, whether intended or otherwise. Italian government censors, for their part, were presumably too disoriented by Joyce's Italo-Wakean convolutions to notice anything amiss.

The "foostherfather of fingalls and dotthergills," to return to the quare old buntz, is now a more sinister "padre saturno di quinti e quante," a Saturnian father, devouring his own offspring, whether male ("quinti") freshmen (*quinta* "freshman year") or an equivalent number of females (*quante*). The phrase, a decasyllable by the rules of Italian prosody

(Risset 1984, 7), has the rhythm of a truncated dactylic tetrameter for an English ear, "*pa*dre sa- | *tur*no di | *quin*ti e | *quan*te."

***[3] Gammer and gaffer we're all their gangsters.* (*ALP* 34; *FW* 215.14–15)**

OGDEN: Old girl and old boy, their servants are we.

Queer old skeowsha and quare old buntz though the two of them may be, however, archetypal gammer and gaffer, granny and granddad, we are all, says one washerwoman to the other, members of their (alliterative) gang, their progeny, their lineage. Ogden, however, sees that relationship less favourably as actually one of servitude rather than ancestry.

JOYCE: Mémère et pépère, nous sommes toutes de leur bande.

For Joyce's French, while they may likewise merely be granny (*mémère*) and granddad (*pépère*), we all nonetheless belong to their gang (*bande*). The Nigerian Eme and Swiss Emme put in appearances in "mémère," as do the French *mer* and German *Meer*, both meaning "sea," while "pépère" evokes both French *pipi* ("pee") and the Hawaiian Peepee Falls as well as the English Aire. While the English *we* is gender-neutral, Joyce's French washerwoman's "toutes" – in which the Indian Tut and Laotian Ou may be detected – is unambiguously feminine.

JOYCE: Gerarca e gitana, siam pur sempre della ganghera.
SETTANNI: Caporione o gitana, siam sempre della ganghera.

"Gammer and gaffer" in Joyce's English clearly refer (if anything in the *Wake* universe can ever be said to refer "clearly" to anything else) to ALP and HCE as a quasi-mythological ancestral pair, quasi-Adam and quasi-Eve. Joyce may possibly have originally considered the phrase *ganghero e gangherella* ("hook and eye") as an Italian rendering of the interlocking ancestral pair, but finally opted instead, reversing the order of the pair, for "Gerarca e gitana, siam pur sempre della ganghera," roughly, "hierarch (*gerarca*) and gypsy (*gitana*) though they may be, we all still (*pur sempre*) belong to the gang (*ganga*)" – and are thus perhaps equally likely to do things we might later regret (*uscire dai gangheri* "to fly off the handle"). The French Arc and Arques,

Siberian Arka, and Alaskan Tana put in appearances, followed by the Ganges. Unlike Joyce's English, which presents "gammer and gaffer" as a closely comparable pair, his Italian "gerarca e gitana," despite the alliteration linking them, seems to stress the difference between them, one a high official of some kind, the other a gypsy girl, on the fringes of society.

The term *gerarca,* however, is also a highly loaded term politically. Though literally meaning "hierarch," a person holding high rank in a religious hierarchy, the term was in fact used in Mussolini's Italy specifically for a member of the National Fascist Party. The combination of *gerarca* and *gitana* in the Italy of 1940, moreover, was a potentially dangerous joke, since the fascist party systematically persecuted gypsies. Suggesting that the two belonged in the same "ganghera" was therefore not just an amusing alliterative effect but potentially a dangerously provocative word play (Bosinelli 1996, 60). Settanni, more cautious than Joyce, sacrificed the alliteration and discreetly emended "gerarca" to the less potentially offensive "caporione," literally "ringleader." The French Arc and Arques and the Siberian Arka all disappear, modestly compensated for by an Italian *rio* ("brook, canal").

***[4] Hadn't he seven dams to wive him? And every dam had her seven crutches. And every crutch had its seven hues. And each hue had a differing cry.* (*ALP* 34; *FW* 215.15–17)**

OGDEN: Hadn't he his seven women of pleasure? And every woman her seven sticks. And every stick its seven colours. And every colour a different cry.

Here HCE attains to pseudo-mythical status, with seven dams to wive him – and since every dam had her seven crutches, and every crutch its seven hues, and every hue a different cry, there are 49 crutches, 343 hues, and 343 different cries involved.[1] Our hero finds himself situated in a venerable medieval Irish narrative tradition of descriptive excess here: the mythical Irish giant Fergus mac Róich, king of Ulster, had such huge sexual appetites that it took seven women at once to satisfy him. His other appetites were correspondingly gigantic, his standard daily meal consisting of seven deer, seven pigs, seven cows, and seven vats

1 Harriet Weaver reported Joyce's remark that the much-married Ford Madox Ford's six wives were just one fewer than HCE's (Ellmann 1982, 636n).

of alcohol (Green 1992, 96–7).[2] His first name, not inappropriately, combines the Old Irish elements *fer* ("man") and *gus* ("vigour") (Hanks et al. 2002, 758). Ciaran Carson observes that the name could plausibly be rendered as "male ejaculation," while *mac Róich* means "son of superhorse," the latter name possibly referring to a horse-goddess (2008, 210). In our present context the combination of the intensifier *ro* ("super") and the nominative case of *ich*, namely *ech* ("horse"), serendipitously evokes none other than HCE alias ECH. The seven dams, meanwhile, like the backwater sals in general, are also aspects of ALP herself.

HCE also, as Roland McHugh observes, shares the tricky company of a well-known nursery-rhyme traveller: "As I was going to St Ives, / I met a man with seven wives, / Each wife had seven sacks, / Each sack had seven cats, / Each cat had seven kits; / Kits, cats, sacks, and wives, / How many were going to St Ives?" (Baring-Gould 1962, 270–1). The answer in this case is of course just one, namely "I," since all the rest were coming from rather than going to St Ives. Joyce's seven dams and their assorted impedimenta lead a likewise trickily unstable existence. *Dams* may be dams (mother animals) or dames (French *dames*) or feats of civil engineering: Joyce wrote to Harriet Weaver on 7 March 1924 that "the splitting up towards the end (seven dams) is the city abuilding" (*L* 1, 212–13; Ellmann 1982, 564). *To wive* is "to marry," but *to swive* is merely to have sexual intercourse. *Crutch* in British English is a variant of *crotch*, their multiplication here both recalling the fantastic sexual appetites of a Fergus mac Róich and implying the fantasized appetites of the seven pseudo-femmes. A *hue* may be visual, as in a particular shade of a colour (from the Old English *hīw* "beauty"), as in the seven colours of a rainbow, for example, or auditory, as in *hue and cry*, from the Old French *huer* ("to shout"). Fluvial elements are not missing: dams block rivers, Canada boasts a Crutch River, and Vietnam has a Hue. Ogden, for his part, reduces the dams to "women of pleasure," reduces the crutches to mere sticks, and abandons the play on *hue and cry*.

> JOYCE: N'avait-il pas eu sept fem pour le femer? Et chacune des fems avait sept crochettes. Et chaque crochette ses sept couleurs. Et toutes les couleurs des cris différents.

2 The number seven plays a decidedly baroque role in some early Irish tales. Among his other physical charms, for instance, the legendary hero Cúchulainn had "seven pupils in each of his eyes, seven toes on each foot, seven fingers on each hand" (Rees and Rees 1989, 60).

The "sept fem" that the Dear Dirty Dumpling is alleged to have had in Joyce's French are not quite *femmes*, neither fully wives nor fully women, just as the original "dams" were not quite dames or *dames*. They are also, oddly enough, not yet plural, "sept fem" rather than "sept fems." Categories slide and bend. Each of the seven "fem" are "pour le femer," the implied sense of which is clearly to "wive" him, but there are clearly (or, rather, darkly) also implications left unspecified. "Fem" puns on *faim* ("hunger"), suggesting in the context a sevenfold sexual voracity on our hero's part. As for the seven "fem" as *femmes*, sexual voracity is even more in evidence, each no longer having just seven "crutches," but rather seven "crochettes," each ominously combining "hook" (*crochet*), "fang" (*crochet*), and "skewer" (*brochette*) as well as English *crotch*, suggesting a pseudo-mythical and dauntingly multiple *vagina dentata*. Each of these dubious pieces of equipment has seven colours, and all the variegated shades, we are assured, playing on the relationship of visual and auditory once again, have different cries, each attraction its different appeal or different terror, each cry its corresponding register.

JOYCE: Non ebbe sette manze a toro? E ogni manza sette cavezzi. E ogni cavezzo sette colori. E ciascun colore un altro suono.
SETTANNI: [*without change*]

In Joyce's Italian, the "seven dams to wive him" become "sette manze a toro," seven "heifers" (*manze*) to his "bull" (*toro*) and to his "marital bed" (*toro*). And every heifer had seven "cavezzi," conflating *cavezze* ("halters") and *vezzi* ("caresses"), and each of the latter had seven "colori" ("colours"), no doubt in the spirit of the colloquialism *farne di tutti i colori* ("to get up to all kinds of tricks"), and each colour had a different "suono" ("sound"), depending again on the nature of the particular trick. Zanotti (2001, 423) points out that *cavezzi* is also Triestine and Venetian for "remnants, the end of a roll," thus potentially suggesting also seven females with seven pieces of fabric, each of seven different colours. All in all, the seven Italian ladies appear to be rather less potentially worrying than their French counterparts.

[5] But at milkidmass who was the spouse? Then all that was was fair. Tys Elvenland! (ALP 34; FW 215.21–2).

OGDEN: But in the animals' time, where was the woman? Then all that was was good. Land that is not?

In medieval England, Michaelmas ("milkidmass"), celebrated on 29 September, marked the end of the harvest and thus the end of the agricultural year. The feast of the archangel Michael, defender of good against evil, protector against the powers of darkness, Michaelmas was also, as one of the four quarter days, a time of reckoning, a time for settling accounts. The weeks before Michaelmas typically see large numbers of baby goats born and given mothers' milk, thus "milkidmass" and Ogden's "the animals' time."

Despite the dubious pleasures of HCE's multiple extra-marital gambollings, when these good and not so good times were over, at summer's end when it was time to settle accounts, ALP retained without question her status as the central woman of his existence. In the end, all was well. Or was that just wishful thinking, a fairytale ending in a fairyland (Dutch *elvenland*), a "land that is not," as Ogden puts it? Rivers evoked include the Canadian Milk, English Ouse, Russian Alle, American Fair, English Aire, Hungarian Tysa or Tisza, and English Tees. The Dutch *elvenland* is watered by a Norwegian *elv* and a Danish *elve*, nouns that in both cases mean "river."

JOYCE: Mais la Saint Cornélie qui était l'espouse? Alors tout ce qui était et était et juste. Royaume des elves?

Joyce's French replaces the English Michaelmas by the French feast of Saint Cornelius, patron saint of domestic animals, especially horned cattle, celebrated on 16 September. A third-century pope and martyr, his name – possibly a derivative of Latin *cornu* ("horn") (Hanks et al. 2002, 731) – ensures that he is frequently represented as either holding a cow's horn or with a cow discreetly in the background. The washerwoman asks the same rhetorical question, repeats the same Panglossian statement – "everything that was both was (*était*) and was right (*juste*)" – and undermines it in a similar way, relegating such a vision to the realm (*royaume*) of the fairies ("elves"). The Finnish Espoo ("l'espouse") puts in a brief appearance, while the fairy realm is still watered by a Norwegian *elv* and a Danish *elve*.

JOYCE: Ma alla Capriellora chi è ita all'ara? Allora che fu, bene fu. Giovava Giove.
SETTANNI: [*without change*]

In Italian, Saint Michael the Archangel is replaced by Saint Gabriel the Archangel, who shares the same feast on 29 September. Usually presented with a lily in his hand, Gabriel (Italian *Gabriele*) is here associated with goats instead (*capra* "goat"), his feast (*ora* "time") becomes the "Capriellora," and the question is rephrased as "alla Capriellora chi è ita all'ara?" ("On Gabriel's Day, who went to the altar, who was the bride?"). Then (*allora,* playing on "-ellora" and "all'ara"), at that time, what was (*che fu*) was good (*bene fu*), and "Giovava Giove" (literally, "Jove was Joving"): in those mythological times, as in a fairytale, Jove was in his heaven, HCE as CHE ("che fu") was in his home, and all was right with the world. Rivers evoked include the South East Asian Ma, the Ugandan Alla, the Indonesian Ello and Norwegian Lora ("Capriellora"), the Irish Ara, and, twice, the Chinese Fu.

***[6] Teems of times and happy returns. The seim anew. Ordovico or viricordo. Anna was, Livia is, Plurabelle's to be.* (*ALP* 34; *FW* 215.22–4)**

> OGDEN: A number of times, coming happily back. The same and new. Vico's order but natural, free. Anna was, Livia is, Plurabelle's to be.

Seven dams or not, there is always ALP, always changing and always the same. History, for that matter, is an endless sequence of times, all different and all ultimately amounting to the same thing, teeming with discrete events and separate peoples and individual lives, transient all. The Ordovician period lasted for some forty million years some 500 million years ago, in time immemorial – but it passed and is remembered only as one geological period among many. It takes its name from the Ordovices, a powerful Celtic people who strenuously resisted the Roman invasion of Britain almost 2,000 years ago – but who were also finally defeated and passed into history as likewise little more than a name, one almost entirely forgotten people among many. Viconian cycles ("ordovico"), one scheme among many to impose even an illusory order on history and time, are in a sense just another way of saying "*Vi ricordo,* I remember you, I have seen you before." Ogden appears to contrast a merely theoretical scheme and (rhymingly anticipating "Plurabelle's to be") a "natural, free" human reaction. There is indeed nothing new under the sun, and "in the *Wake* past, present, and future are always in a state of flux" (Benstock 1985b, 162). As the river of time itself, "Anna was, Livia is, Plurabelle's to be," embodying the "female principle of flux and continuity" (Hart 1962, 202) while simultaneously a reminder of the tidal nature of the Liffey, going, coming, always changing and still always the same. Rivers, by the same token, continue to run: the English Tees and Welsh Teme ("teems"), Ukrainian Seim, Argentine Rico ("viricordo"), Mongolian Ur and Russian Ura ("Plurabelle"), the last two once again in appropriate combination with the Basque *ur* ("water").

JOYCE: Abonbenz des ages, bienheureux retours. Paraleillement. Ordivico et viricordo. Anna fut, Livie est, Plurabelle sera.

"Well then" (*bon ben*), says Joyce's French, remaining close to the original English, and summoning up an "abonbenz des ages," suggesting an "abundance (*abondance*) of ages" and celebrating their "bienheureux retours" ("happy returns") "paraleillement," all "at the same time" (*parallèlement*). The Scottish Abon, German Enz, and Belgian Leie lend appropriate assistance. "Ordovico *or* viricordo" now becomes "Ordivico *et* viricordo," conflated rather than as alternatives, and now also suggesting the Ugandan Ivi. And as before, "Anna fut, Livia est, Plurabelle sera," but now also, geographical space imitating historical time, with glimpses of the Chinese Fu, Ugandan Ivi once again, and, teasingly, the Spanish Ésera and Australian Sara.

JOYCE: Sacco di secoli che mi rallegri. E sempresia. Ordovico e viricordo. Anna fu, Livia è, Plurabella sarà.
SETTANNI: [*without change*]

Joyce's Italian renders "teems of times and happy returns" as "sacco di secoli che mi rallegri," literally, "may a sackful of centuries cheer me up." The wish, expressed as an Italian hendecasyllable and an English dactylic tetrameter, is framed around allusions to the Italian Sacco, Corsican Codi, Spanish Río Seco, Portuguese Mira, and Russian Alle, shortly joined by the Italian Resia in "E sempresia" ("and may it always be so"), translating "the seim anew." As in his French, the original "or" in "Ordovico or viricordo" is replaced by "and" ("e"), while "Anna fu, Livia è, Plurabella sarà" calls up the Chinese Fu, Ugandan Ivi, Belgian Our, Mongolian Ur, Russian Ura, Japanese Asa, and Australian Sara.

[7] Northmen's thing made southfolk's place but howmulty plurators made eachone in person? **(*ALP* 34; *FW* 215.24–6)**

OGDEN: Our Norwegian Thing-seat was where Suffolk Street is, but what number of places will make things into persons?

HCE's role as builder of the city is paralleled by that of the "Northmen," to take just one example of transience from Irish history, who came first as raiders and eventually as settlers to the banks of the Liffey, displaced the natives, and were likewise displaced in their turn. The Northmen (Old Norse *Norðmenn*) are the Scandinavian Vikings from Norway who founded what would later become the city of Dublin in the ninth century and held their assembly or Thing (Old Norse *þing*) in what would later become Suffolk Street. That street took its name ultimately from the "southfolk" who supplanted them, first the Anglo-Normans, followed by the English, and eventually even by the Irish, for whom Dublin was for centuries a city of foreigners. Joyce seized with glee on the relationship between the linguistic history of the word *thing* and the traditional definition of a noun as the name of a person, place, or thing. In both Old Norse and Old English a *þing* denoted an assembly, a coming together of particular persons in a particular place; the concept developed in English in the specific sense of a "thing" to be discussed in such an assembly; and finally, specificity forgotten, a "thing" became just an object among objects (Ayto 1991, 528).

Person, place, and thing are all present in "Northmen's thing made southfolk's place but howmulty plurators made eachone in person?"[3] The question punningly underlines the interpenetration and interplay of past and present. Taking "plurator" as suggesting an agent of multiplication and the paired contractions "howmulty" and "eachone" as suggesting in each case either a singular or a plural referent, the question can be read as implying either "How many individual ancestral progenitors ('plurators') did it take in one generation after another to make each one of us as we are today?" or "How many descendants ('plurators') did each one of them eventually come to have over the centuries, thus multiply replicating some part of himself?" Both readings at once are of course also an option. Ogden sidesteps the issue, concentrating instead on the play of grammatical categories, "what number of places will make things into persons?" Rivers evoked include the Irish Ow and Thai Mul ("howmulty"), Belgian Our, Mongolian Ur, and Russian Ura ("plurators"), and South American Chone ("eachone").

JOYCE: Le Thing des nordiques céda platz au sudvolk, mais combien bien d'incestres pour faire chaque seul nous?

3 The expression "plurators" was substituted for an earlier "creators" (Higginson 1960, 58–9).

In Joyce's French, "le Thing des nordiques" gave place ("céda platz") to the "sudvolk," southfolk who are now evidently Anglo-Saxon, their Germanic origins demonstrated by German *Platz* ("place") and *Süd-volk* ("southern people"). The three elements constituting the definition of a substantive are playfully and translingually retained, Old Norse *Thing*, German *Platz*, German *Volk*. The "plurators" of the original are now, more narrowly, "incestres," involving "ancestors" (*ancêtres*) and not excluding the possibility of incest (*inceste*), and the question is how many of these possibly incestuous ancestors it may well have taken, each on his own ("chaque seul"), to produce each one of us (French *nous*), each individual modern mind (Greek *nous*). "Seul nous" also provides a hint in passing of the Irish *sinn féin* ("we ourselves").

JOYCE: La sforza di Dio fe' l'urbe ad uomo, ma quinquequente pluraglie ne fe' caduno.

SETTANNI: La sforza di Dio fe' l'urbe ad uomo, ma quinquequento pluraglie ne fe' cadauno.

Northmen, southfolk, and their respective thing and place all disappear in Joyce's Italian, which chooses to play instead on the role of the powerful Sforza family of Milan in the complex and troubled relationship between the nobility and the papacy in Renaissance Italy. "La sforza di Dio fe' l'urbe ad uomo" suggests as a surface meaning "the power (*forza*) of God made the city for man (*uomo*)," but the final three words recall the Latin phrase *urbi et orbi*, traditionally applied to papal addresses "to the city (*urbi*) and to the world (*orbi*)," while the combination of Latin *ad* ("for") and Italian *uomo* is a reminder that the Duomo of Milan is the largest cathedral in Italy. The "plurators" of the original are now "pluraglie," conflating *plurale* ("plural") and *raglio* ("bray"), and they are evidently the descendants of those for whom God made the city. The relevant reflection (no longer phrased as a question) now becomes something like "how many (*quanti*) braying cinquecento ("quinquequente") donkeys did each one (*cadauno*) of these men for whom God made the city engender." The grammatical play on persons, places, and things is completely abandoned. Settanni changes Joyce's "quinquequente" to "quinquequento" to make the reference to the 1500s more obvious and alters "caduno" to a more standard "cadauno," replacing Joyce's fluvial reference to the Irish Dun with an evocation of the New Zealand Ada. Hints of the Danube (German Donau, Hungarian Duna) are apparent in both versions.

***[8] Latin me that, my trinity scholard, out of eure sanscreed into oure eryan!* (*ALP* 34; *FW* 215.26–7)**

OGDEN: Put that into Latin, my Trinity man, out of your Sanscrit into our Aryan.

Patrick McCarthy observes that here "Joyce openly alludes to the problem of translating from one language to another as the washerwomen refer sardonically to the pretensions of linguistic scholars" (2007, 172). Languages too have their day and fade away, preceded and succeeded by other languages. Words and languages slip and shift, and in colloquial Irish English, for example, the phrase "latin me that," frequently poking fun at what might pass for arcane learning, has nothing at all to do with Latin any more, the expression simply meaning "explain that to me, if you can." Languages once viewed as pure and sacred, such as Sanskrit or Latin, come to need interpretation and explanation in languages profane and prone to error, such as the "eryan" encountered in Erin's green and pleasant land. Nor do religions have any greater claim to permanency. "My trinity scholard," with its aquatic hint of the Scottish Loch Ard, is one washerwoman's mocking title for the other, highly unlikely ever to have been a student at Trinity College, Dublin, but it also allows a reading as referring to a student of theology who studies the nature of the Trinity, momentarily deprived of its conventional initial capital. Ogden's scholar is unambiguously a student of Trinity College – and unambiguously male.

Joyce's "eryan" is understood by Ogden to be simply "Aryan." Sanskrit is itself one of the most important Indo-European or Aryan languages (the term deriving from Sanskrit *āryas* "noble"), and just as Sanskrit, proud of its own *saṃskṛtā vāk* ("refined speech"), has been seen as disintegrating into a plethora of vernacular Indo-Aryan languages, so the Holy Trinity itself was denied by the Arian heresy, which denied the divinity of Christ and thus the nature of the Trinity (Hodgart 1978, 154; Eco 2001, 110–11). Arianism was condemned by the First Council of Nicaea in 325, which formulated the Nicene Creed and thus turned Arianism into a "sanscreed" sans institutionally authorized creed. McCarthy notes that "the pernicious and historically inaccurate use of 'Aryan' to mean 'Nordic' in Nazi propaganda may also be satirized in this passage" (2007, 172). Fluvial references are not lacking, to the American Trinity, English Ure and French Eure ("eure"), Belgian Our ("oure"), and the Australian Eyre and Chinese Yan ("eryan"), as well as the American Lard Lake ("scholard").

JOYCE: Latine-moi ça mon prieux escholier, des vostres sanscroi en notre erryen.

The "trinity scholard" becomes for French Joyce a "prieux escholier," the Middle French form of *écolier* ("schoolboy") reflecting the Irish English "scholard" for *scholar*. Direct access to divine, educational, and fluvial resonances of "trinity" are no longer available, replaced by "prieux," conflating *preux* ("valiant") and *pieux* ("pious"), parodically evocative of medieval chivalry. The distorted and misshapen trio of languages are present. "Latine-moi" as an invented French verb refers at only a distant remove to Latin. Sanskrit is "vostres sanscroi," its antiquity evoked by the archaic possessive adjective "vostres" (modern French *votre* "your") and its alleged association with heresy adumbrated in the play on an English "sans creed" (*croire* "to believe") and a corresponding French *sans croix* ("without a cross"), thus lacking any connection to the Christian one true cross. The suggestion of Irish error is reinforced in "erryen," though the disappearance of any direct reference to Trinity weakens any suggestion of Arianism. Fluvial references include the English Esk and Irish Eske ("escholier") as well as the German Esse and Polish San, abetted by the water-related Polish noun *ostrów* ("island") ("vostres sanscroi").

JOYCE: Latinami ciò, laureata di Cuneo, di lingua aveta in gargarigliano.
SETTANNI: Latinami ciò, laureata di Cuneo, da lingua aveta in gergarigliana.

Joyce's Italian summarily replaces the "trinity scholard" with a "laureata di Cuneo," a female graduate student from a fictional university of Cuneo, an actual small city in northern Italy. References to any variation on "trinity" are abandoned for a very different range of references. In Italian, the noun *cuneo*, from the Latin *cuneus*, means "wedge," and the particular choice of location for the fictional seat of learning undoubtedly derives from the suggested interplay of Latin *cuneus* and *cunnus* ("cunt"). While the former might suggest the scholarly deciphering of cuneiform writing, appropriate for an institution of higher learning, the latter certainly suggests much more earthy connotations. The graduate is now required to "translate" ("latinami ciò") from "lingua aveta," from an ancestral (*avito*) Avestan (*lingua avestica*), the sacred language of Zoroastrianism, distantly related to Sanskrit. The target language for her efforts is now no longer "eryan" but "gargarigliano," evoking two Italian rivers, the Gari and the Garigliano.

None of the resonances of "eryan" survive. Bosinelli suggests (1998b, 197) that "gargarigliano" refers to a local dialect from Gargano in Apulia, in the heel of the Italian boot, enriched by the aquatic effects generated by *gargarismo* ("gargling"), *gorgogliare* ("to gurgle"), and *rigoglio* ("gurgling"). Umberto Eco proposes a flamboyantly robust alternative, observing that the conjunction of *Cuneo* and *lingua* ("language, tongue") suggests a perceptible echo of *cunnilingus*, "reinforced by the allusion to gargling." In Italian, Eco writes, Joyce "has evidently decided that the linguistic references had to pass, so to speak, from linguistics to the glossa or from language to tongue, understood as a physical organ; and that any theological errancy had to become sexual errancy." Whether or not one subscribes to this assessment, one certainly has little difficulty in agreeing with Eco's overall conclusion: "Any translator who was not Joyce himself would have been accused of intolerable licence" (2001, 111–12).

Settanni emends Joyce's "gargarigliano" to "gergarigliano," thus replacing gurgling, gargling, and their alleged causes and implications by *gergo* ("slang") and suggesting a considerably more restrained and more restrictedly linguistic reading as merely "the jargon of the Garigliano," the central Italian region on the border of Lazio and Campania.

[9] Comments and Contexts

ALP's toes provoke a rather surprising amount of translational excitement [9.1]. Joyce's original "trinkettoes" is rendered by Ogden as "with drops from her toes." Joyce's French "petontintamahr" ignores the drops and endows her, despite the length of the descriptor, with a "tiny little foot" (*peton*). He changes his mind in Italian and instead, ungallantly, gives her a "great big foot" (*zampolona*). Settanni more chivalrously, and more in line with the original, reverts to celebrating her "tiny little foot" (*zampilina*).

Dear Dirty Dumpling, a "quare old buntz" in Joyce's English, a "strange fat old father" for Ogden [9.2], becomes a great stuffed sausage (*andouille*) in Joyce's French and, transgendered, a "sugna purca," a fat sow, in his Italian. His English "gammer and gaffer," Ogden's "old girl and old boy" [9.3], is rendered idiomatically but unremarkably as "mémère et pépère" in his French but, abandoning any semblance of semantic fidelity, by the Italian "gerarca e gitana." Settanni, abandoning the alliteration, emends this to "caporione e gitana," undoubtedly with an eye to possible political repercussions.

HCE's "seven dams to wive him" [9.4], each with her seven crutches, are ominously transformed in his French into "sept fem pour le femer," each with her "sept crochettes" that humorously suggest a pseudo-mythical and dauntingly multiple *vagina dentata*. For once, his Italian is rather less extravagant than his French, and in this case distinctly less threatening, the seven dams now become merely "sette manze a toro," seven heifers to his bull and to his marital bed. The archangel Michael of his English original [9.5] is transformed into the archangel Gabriel in his Italian and into a lesser known Saint Cornelius, patron saint of horned cattle (and thus punningly also of cuckolds), in his French.

"Northmen's thing made southfolk's place" in English [9.7] becomes, relatively unremarkably, "le Thing des nordiques céda platz au sud-volk" in French. Northmen, southfolk, and thing all disappear in Italian, however, where the locution "La sforza di Dio fe' l'urbe ad uomo" plays instead on a very different place and the role of the powerful Sforza family of Milan in Renaissance Italy. The "trinity scholard" of his English [9.8] becomes the "prieux escholier," at once pious and valiant, of his French, only to be drastically transformed into an Italian "laureata di Cuneo" whose qualifications, remarkable though they may be, appear to be in an entirely different field of endeavour.

Settanni, with a view to the delicacy of the original English "trinkettoes," alters Joyce's augmentative "zampolona" to the diminutive "zampilina," dismissing in the process the Olona and Ona rivers in favour of the Pili and Lin [9.1]. He neglects any intervention in the case of Joyce's "Sugna Purca Qua Ramengo," potentially a highly offensive reference to Mussolini [9.2], while emending Joyce's likewise politically laden "gerarca" to the inoffensive "caporione" [9.3]. He changes Joyce's "quinquequente" to "quinquequento" to make the reference to the 1500s more obvious and alters "caduno" to "cadauno," fluvially replacing the Irish Dun by the New Zealand Ada [9.7]. His emendation of Joyce's "gargarigliano" to "gergarigliano" for the original "eryan" [9.8] reduces the sexual charge of the former and invites a more restrictedly linguistic reading.

10 Night Now

Is that the Poolbeg flasher beyant, pharphar, or a fireboat coasting nyar the Kishtna ... ? ... My sights are swimming thicker on me by the shadows to this place. I sow home slowly now by own way, moyvalley way. Towy I too, rathmine. ... Can't hear with the waters of. The chittering waters of. Flittering bats, fieldmice bawk talk. Ho! Are you not gone ahome? What Tom Malone? Can't hear with bawk of bats, all the liffeying waters of. Ho, talk save us! My foos won't moos. I feel as old as yonder elm. A tale told of Shaun or Shem? All Livia's daughtersons. Dark hawks hear us. Night! Night! My ho head halls. I feel as heavy as yonder stone. Tell me of John or Shaun? Who were Shem and Shaun the living sons or daughters of? Night now! Tell me, tell me, tell me, elm! Night night! Telmetale of stem or stone. Beside the rivering waters of, hitherandthithering waters of. Night! (*ALP* 33–4, 34–5; *FW* 215.01–3, 09–11, 31–216.05)

[1] Is that the Poolbeg flasher beyant, pharphar, or a fireboat coasting nyar the Kishtna ...? (*ALP* 33; *FW* 215.01–3)

OGDEN: Is that the Poolbeg light-house over there, far, far, or a steamer sailing near the Kish sands ...?

As dusk gathers and darkness falls, the two washerwomen's sight and hearing become less reliable, and the world around them, increasingly dimly discerned, becomes an increasingly confused and confusing one. "The de-formations and re-formations of words give us the murk of the evening," as Padraic Colum wrote (1928a, 321). The Poolbeg lighthouse (Irish *poll beag* "little pool"), on the South Bull Wall in Dublin Bay, and the Kish lightship (replaced after Joyce's time by today's Kish lighthouse), marking the sand bank known as the Kish Bank, were designed to provide navigational assistance in the darkness but merely add to the confusion of the two watchers. The faint far light the watchers dimly see may be, they think, "the Poolbeg flasher beyant, pharphar, or a fireboat coasting nyar the Kishtna," possibly the lighthouse (Greek *pharos*, French *phare*), far far away, possibly a far fireboat sailing along the coast (German *Küste*), coasting near the Kish – or, even farther away, near the Russian river Nyar, perhaps, or the Indian river Kistna (also called the Krishna). Other rivers are dimly discernable, the Italian Po, English Pool, German Olbe, Romanian Beg, Indian Sher ("flasher"), Chinese Yan ("beyant"), and even the biblical Pharphar of ancient Syria (2 Kings 5:12). Clive Hart observes (1962, 214) that the phallic *phare* doubles as a Danish *far* ("father"), a signal from the faraway father sea towards which ALP as river is flowing and with which she will eventually merge. In Ogden's version, the echo of the *phare* is retained, while the fireboat (also a flasher) is domesticated into a steamer, and the exotic shimmer of the Kishtna is sternly abandoned for the geographically verifiable Kish sands.

JOYCE: Est-ce Gris-naze Poulbeg au phare-ouest, là, là-bas ou un bateau à feu qui côtoie preto Kishtna ...?

In Joyce's French, the washerwomen become even more confused, as does European geography. The "flasher" of Poolbeg now becomes the "Poulbeg," as if the (adjusted) name itself were synonymous with "lighthouse," of "Gris-naze," a Joycean headland conflating Cap Gris Nez on the northern French coast and the Naze headland on the Essex coast of England, each of which boasts its own lighthouse. Unlike the Poolbeg flasher, situated to the east of the river Liffey, the lighthouse (French *phare*) of "Poulbeg," the revised spelling providing the correct pronunciation for French readers, is now situated in the far west ("phare-ouest"), all the more easily to be confused with a fireboat ("bateau à feu") coasting (*côtoyer* "to run alongside") near (*près de*) the Kishtna, conflating Kish and Kistna again – or, for that matter, near the Brazilian river Preto. The English Pool continues to flow, joined by the Finnish Oulu and Canadian Owl, but without the German Olbe.

JOYCE: È il baleneone di Pulberg che scorgo, lontanalanterna, o una vegliera che costeggia la Kishtna ...?

SETTANNI: È il baleneone di Pulbeg che scorgo, lontanlanterna, o una vegliera che costeggia la Kishtna ...?

Joyce's Italian washerwoman, playing on *balenare* ("to flash"), wonders "Is it the Pulberg flasher ('baleneone') I see (*scorgere* 'to perceive'), a lighthouse (*lanterna*) afar (*lontano*), or a guard boat (*vegliare* 'to guard') sailing along (*costeggiare* 'to sail along') the Kishtna?" "Poolbeg" is now italianized as "Pulberg," ignoring Irish geography but retaining the English Pool while offering complementary access to the South African Berg River, shortly followed by the Portuguese Corgo, Norwegian Tana, and Italian Era. The fireboat is now sailing not "near" the Kishtna (whatever the latter may be) but on it. Settanni's version corrects "Pulberg" to "Pulbeg," substituting the Romanian Beg for the Berg, and reduces "lontanalanterna" by a syllable to "lontanlanterna," abandoning the Norwegian Tana in favour of the Philippine Tanla.

[2] *My sights are swimming thicker on me by the shadows to this place. I sow home slowly now by own way, moyvalley way. Towy I too, rathmine.* (*ALP* 33–4; *FW* 215.09–11)

OGDEN: What I see gets feebler among these shades. I'll go home slowly now by my way, to Moyvalley. And so will I, to Rathmines.

With evening falling, shadows deepening around them, sights swimming before their eyes, and tongues growing heavier, confusing one consonant with another, the two weary washerwomen decide to set off slowly for home, one on her "own way" in the direction of the Kildare village of Moyvalley ("my valley"), on the Royal Canal, the other, her "so will I too" wearily slurred to an alliterative "towy I too," to "rathmine" and the Dublin suburb of Rathmines. Rivers continue to flow around them, the English Sow, New Zealand Owen, Irish Moy, American Valley, Welsh Towy, and German Main. Ogden once again deprives the place names of any additional resonances beyond immediate geographical verifiability.

JOYCE: Mes vues nagent grosses par les ombres pour ici. Je vaga vhez moi voucement par ma valley. Et moi de memel du côté de chez tertre.

Joyce's French washerwoman's eyesight (*vue*) and her view (*vue*) of the world around her are swimming (*nager* "to swim") and blurring (*gros* "thick") among the shadows (*ombres*) around her. Her language likewise begins to swim and blur, "Je vaga vhez moi voucement par ma valley" deforms the normal French statement *Je vais chez moi doucement par ma vallée* ("I'll go home slowly by my valley") under the alliterative influence of the Russian river Vaga and the attraction of her own valley (*vallée*), not necessarily Moyvalley, accompanied by the Laotian Ou and English Ouse. "Me too (*de même* 'likewise')," responds her colleague, "along the way by the mound (*tertre*)." She has a long trek ahead of her, for her residence appears to have moved from the Rathmines of the original to the Parisian Place du Tertre, a haunt of artists in Montmartre, evidently under the influence of Proust's *Du côté de chez Swann* (1913; *Swann's Way*, 1922) – which, as Dirk Van Hulle notes (2007, 97), Joyce had read while making his first notes for *Finnegans Wake*. Joyce's play in English on *my* and *moy* and *mine* is replaced in his French by the play on the valley that is ALP and the mound that is HCE. The move to Paris is accompanied by the Irish river Moy ("moi"), East Prussian Memel, English Mel ("memel") and Ter ("tertre"), and even the Canadian Swan, translingually evoked by the title of Proust's novel. The characteristic dactylic rhythm of *ALP* resurfaces in "Et | *moi* de me- | *mel* du cô- | *té* de chez | *ter*tre," which also approximates closely to a French alexandrine.

JOYCE: Nelle nebbie, per a qui ora traveggolo. Vado a piano per il mio santerno di vellembrosa. E io lo stesso, per Monselvata.
SETTANNI: Nelle nebbie per a chi ora traveggolo. Vado a piano per il mio santerno di vallombrosa. E io lo stesso per Monselvata.

Joyce's Italian begins with the mists (*nebbie*) in which, says his washerwoman, "I am here (*qui*) and now (*ora*) seeing things, but distortedly," just as a noun can be distorted into a verb (*avere le traveggole* "to see things distortedly") or the Ugandan river Ora made to flow through an Italian adverb. "I'm going (*vado*), slowly (*piano*), on my pathway (*sentiero*) through the shady (*ombroso*) valley (*valle*)," she volunteers, where the pathway is now also the Italian river Santerno and the shady valley doubles distortedly as the Benedictine abbey of Vallombrosa, in Tuscany, but evidently also close to the French river Elle and the Velle reservoir on the Portuguese river Minho. Her colleague is also departing, by "Monselvata," a name that economically conflates French *mon* ("my"), Italian *selva* ("forest") and *selvato* ("woodland"), the Grail Castle of Montsalvat in Richard Wagner's *Parsifal*, and the likewise Benedictine abbey of Montserrat, in Catalonia. The symbolic relationship of ALP and HCE as valley and mountain is once more adumbrated, as in Joyce's French. Settanni inadvertently deflates Joyce's wordplay on "per a qui" by adjusting it to "per a chi" ("through which") and explains that "vellembrosa" is really "vallombrosa." The latter change eliminates the Elle and the Velle reservoir, replacing them by the Irish river Allow.

***[3] Can't hear with the waters of. The chittering waters of. Flittering bats, fieldmice bawk talk.* (*ALP* 34–5; *FW* 215.31–2)**

OGDEN: No sound but the waters of. The dancing waters of. Winged things in flight, field-rats louder than talk.

The final passage of *ALP* has been aptly called "a paean to the life-giving properties of the river of life which carries the past into the future and makes the 'seim anew'" (Spinks 2009, 142). The concluding lines, Joyce wrote to Harriet Weaver on 1 February 1927, were truly "something," or else, he added, "I am an imbecile in my judgment of language" (*L* 1, 249; Ellmann 1982, 589). The famous finale is marked by a strongly dactylic underlying rhythm, introduced already in its opening words, by striking effects of rhyme and assonance, and by a sense of growing darkness, blurred outlines, inability to hear or see or communicate properly, and general confusion and disintegration. The waters are "chittering," chattering like the washerwomen, twittering like birds. Bats, rhymingly, are "flittering," flitting and fluttering to and fro. They are joined by fieldmice, a combination motivated by linguistics rather than biology, since in early modern English a bat was a *flittermouse* (Onions 1966, 79), already blurring the boundaries of species. The bats and the mice together "bawk talk," baulking talk with their own incongruously barking talk, as if they were great hounds instead, as if the boundaries of species and size and behaviour were blurring also, as if visual confusion were now matched by auditory confusion. Ogden changes the auditory image of the "chittering waters" to a visual "dancing waters," while the fieldmice become fieldrats, and the bats become undifferentiated but rhyming "winged things."

JOYCE: N'entends pas cause les ondes de. Le bébé babil des ondes de. Souris chauve, trottinette cause pause.

Joyce's French begins with a punning "N'entends pas cause les ondes de," unable to hear (*entendre*), for good reason (*pour cause*), because of (*à cause de*) the chatter (*causer* "to chat") of the waves – waves (*ondes*) rather than waters to accommodate a stuttering dactylic "ondes de" and a reference to the French river Onde. The chittering waters now produce a "bébé babil," the stuttering babylike "prattling" /bebebabi/ of the stuttering waves – reminding us, perhaps, that one of Joyce's French washerwomen earlier calls the other an "antibabébibobu" [7.2]. In a scene evocative of *Alice in Wonderland*, and once again blurring the boundaries of species, an occasional "bald mouse" ("souris chauve"), or perhaps it is just a discombobulated bat (*chauve-souris*) forgetting that it can fly, scurries along (*trottiner* "to scurry along") as if on wheels (*trottinette* "scooter"), sometimes causing a pause ("cause pause"), perhaps by baulking talk, and sometimes, on the contrary, just stopping to chat (*causer*). The scenario plays on the colloquial phrase *on entendrait trotter une souris*, "you could hear a pin drop" – literally, "one could hear a mouse trotting."

JOYCE: Non odo piú per le acque di. Le chiacchiericcianti acque di. Nottole qua, topi là fan pian.

SETTANNI: Non odo più per le acque di. Le chiacchiericcianti acque di. Nottole qua, topi là fan piano.

Joyce's Italian speaker, now evoking the Nigerian Odo and the Yoruba noun *odò* ("river"), can also no longer hear with the waters that "chatter" (*chiacchierare* "to chatter, gossip"), more or less (the Italian suffix *-iccio* operating like the English suffix *-ish*), and "curl" (*riccio* "curl, curly"), lapping in tiny waves. Creatures of the night (*notte*), bats (*nottole*) and, blurring species boundaries yet again, perhaps even owls (*nottole*) on the one hand, mice (*topi*) and perhaps even rats (*topi*) on the other, now go softly rather than baulking talk, "Nottole qua, topi là fan pian." Settanni, without altering the sense, finds it necessary to normalize the final spondaic "fan pian," echoing that of the original "bawk talk" (and the French "cause pause"), to a pedestrian "fan piano."

[4] *Ho! Are you not gone ahome? What Tom Malone? Can't hear with bawk of bats, all the liffeying waters of. Ho, talk save us! My foos won't moos.* (*ALP* 35; cf. *FW* 215.32–4: "Thom Malone"; "all thim")

OGDEN: Ho! Are you not gone, ho! What Tom Malone? No sound but the noise of these things, the Liffey and all its waters of. Ho, talk safe keep us! There's no moving this my foot.

Linguistic confusion reigns. One washerwoman's question of the other, "Are you not gone ahome?" is misheard and misunderstood to be a question about one Tom Malone. The confusion extends to include the reader. Is Tom Malone at all related to that famous Dubliner Molly Malone? Is it relevant that Little Chandler in *Dubliners* considers adopting the name Thomas Malone Chandler? (*D* 69). The relevance of the Russian river Tom and the (trisyllabic) Italian river Malone, on the other hand, is beyond question. The bawk of bats prevents properly hearing the liffeying waters. Talk, God save us, may or may not save us, but feet at any rate refuse to move and, as if in a process of Ovidian metamorphosis, become one with the unmoving moss underfoot. Ogden rather oddly reduces "gone ahome" to "gone, ho" rather than the more obvious "gone home," while his "There's no moving this my foot" introduces a consciously more poetic note than Joyce's original. The liffeying waters, meanwhile, are swollen by those of the African Save, German Oos, and various North American Moose Rivers.

> JOYCE: Hein! Tu n'es pas rentré? Quel père André? N'entends pas cause les fuisouris, les liffeyantes ondes de. Eh! Bruit nous aide! Mon pied à pied se lie lierré.

Joyce's French speaker, substituting "hein!" ("hey!") for "ho!" and the Chinese river Hei for the Chinese noun *ho*, asks "Tu n'es pas rentré?" ("Haven't you gone back?") but is misheard as referring to an otherwise undocumented Père André, possibly a priest, Father André, possibly just an old man, Old André, who owes his name and his existence, like Tom Malone, entirely to misheard information and the requirements of rhyme. One can't hear because of (*à cause de*) the chatter (*causer* "to chat") of the "fuisouris," mice (*souris*) scurrying and fleeing (*fuir* "to flee"), and the liffeying waves. God (*Dieu*) may not save us, but "noise" (*bruit*) may. Meanwhile, in a play on *lier* ("to bind") and *lierre* ("ivy"), strengthening the note of Ovidian metamorphosis, and introducing a doubly alliterating French octosyllable with internal rhyme, "Mon pied à pied se lie lierré" ("My foot to ivied foot is bound").

> JOYCE: Oh! Non sei andata a casa? Che Renata la Masa? Non odo piú il nottolio, le liffeyanti acque di. Rio ci scampi! Al mio piè ledra v'è.
>
> SETTANNI: Oh! Non sei andata a casa? Che Renata La Masa? Non odo più per il nottolio, le liffeyanti acque di. Lio ci scampi! Al mio piè ledra v'è.

Joyce's Italian washerwoman's question, "Non sei andata a casa?" ("Haven't you gone home?"), introduced by an "Oh!" that puns on

French *eau* ("water"), elicits the counterquestion "Che Renata la Masa?," linguistic confusion now inventing a Renata, named either for her mother Tommasa, colloquially "Masa," or an also generically confused version of her father Tommaso, colloquially "Maso." Lobner (1989, 41) sees the name of this transgendered Tom Malone, in which the vowel *a* now occurs five times, as one example of a sustained strategy throughout the Italian *ALP* that "ensures the predominance of the vowel *a*, an indicator in Italian of feminine gender," a strategy that begins with the elimination of Joyce's original opening "O."

Renata unleashes a fluvial deluge: the German Rhine, disguised in Polish as the Ren, is tumultuously joined by the Norwegian Rena, Canadian Ena, African Nata, Indonesian Tala, Russian Lama, Dutch Maas, the Arabic *ma* ("water"), and the Japanese Asa. One can no longer hear the bats (*nottole*) or see the loopings (*rotolio* "rolling") of their swooping flight or hear the liffeying waters, or even those of the Nigerian Oli. May God (*Dio*) and the river (Spanish *río*) together save us (*scampare* "to save"), but just look here (*vi*), even if short-sightedly (*miope*), at the ivy (*l'edera*) growing on my foot ("al mio piè"). That final sentence allows access to the Canadian Edra Creek, Algerian Dra, and central European Drave. The Ovidian context of the invitation, meanwhile – the fleeing nymph Daphne transformed into a laurel tree (Greek *daphnê*) to avoid Apollo's amorous attentions – allows implied supplementary access to Kentucky's Laurel River and Australia's Apollo Bay.

Settanni makes one correction to Joyce's text, changing "Non odo piú il nottolio" to "Non odo piú *per* il nottolio," now, with the washerwoman's vision and hearing confused, more appropriately meaning "I can no longer hear *because of* the bats' swooping flight." Other than adding a capital letter to Renata La Masa's name, he also improves Joyce's "Rio ci scampi" to "Lio ci scampi," conflating the conventional phrase *Dio ci scampi* ("God save us"), a general Spanish *río*, and the specific Chinese river Li, while humorously playing also on the first-person pronoun *io*, which doubles in Italian for the English noun *ego*, to suggest, tongue in cheek, "May our ego (*l'io*) save us."

***[5] I feel as old as yonder elm. A tale told of Shaun or Shem? All Livia's daughtersons. Dark hawks hear us. Night! Night! My ho head halls.* (*ALP* 35; *FW* 215.34–6)**

OGDEN: I seem as old as that tree over there. A story of Shaun or Shem but where? All Livia's daughters and sons. Dark birds are hearing. Night! Night! My old head's bent.

As Campbell and Robinson put it, the two washerwomen function as symbols of change and permanence, time and space, and implicitly as ALP and HCE (1961, 140). In the final lines, the two figures, who in *Finnegans Wake* will much later be named as "Queer Mrs Quickenough and odd Miss Doddpebble (*FW* 620.19–20), and who in one sense are just personifications of a tree on one bank and a rock on the other, fade respectively back into tree (as in "quicken," otherwise the rowan or mountain ash) and stone (as in "pebble"). Tree and stone in turn become cloudily identified with Shem ("stem") and Shaun ("stone"), sons (or was it daughters, female like the confused washerwomen?) or "daughtersons" of ALP and HCE.

One woman's "I feel as old as yonder elm" is misheard by the other as "A tale told of Shaun or Shem?" A similar misperception seems to derive "all Livia's daughtersons" rhymingly from the preceding "all the liffeying waters of" [10.3]. The distinctions between day and night, light and darkness, are likewise increasingly blurred. Ogden changes the elm to an unidentified tree and the hawks to unidentified birds, the change from hyponyms to hyperonyms contributing to the general blurring of distinctions. "I seem as old as that tree over there. A story of Shaun or Shem but where?" introduces a compensatory rhyming couplet in mixed metre. The yawning alliteration of "My ho head halls" disappears in "My old head's bent."

More rivers run. The appearance of the American Elm may remind some readers that the first letter of the Irish alphabet, *a* (also the first and last letter of *Anna*), was traditionally known by the name *ailm* ("elm"). The "dark hawks" of night, partially evoked by the vowel sound of "daughter," evoke the Canadian Hawk River. The yawned "My ho head halls," suggesting "My old head falls," also evokes (German *hallen* "to echo") the New Caledonian Ho, the Canadian Head River, and the Australian Halls Creek, while simultaneously conflating the promontory that is HCE and the river (Chinese *ho*) that is ALP.

> JOYCE: Je me sens vieille comme mon orme même. Un conte conté de Shaun ou Shem? De Livie tous les fillefils. Sombres faucons écoutent l'ombre. Nuit. Nuit. Ma taute tête tombe.

As Joyce's English "I feel as old" rhymes with "a tale told" in English, "Je me sens vieille" ("I feel old") rhymes with "un conte conté" ("a tale told") in his French rendering. Similarly, "yonder elm" becomes a French "mon orme même" ("my own elm"), evoking the African Mono and French Orme, facilitating the corresponding rhyme on "Shaun ou Shem," and implying that the speaker has in fact already almost become the elm. "Livia" becomes "Livie," suggesting a pun on "la vie" ("life") and suggesting once again a translingual pun on *Life*, the Irish name of the Liffey, while Livia's "daughtersons" become a literal "fillefils." The "dark hawks" that hear "us" become rhyming "sombres faucons" ("dark hawks") who, blurring sight and sound, "écoutent l'ombre" ("listen to the shade"). The "ho head" that "halls," evoking Howth Head and alliterating in /h/, becomes "Ma taute tête tombe," with a new alliterative sequence in /t/ causing *haute* ("high") to become "taute," thus suggesting "My high head is falling," while evoking the French rivers Taute and Têt, with echoes of the English Thet, Russian Tom, and African Ombe. The echo of German *hallen* ("to echo") disappears.

JOYCE: Mi sento vecchia come l'elmo tasso. Fiaba detta di Gionni e Giace? D'Anna Livia i figlifiglie. Corvo scuro ode. Notte! Notte! Il mio cupo capo cade.

SETTANNI: Mi sento vecchia come l'olmo tasso. Fiaba detta di Gionno e Giaco? D'Anna Livia i figlifiglie. Corvo scuro ode. Notte! Notte! Il mio cupo capo cade.

Joyce's Italian washerwoman feels "vecchia come l'elmo tasso," playing first on *elmo* ("helmet") for *olmo* ("elm") in order to evoke the American river Elm, then on *adesso* ("just now") and *tasso* ("yew") and the Indian river Tasso, and implicitly on space ("yonder") and time ("just now"); she feels "old like that elm just now." Lobner has observed (1989, 83) that as well as the arboreal play on elm and yew, the combination of a possibly military *elmo* ("helmet") and *tasso* suggests a passing Italian cultural reference to Torquato Tasso (1511–1595), whose epic *Gerusalemme liberata* (1574) celebrates the fight to liberate Jerusalem during the First Crusade.

The "tale told of Shaun or Shem" becomes an Italian fairy tale (*fiaba*) evoking the Ghanaian river Fia and told of "Gionni e Giace," pet forms of *Giovanni* and *Giacomo*, italianized versions of the given names of John Joyce and James Joyce, as also of Shaun and Shem, "figlifiglie" ("sonsdaughters") of Anna Livia. The plural "dark hawks" of Joyce's English give way to a singular "corvo scuro" ("dark raven") that likewise "ode" ("hears"), while simultaneously evoking the Portuguese Rio Corvo, Belgian Our, Mongolian Ur, and French Odet, followed by the German Notte. Fading out with the fading day, her "sad (*cupo*) head (*capo*) falls (*cade*)" in alliterative trochees. Risset (1973, 56) points out the intertextual play here on a similarly alliterative reaction to the tragic narrative of Paolo and Francesca in the fifth canto of the *Inferno*: overcome by emotion, Dante as character faints dead away and "caddi come corpo morto cade" (*Inferno* 5.142), "I fell as a dead body falls" (Mandelbaum 1982, 47). Dante's Italian decasyllable is adjusted to Joyce's Italian octosyllable.

Settanni, schoolmasterly once again, emends Joyce's "vecchia come l'elmo tasso" to "vecchia come l'olmo tasso," rescuing the elm (*olmo*) for struggling Italian readers while exchanging the American river Elm for the South Sudanese river Lol. He likewise alters Joyce's "Gionni e Giace," which evokes the English river Onny and the Nigerian Acha, to a more normal "Gionno e Giaco," thus hinting instead at the Japanese Ono and Brazilian Iaco, while diminishing the sense of increasing confusion, linguistic and otherwise.

***[6] I feel as heavy as yonder stone. Tell me of John or Shaun? Who were Shem and Shaun the living sons or daughters of? Night now!* (*ALP* 35; *FW* 215.36–216.02)**

OGDEN: My weight is like that stone you see. What may the John Shaun story be? Or who were Shem and Shaun the living sons and daughters of? Night now!

The final lines involve two different forms of confusion, as Patrick McCarthy has observed, on the one hand a blurring of distinctions and on the other a tendency toward fragmentation or incompletion. "The chapter attempts to tell us 'all about Anna Livia,' yet the totalizing impulse implied by this phrase leads inevitably to a breakdown of narrative, to fragmentation, in part because one story constantly runs into another as tidiness gives way to tidalness" (2007, 173–4). "Yonder stone" is misheard as "John or Shaun." Confusion of sexual and generational identity is added to linguistic confusion. Should "Livia's daughtersons" be understood as her children or her grandchildren? Are Shem and Shaun her sons or her daughters? The "daughters of" is rhymingly generated by the "waters of," and McCarthy observes that "this element of hermaphroditism is a prominent aspect of the conclusion from the earliest drafts on" (2007, 173). As Beckett puts it, "When the sense is sleep, the words go to sleep" (1972, 14). As John Gordon puts it, "oblivion has won out" (1986, 169). As Joyce puts it, "Night now!" Rivers continue to run, including the French Yon, American Stone, and Indian Tel.

Ogden changes "the living sons *or* daughters" to "the living sons *and* daughters," and his washerwoman understandably wonders "What may the John Shaun story be?" Her next observation, "My weight is like that stone you see," completes a rhyming pair of iambic tetrameters, once again employing a compensatory strategy to offset the inevitable losses incurred by attempting to translate only the "simple sense."

> JOYCE: Je me sens lourde comme ma pierrestone. Conte moi de John ou Shaun. Qui furent Shem et Shaun en vie les fils ou filles de. Là-dessus nuit.

Joyce's French washerwoman feels "lourde" ("heavy") as a stone, linguistically even doubled as "ma pierrestone," the phrase evoking the Belgian Our, South East Asian Ma, Canadian Rivière-à-Pierre, and American Stone, while the possessive adjective *ma* ("my") once again suggests that the speaker, as if in an Ovidian metamorphosis, is already partly stone. The Arabic *ma* ("water") is very appropriately present once again. Shem and Shaun as "the living sons" become Shem and Shaun "en vie" ("in life"), as if already dead, while punning on *Livie*. "Là-dessus nuit" evokes a primarily spatial rather than temporal image, night falling as a dark all-obscuring cover "over" the scene, while "nuit" concludes the rhyming sequence of "en vie les fils ou filles."

> JOYCE: Mi sento pesa come quel sasso. Dimmi di Giaco e Giaso! Chi fur Giac e Gion i vivi figli e figlie di? Notte addenso!
> SETTANNI: [*without change*]

Our Italian washerwoman, in an Italian decasyllable, feels "pesa" ("heavy") as "quel sasso" ("that stone"), while the singular "John or Shaun" becomes a plural "Giaco e Giaso," the latter rhyming with "sasso." Giaco (Giacomo, James, Shem) fades confusedly into an otherwise unheard of Giaso (Giasone, Jason), while "Shem and Shaun" becomes "Giac e Gion," with Shaun reverting to the Gion (Giovanni) one might have expected. In a further element of interlinguistic confusion, English *Jack* and *John* and *Shaun* are three forms of the same name. The hint of "Livia" in "living" survives rather more faintly in "i vivi figli e figlie," blurred and blended in the gathering dusk. It is dark night now, "notte addenso," the adverb conflating *adesso* ("now"), *denso* ("dense, dark"), and a hint of the Italian river Adda following the German Notte.

***[7] Tell me, tell me, tell me, elm! Night night! Tell me tale of stem or stone. Beside the rivering waters of, hitherandthithering waters of. Night!* (*ALP* 35; cf. *FW* 216.03–5, "telmetale")**

> OGDEN: Say it, say it, say it, tree! Night night! The story say of stem or stone. By the side of the river waters of, this way and that way waters of. Night!

The overtly poetic effect of the concluding lines is striking. "Tell me, tell me, tell me, elm!," a truncated trochaic tetrameter, is followed by a spondee ("Night night!") and a second truncated trochaic tetrameter ("Tell me tale of stem or stone"), before a single amphibrach ("Be*side* the") introduces a final truncated dactylic hexameter – "*riv*ering | *wa*ters of, | *hith*erand- | *thith*ering | *wa*ters of | *Night*!" The effect of the final foot in each of the truncated lines is to emphasize the final monosyllable, "elm," "stone," "Night!" While Ogden's version retains the rhythm in the opening clauses, Joyce's "elm" has to become a hyperonymous "tree" – while the possibility of alliteratively combining "tree" and "tell" is excluded because *tell* is not one of the only eighteen verbs included in the extremely reduced list of verbs employed in Basic English. Rhythm is abandoned in Ogden's penultimate sentence, one of Joyce's most musical in the original.

> JOYCE: Dis-mor, dis-mor, dis-mor, orme. Nuit, nuit! Contemoiconte soit tronc ou pierre. Tant rivièrantes ondes de, couretcourantes ondes de. Nuit!

In French, the Indian Tel and American Elm evoked in "Tell me, tell me, tell me, elm!," with its play on /l/ and /m/, are replaced by the Scottish Dee and Indian Mor (conflated with *moi* "me") and French Orme in "Dis-mor, dis-mor, dis-mor, orme," with its corresponding play on /r/ and /m/ suggesting the uninterrupted murmur of the river. Serendipitously, the Scottish Dee takes its name from a British Celtic *deva* ("goddess"), while the Irish adjective *mór* ("great") and the Scandinavian noun *mor* ("mother") translingually combine to evoke Anna (Hungarian *anya*, Turkish *anne* "mother") as fluvial Great Mother, the river of rivers on its widening way to the sea (Breton *mor*, Cornish *mor*, Welsh *môr* "sea"). "Contemoiconte," while allowing for hints of the Irish Moy and French Onde, is a quite literal rendering of "tell" (*conter*) and "tale" (*conte*) as "tronc ou pierre" is of "stem or stone," though the echo of "Shem or Shaun" is abandoned in favour of the two Canadian rivers Grand Tronc and Pierre. The "rivering" and "hitherandthithering waters" become "rivièrantes ondes" ("rivering waves") and, drawing on the verb *courir* ("to run"), while playing on approximately rhyming nasal vowels, "couretcourantes ondes" ("runandrunning waves").

JOYCE: Dimmi, dimmi, dimmi, olm! Nottenot! Dimmifiaba d'alberoccia. Presso le frusciacque di, le quinciequindi acque di. Not!
SETTANNI: Diddmi, dimmi, dimmi, olm! Nottenot! Dimmifiaba d'alberoccia. Presso le frusciacque di, le quinciequindi acque di. Notte!

Joyce's Italian "Dimmi, dimmi, dimmi, olm!," evoking the Turkish Dim, Dutch Diem, and Sudanese Immi, adheres closely to both the semantic meaning and the trochaic rhythm of the original, with *olmo* ("elm") reduced to a monosyllabic "olm" for the purposes of that rhythm. The German Notte continues to flow, now accompanied by the Finnish Teno and American Eno ("Nottenot"). The conflated "dimmifiaba," with the *fiaba* ("tale") watered by the Ghanaian Fia, anticipates the later conflation in *Finnegans Wake* of "tell me tale" to "telmetale." "Stem or stone" generates a new Italian conflation, "alberoccia" conjoining *albero* ("tree") and *roccia* ("stone") – and completing an Italian octosyllable (Risset 1984, 7) – while evoking the Romanian Apele Albe, Angolan Bero, and English Roch. The "rivering waters" become, evoking the Belarussian Usha, a likewise conjoined "frusciacque," literally "rustling (*frusciare* 'to rustle') waters (*acque*)," while the "hitherandthithering waters" become the "quinciequindi acque," literally, while evoking the English Quin,"waters from here (*quinci*) and from there (*quindi*)." Settanni's emendation of the opening "dimmi" to "diddmi" spoils the effect of repetition, though incorporating the Alsatian river Idd, while his alteration of "Not!" to the more conventional "Notte!" undoes Joyce's choice of a final monosyllable.

[8] Comments and Contexts

The washerwomen's exhaustion, already evident in Joyce's English, is conveyed more strongly in his French, with a series of standard French words strangely deformed by alliterating in /v/, as if the speaker were no longer able to make the effort to move her lips in order to pronounce other consonants. Two geographical references in his English to locations in or near Dublin become a reference to Proust and Paris in his French and to two Benedictine abbeys, Tuscan and Catalan respectively, in his Italian [10.2]. Bats flitter and fieldmice bark like great dogs in his English, while the distinction between a bald mouse ("souris chauve") and a bat (*chauve-souris*) is blurred in French and the distinction between bats (*nottole*) and owls (*nottole*), both creatures of the night (*notte*), disappears in Italian [10.3]. The English-language Tom Malone, himself just a linguistic figment of the moment, becomes a Père André, perhaps a cleric, perhaps just an old man, perhaps both, in French, and changes gender to become a Renata la Masa in Italian [10.4]. Gender difference continues to be blurred as Shaun and Shem become ALP's "daughtersons" in English, "fillefils" in French, but "figlifiglie" ("sonsdaughters") in Italian, their names also italianized as "Gionni e Giace" [10.5] and later "Giac e Gion" [10.6]. All distinctions finally drown in the darkness of night and the murmur of the "hitherandthithering waters," the "couretcourantes ondes," the "quinciequindi acque" [10.7].

Settanni takes on Joyce at his own game in fluvially substituting the Beg for the Berg and the Tanla for the Tana [10.1]. He deflates Joyce's wordplay on "per a qui" by correcting it to "per a chi" and explains that "vellembrosa" is really "vallombrosa," thereby eliminating the Elle and the Velle reservoir in favour of the Irish Allow [10.2]. He normalizes Joyce's final spondaic "fan pian," echoing that of the original "bawk talk" (and the French "cause pause"), to a pedestrian "fan piano" [10.3]. One of his occasional improvements has him emending Joyce's "Rio ci scampi" to "Lio ci scampi," conflating *Dio ci scampi* ("God save us"), a Spanish *río*, and the Chinese river Li, to suggest, tongue in cheek, "May our ego (*l'io*) save us" [10.4]. He quite unnecessarily emends Joyce's "vecchia come l'elmo tasso" to "vecchia come l'olmo tasso," fluvially exchanging the Elm for the Lol. He alters Joyce's "Gionni e Giace" to a superficially more reasonable "Gionno e Giaco," trading the Onny and Acha for the Ono and Iaco, while diminishing the sense of increasing confusion, linguistic and otherwise [10.5]. His substitution of "diddmi" for the opening "dimmi" in Joyce's "Dimmi, dimmi, dimmi, olm!," spoils the cumulative effect of the repetition, while his final substitution of "Notte!" for Joyce's monosyllabic "Not!" undoes a carefully structured textual effect [10.7].

Klaus Reichert has observed that *ALP* not only opens with an "O" that can be read as omega, the last letter of the Greek alphabet, but closes ("Night!") with a *t* that can likewise be read as tau, the last letter of the Hebrew alphabet (Reichert and Senn 1970, 31). The latter effect is replicated by Joyce both in French "Nuit!" (even if only visually) and in Italian, where a standard Italian *notte* is replaced, replicating the monosyllabic finale of the original, by a monosyllabic "Not!" – an effect Settanni chooses to reverse. Readers may or may not feel justified in seeing that final "Not!" as a humorous intertextual and translingual play on Molly Bloom's final "Yes."

Conclusion

Five lines of text and ten pages of notes (*U* 1.365–6)

This project has compared in considerable detail slightly more than half of Joyce's French and Italian versions of *Anna Livia Plurabelle,* as well as the corresponding portions of Beckett's French, Settanni's Italian, and Ogden's Basic English variations, with Joyce's original English. The chosen method has been a series of comparative microanalyses of roughly fifty selected excerpts, usually short, and sometimes very short, ranging from a single sentence of a few words to seldom more than half a dozen sentences. The need to keep the project within reasonable limits made any attempt to deal with the entire text at a similar degree of detail unrealistic. The resulting overall focus has thus not at all been on would-be overarching interpretation but rather on closely scrutinized details of individual textual features, an unapologetic example of "pedestrian semantic rummaging," in Fritz Senn's phrase (1995, 226), attempting to examine every word and resonance, and, at least in principle, every letter, in a limited range of exemplary passages in all three languages. By the same token, the focus has also not been on larger questions of translation theory – including notably the question as to whether these renderings even qualify in the first place to be considered translations properly so called – but rather on the very frequently subtle and sometimes drastic new shades of meaning and implication introduced by the linguistic and cultural transposition of individual words and phrases.

An implicit guiding principle throughout has been to consider Joyce's French *ALP* and Italian *ALP* not as mere secondary versions, successful or otherwise, of a primary English *ALP*, but rather to consider each of the three as being at once both a separate individual text *and* a separate individual component of a combined trilingual macrotextual *ALP*.

1 English *ALP*

Three areas that suggest themselves as appropriate points of overall comparison between the three variations of a trilingual *ALP* are, first, the specifically Wakean nature of the language and languages employed; second, the specific nature of the multifarious cultural references woven into the text; and, third, the comparative degree of the pervasive fluvial references.

Finnegans Wake as a whole has aptly been described as "English in syntax, Irish in cadence, and multilingual in vocabulary" (Reynolds 1981, 202), and the description certainly also holds for *ALP*. The two washerwomen, whose dialogue constitutes the entire text of *ALP*, converse animatedly in a language whose base is immediately recognizable as colloquial Irish English, with its characteristic rhythms and expressions and idiomatic turns of phrase. This base appears either entirely unmodified, as in the humorous description of HCE "with a hump of grandeur on him like a walking rat" [5.2], or with its natural alliterative and rhythmical tendencies needing little or no authorial enhancement to achieve poetic effect, as in "How many goes is it I wonder I washed it?" [3.3]. Metrical effects, most often involving dactylic rhythms, are omnipresent. The predominant dactyls are occasionally and temporarily replaced for particular effect by anapestic [1.3] or iambic [4.4] or trochaic [5.2] rhythms. Tindall's opinion is entirely warranted: *ALP* is indeed "a triumph of sequence, rhythm, and sound" (1996, 140).

The colloquial Irish English base is very frequently and to different degrees deliberately deformed, Wakeanized, as in "What was it he did a tail at all?" [4.1], with the idiomatic *at all at all* modified to include an overtly sexual implication, or when Anna Livia is called a "queer old skeowsha" [9.1], with the colloquial *segocia* restructured to include half a dozen fluvial references, or when one of the washerwomen's "I sow home slowly now by own way" [10.2] concisely invokes the effect of physical exhaustion. And sometimes the base is humorously abandoned altogether, as when "it was put in the newses what he did, nicies and priers, the King fierceas Humphrey" [4.3], burlesquing legalese, or as when an uneducated Dublin washerwoman offers the opinion that

Anna Livia is nothing less than a "proxenete" [7.2], a term not overtly Wakean but rarely if ever heard either before or since on the banks of the Liffey.

All of this is of course part of what Robert Sage called "the breathtaking complexity of the text" (1928, 172). As another major part of that complexity, multiple and manifold cultural references abound throughout the text, and include at least the following fifty or so instances in the excerpts considered here, some overt, some covert, some only minimally and obliquely implied: Dublin [2.1], Isaac Butt [2.2], Parnell [2.2, 7.1], the Phoenix Park [2.3, 6.1], the Garden of Eden [2.3], Lough Neagh [4.2], Thomas Moore [4.2], possibly T.S. Eliot [4.4], the prophet Hosea [4.4], various proverbs and popular maxims [4.4, 8.2], the town of Drogheda [5.1], Deucalion [5.2], Noah [5.2, 6.1], Howth [5.2], the Duke of Wellington [5.2], Derry, Cork, Dublin, and Galway [5.3], the Garda Síochána or Irish police force [5.4], Gilbert and Sullivan [5.4], Hugh Capet and Henry the Fowler [5.5], the ancient Greek geographer Ptolemy [6.1, 6.3], Dante [6.1], Finn MacCool [6.1, 6.3, 8.1, 9.2], Solomon and Sheba [6.3], the biblical Saul of Rehoboth [6.3], Johnson's dictionary [7.3], Irish musicians Michael Kelly, Michael Balfe, and Joseph Robinson [7.4], Rossini [7.4], Finn MacCool's bevy of seven legendary female admirers [8.1], the biblical Tamar [8.3], Abraham [8.3], Lady Morgan [9.2], Norwegian Vikings [9.2, 9.7], Michaelmas [9.5], Giambattista Vico [9.6], the Ordovices [9.6], Trinity College and the Holy Trinity [9.8], Wagner [10.2], and Ovid [10.4].

As for specifically fluvial references, Joyce, as is well known, devoted an extraordinary amount of time, labour, and ingenuity in obsessively collecting and incorporating many hundreds of river names and associated aquatic features in his text, increasing the number with every further revision – and it has therefore seemed entirely appropriate to devote a considerable degree of attention also to identifying those elements in the text in its threefold manifestation. The English *ALP* includes numerous individual feats of Wakean hydronymy. Many of these involve deliberate verbal deformations, from the relatively simple, such as "the old cheb" [2.1] or "an awful old reppe" [3.1], evoking the Czech Cheb and French Reppe respectively, to the considerably more complicated, such as "illyssus distilling" [4.3], evoking the Greek Ilissos, Austrian Ill, French Ill and Lys, and the Hyssus of ancient Pontus, or "the gran Phenician rover" [6.1], evoking the Slovak Gran, Chinese Fen, Indian Feni, Cornish Enni, Japanese Nishi, the Rove River of the Solomon Islands, the Zimbabwean Ove, and the English Ver.

One of the most interesting forms of fluvial evocation, however, involves plain English being seduced by the Wakean context into functioning to Wakean effect. The opening six-word invitation to "tell me all about Anna Livia" [1.1] thus effortlessly evokes, as mentioned, more than a dozen other rivers as well as the Irish Liffey, including the Indian Tel, American Elm, Ugandan Alla, South American Abou, Nigerian Bou, Laotian Ou, Norwegian Tana, American Ana, Scottish Annan, Thai Na, the Nali of Bangladesh, the Lyvia of New Zealand, and the Ugandan Ivi. To take just one more example, "Yes, I know, go on" [2.1] is once again a perfectly plain English phrase, but it also manages to evoke the Italian Esino, New Zealand Ino, English Noe, Australian Nogo, and Nigerian Ogun rivers. In both phrases, plain English has Wakean thrust upon it, thanks both to linguistic serendipity and to the river-obsessed Annalivian context, without which readers simply would not think it at all appropriate to look for such fluvial overtones. Whether Joyce intended such a reading (though he almost certainly did) is essentially irrelevant; the text itself, the machine that Joyce built for the discovery, revelation, and joyous flaunting of subtextual rivers, certainly intends it. *ALP* insistently challenges its readers to join in Joyce's gleeful hydronymous game, overtly turning them in the process into his voluntary assistants as literary water diviners and thus as co-producers of the Joycean text. The actual number of rivers and other aquatic features evoked, depending as it thus also does on individual readers' aptitude and enthusiasm and investigative stamina, is consequently essentially incalculable.

2 Ogden's *ALP*

In literary terms, Ogden's Basic English rendering was of necessity doomed from the start to inescapable failure, as both Ogden and Joyce were certainly well aware. The fundamental reason for this was of course that the very nature of Basic English, with its ambition to convey nothing more than "simple sense," required the translation to treat the language of *ALP* as if it were nothing more than plain English and attempting to convey nothing more than unambiguous message information, to the exclusion of any signal information (Van Hulle 2004, 79). Polysemy, ambivalence, connotation, allusiveness, and linguistic indeterminacy had thus all by definition to be eradicated. Joyce, however, while thus faced with inevitable failure, was evidently keenly interested in the degree (if any) to which that failure could be mitigated.

The few excerpts from the Basic English rendering considered above are insufficient in number to warrant comprehensive statements about Ogden's rendering as a whole, but certain features emerge clearly enough. Hyperonyms ("tree," "birds," "winged things") substituted for hyponyms ("elm," "hawks," "bats") necessarily involve a serious loss of specificity – though it could of course be argued that the loss of specificity and definition is in fact entirely appropriate at least for the final paragraphs of the washerwomen's discourse. As a would-be compensatory strategy, a very sparing use of rhyme in combination with loose iambic tetrameters contributes at least occasionally a faint patina of literariness: "I seem as old as that tree over there. A story of Shaun or Shem but where?" [10.5]; "My weight is like that stone you see. What may the John Shaun story be?" [10.6]. One rather odd decision has a trochaic tetrameter self-consciously and quite unnecessarily introduced, "There's no moving this my foot" for the original straightforward iambic dimeter "My foos won't moos" [10.4].

Ogden reports that Joyce himself was involved in the translation and that he paid particular attention above all to retaining the original rhythm (1931, 95; 1932a, 259). Alliteration, assonance, sonority, and ambiguity were in this case evidently not as important to him. New cultural references or allusions of any sort are almost non-existent: a single exception in the passages considered is a reference to the Danes [9.2]. Ogden also evidently did not consider fluvial evocations to be any part of the "simple sense" he aimed to recuperate. Joyce's "Kishtna," for example, is reduced to Ogden's "Kish sands" [10.1], rejecting the exotic river name and its resonances and explaining it bluntly as really meaning the Kish sands; HCE's "seven dams" is reduced to his "seven women of pleasure" [9.4], erasing any aquatic resonance; "the seim anew" becomes "the same and new" [9.6], abandoning the reference to the Ukrainian Seim. A rare exception is the presence of the Chinese Yan, which survives the transition from "eryan" to "Aryan" [9.8].

Given his willing participation in the project, which he himself even initiated, we must assume that Joyce agreed, for the purposes of the experiment, with Ogden's overall translational strategy. In the end, however, for all that the experiment was in its way an intriguing one, exploring the difficulties in transposing the most complex English into the least complex, one has to agree with Harry Levin's comment that not much is left (1960, 196). What is most importantly lost is of course the literary richness and allusiveness and polysemy of the original *ALP*. While Joyce's text demands a reader's concentrated attention and unflagging commitment to participation in the literary game, Ogden's text requires only a very minimal readerly reaction. To some degree, Ogden's rendering constitutes a proleptic response to those critics who would object that Joyce's French and Italian renderings ignore "sense." Ogden dutifully reports the "simple sense" – and very little else.

3 Beckett's *ALP*

Completed in 1930, and subsequently lost for more than half a century, Beckett and Péron's French *ALP* has had surprisingly little detailed attention since its first publication by Jacques Aubert in 1985. Some of the few reactions have been decidedly surprising. Beckett himself asserted, quite wrongly, that "practically nothing" of his and Péron's rendering survived into Joyce's team's version (Aubert 1985, 417). Kim Allen asserted, quite wrongly, that "Beckett's strengths lie in his keeping the translation fairly literal," while "his weakness is that he does not play as much with the French language as the reader might like and the text might require" (2000, 430). Megan Quigley (2004, 477) differs from both Beckett and Allen in asserting, quite wrongly once again, that almost *all* of Joyce's version of the opening pages is in fact the work of Beckett and, more particularly, Péron.

Beckett's claim after more than half a century that practically nothing of his original French rendering survived in Joyce's published version evidently results partly from the passage of fifty-odd years and partly from the memory of his original resentment at Joyce's cavalier treatment and Soupault's insulting attitude. Of the thirty-three relevant excerpts examined in the present book, Beckett's rendering was adopted entirely unchanged by Joyce in two cases, adopted with only minor changes in eleven, adopted with major changes in fourteen, and not adopted at all in only six. The influence of Beckett's rendering is thus to be felt to a considerable degree in thirteen (39 percent) and to at least some degree in a further fourteen (42 percent) of all excerpts considered. While these ratios do not necessarily hold for Beckett's entire rendering (of which the thirty-three excerpts examined constitute just under half) they are certainly more than enough to disprove Beckett's irritated claim that his and Péron's original rendering had been almost completely ignored.

As a whole, Beckett's rendering is indeed, and not at all surprisingly, more literal than Joyce's. His "Je sais par coeur les endroits qu'il aime à saalir, le misérable" thus becomes Joyce's "Je sais paroker les endroits qu'il aime à seillir, le mymyserable" [3.3]; his "Mais, derrière tout, qu'est-ce qu'il fit?" becomes "Mais queue fit-il comme histoire?" [4.1]; his "Rive gauche était droite et rive druite était sinistre" becomes "Sbire Kauche était droit mais Sbire Troyt senestre" [5.1]. But while Joyce, exercising authorial licence even as a translator, certainly played more flamboyantly and to a greater extent on the French language than did Beckett, the suggestion that Beckett somehow failed to play adequately on the language is directly contradicted by such examples as "Ou quel quel que fût le tréfleuve qu'il aurait trouvé dans le parc de l'Inphernix" [2.3] or "Sa crête couronne le bec de l'aigle, le vieux deuc alien célèbre" [5.2] or "sa bouche onflée de mots corquets et tous ses bégaiements à dublintente, le farceur qu'il est sans égalouégaux" [5.3] or "ses brisons qui meuseglaient asseillis sans mersey" [6.3] or the splendid invented title "*Le Gouronnement de la Buse*" [7.4].

His rendering also contributes several new cultural references not found in Joyce's English, including at various levels of obliquity to St Patrick [2.3], Dante [2.3], Proust [4.4], the Bec de l'Aigle peak [5.2], Moses [6.1], Finn MacCool [6.2], possibly James Stephens [6.3], the French composer Robert Planquette [7.4], and the French pirate Olivier Levasseur [7.4].

In the realm of hydronymy, meanwhile, Beckett's "espèce d'analphabête" [7.2] evokes the American Peace River and the Irish Lough Dan as well as the Israeli Dan, American Ana, Pakistani Nal and Hab, the Japanese Abe, and Alph the sacred river of Xanadu. He also achieves one remarkable (and otherwise quite unparalleled) feat, with no fewer than nineteen aquatic references (thirteen rivers, two lakes, four nouns) generated by the single word "dandelinant" [7.3], including the Israeli Dan, Angolan Dande, Russian Delin, French Elle, Chinese Li, Irish Lee, English Lea, Lean, Leen, and Lin, Polish Ina, Thai Nan, and Scottish Nant as well as the Irish Lough Dan and Scottish Loch Nant and four aquatic nouns, Irish *linn* ("lake"), Scots *linn* ("waterfall"), Cornish *lyn* ("lake"), and Welsh *nant* ("stream"). It could of course be objected that this is purely serendipitous, since *dandelinant* is an already existing and not particularly unusual item of colloquial French vocabulary, but the achievement, as with the proverbial egg of Columbus, is in both the fortuitous discovery and the adroit utilization of exactly the right word for the context. Joyce's rendering happily adopts the suggestion without change.

There are cases in which Beckett's French was arguably not improved in being adjusted by Joyce, as when his "Comment s'preenomme-t-il encore?" was altered to "Comment le préenomme-t-on encore?" [5.5] – which may indeed be rather more normal French but loses a pleasingly unexpected reference to the German river Spree. Joyce's unexpected and otherwise unmotivated introduction in the Italian *ALP* of Manzoni's novel *I promessi sposi*, meanwhile, is not at all suggested by his own original English "the loom of his landfall," but rather by Beckett's French "la promasse de son atterritoire" [6.1]. Joyce's description of HCE in the Italian *ALP* as "il gran fenicio lope de mara" is likewise clearly prompted less by his own original English "the gran Phenician rover" than by Beckett's French "le grand loup de mer Phénicien" [6.1].

Despite Joyce's highhanded decree that Beckett and Péron's rendering should be withdrawn even though already accepted for publication, and despite Soupault's subsequent dismissal of it as merely a rough first draft, it is clearly preliminary only in the sense that it precedes Joyce's version. Eugene Jolas was no less than accurate in judging that "in reality, this version was already quite remarkable, when one considers the almost insuperable difficulties involved" (Maria Jolas 1949, 172).

4 French Joyce

Joyce's French *ALP*, incorporating Beckett and Péron's work to a much greater degree than suggested by Soupault's slighting characterization (though not at all to the degree suggested by Megan Quigley), was the result of a complex and multi-layered process of group translation – which can thus be seen as functioning to some degree as the ancestor of future *Finnegans Wake* reading groups. Joyce himself was clearly delighted with the result, and he may or may not have been writing tongue in cheek when he informed Harriet Weaver just before its appearance in print that the French *ALP* was indeed finished, "and I think it must be one of the masterpieces of translation" (*L* 1, 302). He was not alone in his opinion, and Richard Ellmann speaks for many later readers in declaring that the French *ALP*, as published in the *Nouvelle Revue Française* in May 1931, is "even more than the French translation of *Ulysses* a triumph over seemingly impossible obstacles" (1982, 633).

Joyce's collaborators were struck by his obvious and apparently unhesitating willingness to abandon literal fidelity to the surface meaning of his own English text in favour of a possible textual effect in French whose relevance to the original was not always immediately apparent to them. Ellmann reports Soupault's later observation that "Joyce's great emphasis was upon the flow of the line, and he sometimes astonished them ... by caring more for sound and rhythm than sense" (1982, 632–3). As Klaus Reichert puts it, his collaborators gained the distinct impression that he was far more interested in exploring and exploiting the linguistic and textual possibilities of the French language itself rather than in a mere would-be literal replication in that language of his original English text (1989, 94). Very justifiably, Philippe Soupault later asserted that the French version was far less a translation than a recreation (1943; Ferrer and Aubert 1998, 181).

The French *ALP* thus contains a number of particularly striking formulations that are clearly more Wakean than their English original. "And how long was he under loch and neagh?" [4.2], for example, with its conflation of "under Lough Neagh" and "under lock and key," becomes a considerably more complex "Combien resta-t-il au bloch et sous nlefs?," playing first on *rester* ("to stay") and *gonfler à bloc* ("raring to go"), and then conflating French *bloc* ("prison, nick"), German *Loch* ("hole, prison"), and English *loch* and *lock*, before combining *sous clé* ("locked up"), and, since the noun *clé* ("key") was formerly spelled *clef*, a complementary maritime *nef* ("ship)," the latter usually pronounced /nɛf/, but here, by linguistic attraction, pronounced as /nɛ/, a near homophone of "Neagh."

On occasion too, Joyce's French gleefully gilds the already very adequately decorated linguistic lily offered by Beckett, as when Beckett's "Ou quel quel que fût le tréfleuve qu'il aurait trouvé" becomes Joyce's "Ou quelque fut le tréfleuve que le triplepatte qu'on dit qu'il trouva" [2.3]. Another example is provided by Beckett's already baroque formulation "On a lu dans les jurneaux ce qu'il fit, nisi et prius, le roi contre Husparey, avec toute l'histoire du faux saônage et des exploits," which becomes Joyce's even more extraordinary "C'était dans les jurnaux le grabuge qu'il fit, les attendus qhuantes et les lus approuvés, le roi fiersus Onfroy avec toute l'histoire du faux saônage, les exploits illycite et le reste" [4.3], extravagantly mixing and mangling a convoluted Wakean clutter of French and Latin legal terminology.

Among a number of new cultural references not encountered in the original, most of them specifically French, we find the dramatist Victor Hugo [5.4], the journalist Victor Noir [5.4], the poet Gérard de Nerval [5.4], the politician Boissy d'Anglas [7.2], Rabelais [8.3], the château of Azay-le-Rideau [9.2], and Proust [10.2], as well as the English soldier Sir Frederick Browning [5.4].

Ferrer and Aubert suggest (1998, 184) that one of the main differences between Beckett's and Joyce's French versions is the greater number of river puns in the latter, reflecting Joyce's increasing insistence that the aquatic allusions should be densified as much as possible. This tendency is certainly apparent in many small details, as when Beckett's "C'est un beau salaud" becomes "C'est un beau saalaud," adding the German Saale [3.1]; or when his "Il a noirci toute mon eau" becomes "Il m'a noirci toute mon eau," adding the German Ilm [3.2]. But Joyce also gratefully incorporated in his own rendering several of Beckett's most striking hydronymous achievements, such as the single word "dandelinant" [7.3] with its highly impressive nineteen separate aquatic references. Among various other feats of hydronymy, Joyce's formulation "au bloch et sous nlefs" [4.2] enlists the help of a pair of prepositions to summon up the French rivers Aube ("au b-") and Saône ("sous n-"). His "margottons" [7.1] conflates references to the Austrian Mahr, German Ahr, Swiss Aar, American Argo Pond, the Otto of New Zealand, and the Indian Tons, while the single word "aarand" [7.1] succinctly evokes the French Aa, Swiss Aar, German Ahr, Irish Ara, French Aran, and Nigerian Randa.

Joyce's Italian is certainly more extravagant than his French, but occasionally the French *ALP* anticipates the flamboyance of the Italian, as, for example, when "Ask Lictor Hackett or Lector Reade or Garda Growley or the Boy with the Billyclub" is rendered as "Demande à Lictor Huckett ou à Lector Noiret ou à Gardar de Norval ou au Boy dit Browning" [5.4]. The iconic opposition of the rival brothers Shem and Shaun, sons of ALP and HCE, fluvially implied as that of *rive gauche* and *rive droite*, is transformed into a play on linguistic rather than interpersonal opposition, namely that of voiced and unvoiced stops, Reeve Gootch and Reeve Drughad becoming "Sbire Kauche" and "Sbire Troyt" [5.1]. The pronounced dactylic rhythms of the English *ALP*, meanwhile, recur at various points in the French *ALP*, at least to the ear of an English-speaker, "*Mais* queue fit-*il* comme his*toire* quelle his*toire* la fête *Fauve*?" [4.1] or "Com*bien* resta-*t-il* au *bloch* et sous *nlefs*?" [4.2], or again, reinforced by internal rhyme and near-rhyme, "Le *tomps* qu'on ne *dompte* n'at*tend* pour per*sonne*" [4.4], or yet again,"Et *moi* de me*mel* du cô*té* de chez *ter*tre" [10.2].

5 Italian Joyce

"The *Wake* is the last text on earth to set limits on its translators," writes Carol O'Sullivan (2006, 182). Joyce takes full advantage of this freedom in his Italian *ALP* – on which considerably more has been written than on the French *ALP*, particularly of course by Italian scholars. Among these scholars there is unanimous and enthusiastic admiration of Joyce's flamboyant exploitation of the Italian language. The Italian *ALP*, Jacqueline Risset writes, is "an exploration of the furthest limits of the Italian language," a sustained play on "the essentially plural quality" of Italian, in which the multiple intersecting layers of the language are "understood not as fixed stratifications, but as moving planes" (1984, 3, 4). The Italian rendering, as Rosa Maria Bosinelli summarizes, is "a recodification of the washerwomen's dialogue into an Italian-like language, full of Italian proverbs, idioms, fixed expressions, literary allusions (mainly Dante and D'Annunzio), songs, opera arias, regional accents, dialects (from Trieste to Florence to Naples to Sicily to Sardinia), Italian place names, Italian river names, Italian proper names" (1998b, 194–5). Massimo Bacigalupo writes of Joyce's "mastery of the secrets of Italian," characterizing the Italian *ALP* as extraordinary in its "reinvention of passages that were particularly important to him" (2009, 367–8; my translation).

There is also unanimous agreement that the Italian *ALP* should more appropriately be regarded as an original work rather than a translation. Risset, the French translator of Dante, thus asserts that the Italian *ALP* "cannot really be called – in the usual sense of the word – a translation at all; for what takes place is a complete rewriting, a later elaboration of the original, which consequently does not stand opposite the new version as 'original text,' but as 'work in progress'" (1984, 3) – and, she adds, "a more daring variation on it" (6). Corinna del Greco Lobner even maintains that "actually it is a mistake, and contrary to Joyce's wishes, to consider the Italian version of *ALP* a translation" (1989, 38). Rosa Maria Bosinelli similarly argues that Joyce functions essentially as author rather than as translator of the Italian *ALP* while he is rather a collaborator and supervisor of the French version (1996, 46). The Italian *ALP*, she argues, should more properly be regarded as an autonomous parallel text, a recreation or rewriting rather than a translation in any traditional sense. Serenella Zanotti writes in similar vein that the Italian translation was done when Joyce "was out of the writing process [of *ALP*] and thus tended to recreate rather than to reproduce the original text" (2001, 422). Umberto Eco calls the Italian *ALP* "a most particular case of rewriting, taken to extremes" (2001, 107). Bosinelli memorably describes the Italian *ALP* as not only an original work but "the last page of great prose that Joyce left us shortly before dying" (1998b, 197).

In the excerpts considered, the Italian *ALP* distinguishes itself from the French *ALP* in its far greater integration of Italian proverbs [4.4], colloquial turns of speech [1.3], colourful oaths [4.5, 6.1, 7.3], dialect forms [1.3, 3.1, 7.3], and play on language levels in general. There is also far more overtly sexual boldness to be found than in either English or French, as in the very robust "Ma che cozzo ha fotto?" as opposed to the very mild "What was it he did a tail at all?" and the only slightly less mild "Mais queue fit-il comme histoire?" [4.1]. The "sullyport" to be entered by the "siligirls" [8.1] is rendered by the ostensibly innocuous term "usciolino" ("tiny little door"), which, as Lobner suggests, punningly allows for the penetration of any such tiny aperture by a Tuscan *uccellino* ("cock, penis") (1989, 38). A Dublin "trinity scholard" becomes an Italian "laureata di Cuneo" [9.8], a female graduate of a fictional university in the real Italian city of Cuneo, whose name is certainly chosen because it allows for a punning reference to the interplay of a Latin *cuneus* ("wedge") and a Latin *cunnus* ("cunt "). Observing that the noun "Cuneo" is followed just two words later by the noun "lingua," the eagle-eyed Umberto Eco is even delightedly able to detect an interlingual reference to cunnilingus (2001, 111).

In the excerpts considered, there is also a considerably greater number of specifically Italian cultural references in the Italian *ALP* than there are French cultural references in the French *ALP*. References are thus introduced to Rossini [3.2], Machiavelli [3.3], the Frati Branca [4.2], the Roman emperor Marcus Aurelius and the journal *Marco Aurelio* [4.3], Mussolini [4.3], Dante [4.4, 6.3, 8.2, 10.3], the Gran Sasso peak [5.2], Ariosto [5.2], D'Annunzio [5.2], the fascist Madonna del Manganello [5.4], Manzoni [6.1], the Sabine women [6.3], Paganini [7.3], Bellini [7.4, 8.1], Puccini [7.4], Pulcinella [7.4], Giulio Cesare Croce

[7.4], Donizetti [7.4], Pietro Bembo [8.3], the city of Rome and the historical acronym SPQR [9.2], the Sforzas and the Duomo of Milan [9.7], the city of Cuneo [9.8], and Tasso [10.5]. References other than specifically Italian occur to the Spanish dramatist Lope de Vega [6.1], the bibulous Noah [7.4], the French fortune-teller Belline [8.1], and St Gabriel the Archangel [9.5].

Considering the almost obsessive efforts made by Joyce to accumulate river names in his English *ALP*, Umberto Eco is struck by what he considers to be the significantly reduced number of such names to be found in the Italian *ALP*, even asserting that by this stage in the development of *ALP* Joyce was essentially "no longer interested in rivers" (2001, 115). There is little evidence to support this contention in the almost fifty excerpts considered here, however, which in fact contain some singularly impressive feats of hydronymy. The "di' di Belvana," for example, translating "Animal Sendai" [4.1], generates no fewer than ten rivers, including the Scottish Dee, Welsh Dee, English Dibb, Canadian Bell and Belle, Estonian Elva, Scottish Elvan, Romanian Vâna, American Ana, and Thai Na rivers, reinforced by the Norwegian noun *elv* ("river"). Similarly, "Renata la Masa" as a replacement for "Tom Malone" [10.4] concisely generates eight rivers, with the German Rhine, disguised in Polish as the Ren, joined by the Norwegian Rena, Canadian Ena, African Nata, Indonesian Tala, Russian Lama, Dutch Maas, and Japanese Asa, reinforced by the Arabic *ma* ("water").

6 Settanni's Emendations

Joyce's Italian rendering as emended by Settanni was considered to be the official Joyce translation for close to forty years. Fifteen years after its appearance, Settanni belatedly revealed Frank's role as translator (1955, 27), but a further twenty-four years were to pass before the original rendering by Joyce and Frank appeared in print, published in 1979 by Jacqueline Risset.

Frank himself reports, with understandable accumulated irritation, that Settanni's emendations involve merely "a dozen slight modifications, most of them absurd" (1979, 102). In fact, however, Settanni occasionally achieves small but not insignificant stylistic improvements. His emendation of "Beh, sai quando" to "Beh, sai allorché" [2.1], for example, improves on Joyce's version in that it includes ("allor*ché*") an initial incriminating reference to HCE. He arguably improves Joyce's "Ma la zucca per te se mai ti pieghi!" by reversing the order of the two clauses, as "Se mai ti pieghi la zucca è per te" in order to accentuate the dactylic rhythm [2.2]. His minimal, one-letter alteration of "quel'infenice di porco nastro" to "quell'infenice di porco nastro" succinctly emphasizes the translingual aquatic reference to a German *Quelle*, while hinting at the French river Elle and the English river Ellen [2.3].

On a number of occasions, Settanni attempts in schoolmasterly vein to correct what he apparently sees as a typographical error on Joyce's part, only to lose a river or two in the process. Correcting "a mostrar" to "per mostrar," for example, loses the Nigerian Amo [8.2]. On at least two occasions, presumably gaining confidence, he challenges Joyce at his own hydronymous game. On one of these, adding a simple "sí o no" to emphasize a question economically allows him to add two new rivers, the Kenyan Sio and the Japanese Ono [8.1]. On another, he decides to offer a different selection of rivers, substituting the Romanian Beg for Joyce's South African Berg and the Philippine Tanla for the Norwegian Tana [10.1].

Settanni also engaged to some extent in censorship of what he evidently considered to be potentially offensive sexual or political references, in principle a not unreasonable precaution in Mussolini's Italy. In the excerpts considered, for example, he defuses Joyce's Rabelaisian "Che cozzo ha fotto?" to "Ma che cospito ha fotto?" [4.1], though limiting himself to removing only one of the two potentially offending sexual terms. His transformation of Joyce's "Frati Branca" to "Fratelli Branca" [4.2] cautiously defuses potential offence both to the police and the clergy – and is a rare example of a humorous emendation on Settanni's part. His cautious alteration of "Gerarca e gitana" to "Caporione o gitana" [9.3] likewise eliminates what he evidently considered to be a too boldly provocative term in the political context.

Perhaps the most interesting aspect of his attempted political censorship, however, in the excerpts we have considered, is the degree to which he appears to overlook references that could certainly have been read as gravely offensive to the political powers of the day. His ostensible reason for suppressing Nino Frank's name as translator was that in 1940 any mention of Frank, who was persona non grata with the fascist regime, could have led to serious consequences for the journal *Prospettive* and its editors. Distinctly oddly in light of this apparent caution, Settanni, inadvertently or otherwise, left unchanged at least three provocative references on Joyce's part that could certainly have attracted such serious consequences.

The reference to "Marco Oraglio" [4.3], though ostensibly merely satirizing the satirical journal *Marco Aurelio*, also overtly mocks Mussolini's imperial ambitions, declares him to be by no means a new Marcus Aurelius, and has him instead, by heavy implication, braying like a donkey. The reference to the fascist Madonna del Manganello [5.4], "Our Lady of the Cudgel," clearly implies a reference also to fascist brutality. Finally, and potentially highly offensive, the tag "Sugna Purca Qua Ramengo" [9.2] once again overtly mocks Mussolini's imperial ambitions while very clearly suggesting that he is in fact just a great fat pig wandering the streets of Rome. Fortunately, government censors appear to have shared Settanni's blindness to political innuendo, for neither the journal nor its editors seem to have suffered any adverse consequences – any more than they did when Frank's name was in fact (and without further explanation) listed as one of the translators of the concluding lines ("I fiumi scorrono"), which appeared separately in the December 1940 issue of the same journal.

New cultural references are naturally limited in Settanni's version, but include the Italian Fratelli Branca distillery [4.2] as well as the implication that HCE, rather than a pillaging (northern) Viking from Scandinavia, is in fact one of the (southern) Milesians from Spain, legendary heroic and semi-divine founding fathers of the Irish race [6.1].

Perhaps the most surprising aspect of Settanni's intervention in Joyce's work is the degree to which Joyce accepted it without any apparent displeasure – Joyce who on other occasions was very prepared to go to great lengths to defend the untouchable sanctity of his literary work. Frank's fury at Settanni's dubious manoeuvring was perfectly understandable. Joyce's calm acceptance both of Frank's unceremonious exclusion and of the emendations undertaken without any prior permission or even consultation is very evidently an unambiguous indication of the delight with which he greeted the appearance in print of his Italian *ALP*, even if it seemed to have required context-appropriate editorial assistance on Settanni's part.

7 Trilingual Joyce

Patrick McCarthy has aptly oberved that "much of the attraction of *Finnegans Wake* lies in its irreducible strangeness and particularly in the rich, complex, comic language of this enduring book" (2007, 176). In the case of Joyce's trilingual *ALP*, the richness, complexity, and comedy are not just triply but exponentially increased. Joyce's practice in both his French and more particularly his Italian version of *ALP* makes it entirely clear that he saw the exercise of translating his own text not so much as an opportunity merely to replicate his original in a different linguistic context but as an opportunity to *extend* that text by confronting it, challenging it, questioning it, and not infrequently subverting it, with what amounts in both French and Italian to a new parallel version. Each of the resulting rewritings may at times be closely coincident in terms of (surface) semantic content, may at other times be radically and unapologetically deviant – but it always functions as both complementary and interrogative, and as an extension of the original text.

Joyce himself, as Ellmann puts it, clearly considered that there is nothing that cannot be translated (1982, 632), but in the case of *ALP* any traditional concept of translation is strained to the breaking point. The present study has concentrated on teasing out the comparative details of the trilingual *ALP*. The cumulative results make it quite clear that it is less appropriate to speak of his French and Italian renderings as translations in any traditional sense than it is to consider them rewritings, recreations, and essentially continuations of Joycean work in progress. While this is true of both renderings, it is much more obviously the case in Italian than in French. French *ALP* adheres for the most part more closely to the apparent literal or surface meaning of the original, while Italian *ALP* demonstrates no hesitation at all in cutting itself flamboyantly loose from it. In fact, to repeat Eco's pithy formulation, "any translator who was not Joyce himself would have been accused of intolerable licence" (2001, 111–12).

Many of the individual plays on words and specific literary or cultural or historical allusions in the English *ALP* do not survive into either French or Italian. Rather they are replaced by functional equivalences (or approximate equivalences) that are calculated, in conjunction with effects of rhythm, assonance, alliteration, sonority, language level, and flow, to generate a similar reading experience (García Tortosa 1992, 113–14; Bosinelli 1998b, 195). Evaluated as translations in accordance with traditional concepts of the relationship of a translation and its source text, a relationship in which semantic fidelity is a key feature, Joyce's renderings are clearly deficient, if not complete failures, the lamentable result of flamboyantly irresponsible disregard for the semantic rights of the source text. Considered as rewritings, as parallel recreations, they emerge as extraordinary examples of what one might call anamorphic reshaping of that source text. Considered as continuations, they vastly expand and extend, in conjunction with that source text, the original textual ramifications and implications and resonances.

"Heaven knows what my prose means," Joyce wrote to his daughter Lucia in 1934, "but it's pleasing to the ear ... That's enough, it seems to me" (*SL* 341). In the unique case of *ALP*, Joyce provided three separate variations of the same text that are all distinctly pleasing to the ear – and together constitute not just three separate texts but a trilingual *ALP* macrotext. In principle, every word in any one of the three variations is subject to comparison with and modification by the corresponding variants in each of the other two versions. ALP is at once a "queer old skeowsha" and a "drôle de drôlesse" and a "stramba duenna," just as HCE is at once a "quare old buntz" and an "andouille azay rideaucul" and a "sugna purca" [9.1]. More productive of epithets than ALP, he is not just an "old cheb," he is also a "vieux gaillarda" and a "messercalzone" [2.1]. The Phoenix Park is simultaneously "the fiendish park" and "le parc de l'Inphernix," evoking Dante, and "il porco nastro" [2.3], equating the park and the *porco* that is *pater noster* HCE himself. Not only "an awful old reppe" but also "un beau saalaud" and a "lughero malandrone" [3.1], he is simultaneously a "gran Phenician rover" and a "raabe rouleur phéniedcien" and a "gran fenicio lope de mara" [6.1], all of these appellations carrying their individual and overlapping and cumulative implications.

The potential degree of that overlapping and its cumulative implications is well illustrated in the shifting constituents of various collections of fluvial evocations, in which waterways of all shapes and kinds converge across languages from all corners of the terraqueous globe. "Wubbling" up in her osiery chair in English [7.3], to take just one example, ALP thus provides her English readers with evocations of five rivers, a quite notable feat in itself; her French readers, finding her "dandelinant" rather than "wubbling," are invited to rediscover two of these and to find as well evocations of eleven further rivers; her Italian readers, reacting instead to the expression "dondolarsi," will find none of these, but are invited to discover six entirely new rivers; while readers of her trilingual wubbling are offered the opportunity to discover no fewer than twenty-two different rivers, seventeen more than in English, fourteen more than in French, sixteen more than in Italian.

Another striking macrotextual effect involves Joyce's interlingual play on English, French, and Italian metrics, involving the generation of poetic lines as defined by the prosodic rules of the relevant language.

The application of the relevant technical labels may or may not be of any particular interest purely for its own sake. What is certainly of interest, however, is the play of metrical effects that can be identified between and across the relevant languages. The Italian phrase "O cosa mai fece bifronte o triforo" [2.3] well illustrates such interlingual metrical effects, the dactylic tetrameter likely to be read by an English-speaking reader simultaneously readable by an Italian-speaking reader as a dodecasyllable, punctiliously composed according to the accepted metrical rule of two hexasyllables, each with an accent on its second and fifth syllable.

Clive Hart once offered the iconic advice that, especially in the case of *Finnegans Wake*, "we must not dismiss too lightly Joyce's delight in the chance meanings of words, the peculiar interaction often caused by their juxtaposition, and the power of verbal circumstance" (1985, 114). The concept of a trilingual macrotext self-evidently increases exponentially the possibility of such chance interactions and responds immediately to Hart's argument for "the validity even of readings which Joyce never had *any possibility* of including. He seems to have wanted meanings to accrete to his text by hindsight as well as by means of his own constant redistortions of the vocabulary" (115). As for the acceptability or otherwise of such readings, Hart's productive rule of thumb is that "a reading is to be accepted if it provides answers" (116).

The evocation of river names once again offers an example of the generation of specifically translingual effects. In the French *ALP*, the word "linge" ("linen") [3.4] may or may not visually generate for a French-speaking reader, who naturally pronounces the word as /lɛ̃ʒ/, the English Lin, Scottish Ling, and Dutch Linge; an English-speaking reader of the French text, less likely to be distracted by the expected pronunciation, may well see not only these but also the visual evocation of the Chinese Li, Austrian Inn, and Thai Ing, as well as the Irish noun *linn* ("pool"). Against the obvious argument that such a reading is merely a case of rampant over-reading, one may advance Hart's assertion that in *Finnegans Wake* "every syllable is meaningful" and that "an explication is lacking unless it accounts for every syllable and justifies every letter" (1985, 119). Hart also asserted that "the danger is not so much that incorrect readings will be offered (ultimately there is, I think, no such thing as an incorrect reading of *FW*), as that we shall lose our sense of proportion in assessing the relative importance of readings" (1985, 112).

As Dirk Van Hulle observes in the same context, "the harder it is to retrieve an intended meaning, the more the reader will be inclined to project meanings into the text" – and readers of *Finnegans Wake* certainly have little alternative but to do exactly that, ensuring that *Finnegans Wake* always remains a work perennially in progress (Van Hulle 2004, 80–1). Arguably, there are as many *Finnegans Wake*s and *ALP*s as there are readings of *Finnegans Wake* and *ALP* – most obviously so in the case of those readers who are also translators, and most intriguingly so when two competing translations are produced by an original author who happens to be James Joyce and who has no qualms whatsoever about projecting his own meanings into his own text.

Appendix

Chronological *ALP*

We may conclude by surveying the international growth, in some twenty different languages, of what we may think of as the multilingual *ALP* macrotext, constituting a progressive polyglot extension of an already very adequately polyglot original text. Full details of all translations mentioned will be found, listed by translator and date, in the final bibliography.

1925 October 1: first printed version of *ALP* appears in Paris (as "From Work in Progress") in Adrienne Monnier's journal *Le Navire d'Argent*, 1.5 (1 October 1925), 59–74.

1927 October: second printed version of *ALP* appears in Paris (as "Continuation of Work in Progress") in Eugene Jolas's journal *transition*, no. 8 (November 1927), 17–35.

1928 October 29: third printed version of *ALP* published in book form (as *Anna Livia Plurabelle*) in New York by Crosby Gaige.

1929 Georg Goyert begins work early in the year on a complete German ALP, the first translation to be undertaken in any language.

August: Joyce records the closing pages of *ALP* (*FW* 213.11–216.05) for C.K. Ogden's Orthological Institute in Cambridge.

November: Joyce writes that he is undertaking a French translation of the closing pages with Léon-Paul Fargue. The plan does not materialize.

December: Joyce invites Samuel Beckett to undertake a French translation of the opening pages.

1930 Beckett and Alfred Péron begin work on their French translation early in the year.

June: fourth printed version of *ALP* published in book form (as *Anna Livia Plurabelle*) in London by Faber and Faber.

October 16: Beckett and Péron's translation, "Anna Lyvia Pluratself" (*FW* 196.01–201.20), reaches page-proof stage for Georges Ribemont-Dessaigne's journal *Bifur*.

November: Joyce instructs Beckett and Péron to withdraw their rendering and begins instead to coordinate a French team translation himself.

1931 May 1: Joyce's French team translation appears in Paris in the *Nouvelle Revue Française* (*FW* 196.01–201.20, 215.11–216.05).

Summer: Joyce collaborates with C.K. Ogden on a Basic English rendering of the closing pages of *ALP*.

October: Ogden's "Anna Livia Plurabelle in Basic" (*FW* 213.11–216.05) appears in Ogden's own journal *Psyche*.

1932 March: Ogden's "Anna Livia Plurabelle in Basic" (*FW* 213.11–216.05) reprinted in Eugene Jolas's journal *transition*.

A complete Czech *ALP*, translated by Maria Weatherall, Vladimír Procházka, and Adolf Hoffmeister, appears in Prague, the first complete translation to be published in any language.

1933 March: Georg Goyert's complete German *ALP* reportedly finished and submitted to Joyce for his approval – but remains unpublished for many years (see 1946, 1970).

Japanese version of the opening and closing pages (*FW* 196, 213–16) by Junzaburo Nishiwaki appears in Tokyo.

1937 Joyce proposes to Nino Frank that they undertake an Italian translation of the same excerpts from *ALP* earlier translated into French.

1938 Joyce and Frank's Italian *ALP* completed early in the year.

1939 May 4: fifth printed version of the English *ALP* appears as chapter I.8 of *Finnegans Wake* (London, Faber and Faber; New York, Viking Press).

1940 February 15: Joyce and Frank's "Anna Livia Plurabella" (*FW* 196.01–201.21) appears in Rome in the journal *Prospettive*, emended by Ettore Settanni, and attributed to Joyce and Settanni without mention of Frank.

December15: Joyce and Frank's "I fiumi scorrono" (*FW* 215.11–216.05), attributed to Joyce, Frank, and Settanni, appears in *Prospettive*.

1946 Excerpts from Goyert's German *ALP* (see 1929, 1933, 1970) appear in Munich in the journal *Die Fähre* and in Salzburg in the journal *das silberboot* (*FW* 196–8, 213–15, 215–16).

1948 Brief excerpts from *FW* (including from *FW* 196), translated into French by Michel Butor in an article on Joyce's work.

1957 Portuguese translations by Haroldo and Augusto de Campos of excerpts from *FW* in the *Jornal do Brasil*, including from *FW* 196, 214–16.

1959 Polish translation by Jerzy Strzetelski of excerpts from *ALP*, including the opening and closing pages (*FW* 196–8, 206–7, 215–16).

1961 Italian translations by J. Rodolfo Wilcock of excerpts from *FW*, including from *FW* 196, 206–7.

1962 Portuguese excerpts from *FW* (including from *FW* 196, 214–16) by Haroldo and Augusto de Campos (see 1957) appear in book form as *Panaroma do Finnegans Wake*.

1964 Hungarian excerpts from *FW* by Endre Bíró (including from *ALP*) in the Yugoslav journal *Híd*.

1968 Japanese translation by Masayoshi Osawa et al. of excerpts from *FW*, including from *FW* 206–7.

1969 German translation by Wolfgang Hildesheimer of the opening pages of *ALP* (*FW* 196–7).

Galician excerpt (*FW* 216) translated by Leopoldo Rodríguez.

1970 Separate complete German translations of *ALP* by Wolfgang Hildesheimer, by Hans Wollschläger, and by Georg Goyert (see 1929, 1933, 1946), in a single volume edited by Klaus Reichert and Fritz Senn.

Japanese translation by Masayoshi Osawa et al. of the first twelve pages of *ALP* (*FW* 196–208), serialized in seven numbers of the Japanese journal *Kikan Paedeia* between 1970 and 1972.

1978 Japanese excerpts from *FW* translated by Kyôko Ono et al. (including from *FW* 206–7).

1979 Joyce and Frank's original Italian "Anna Livia Plurabella," without Settanni's emendations, appears, edited by Jacqueline Risset, in Joyce's *Scritti italiani*.

1982 Complete French translation of *FW* by Philippe Lavergne, the first complete rendering in any language.

Complete Japanese translation of *ALP* by Masayoshi Osawa et al.

Spanish version of the opening and closing pages of *ALP* (*FW* 196–7, 213–16) by Ricardo Silva-Santisteban.

1985 Beckett and Péron's "Anna Lyvia Pluratself" finally published, edited by Jacques Aubert (see 1930).

Complete Korean *ALP* translated by Chong-keon Kim.

Complete Polish *ALP* translated by Maciej Słomczyński.

1991 First volume (parts I–II) of Naoki Yanase's complete Japanese translation of *FW*, including *ALP*.

Complete Spanish translation of *ALP* by Ricardo Silva-Santisteban.

1992 Complete Spanish translation of *ALP* by Francisco García Tortosa et al.

Hungarian translation by Endre Bíró of excerpts from *FW*, including from *ALP*.

1993 Complete German version of *FW* by Dieter Stündel.

Abridged and simplified Spanish version of *FW* by Víctor Pozanco.

1996 Complete Italian translation of *ALP* by Luigi Schenoni.

Romanian translation of *ALP* by Felicia Antip.

1998 Romanian translation of final pages of *ALP* (*FW* 213–16) by Laurent Milesi.

2000 Russian excerpts from *ALP* by Konstantin Aleksandrovich Belyaev (*FW* 196, 209–12).

2001 Revised Italian version of *ALP* by Luigi Schenoni, in his translation of *FW* I.5–8.

Complete Portuguese version of *ALP* by Donaldo Schüler, in his translation of *FW* I.5–8.

Complete Swedish translation of *ALP* by Mario Grut.

2002 Complete Dutch translation of *FW* by Erik Bindervoet and Robbert-Jan Henkes.

Complete Korean translation of *FW* by Chong-keon Kim.

2004 Complete Catalan translation of *ALP* by Marissa Aixàs.

Abridged and simplified Japanese translation of *FW* by Kyôko Miyata.

2007 Spanish version by Leandro Fanzone of selected excerpts, including from *FW* 215–16.

2009 Japanese version by Tatsuo Hamada of *FW* I.1–8.

Complete Portuguese version of *ALP* by Dirce Waltrick do Amarante.

2012 Chinese version by Dai Congrong of *FW* I.1–8.

Complete Polish translation of *FW* by Krzysztof Bartnicki.

2013 Complete Greek translation of *FW* by Eleftherios Anevlavis.

Separately published Dutch translation of *ALP* (with commentary) by Erik Bindervoet and Robbert-Jan Henkes (from their 2002 translation of *FW*).

2015 Complete online French translation of *FW* by Hervé Michel.

Turkish version of *FW* I.1–8 by Umur Çelikyay.

2016 Complete French translation of *ALP* by Philippe Blanchon.

Complete online Spanish translation of *ALP* by Eduardo Lago.

Complete Spanish translation of *FW* by Marcelo Zabaloy.

2017 Online Russian translation of *FW* I.4, 7–8 by Andrey Rene

Complete Turkish translation of *FW* by Fuat Sevimay.

As of December 2017, to summarize, there existed thirty-one complete or substantially complete translations of *ALP*, in sixteen different languages, including Catalan, Chinese, Czech, Dutch, French, German, Greek, Italian, Japanese, Korean, Polish, Portuguese, Romanian, Russian, Spanish, Swedish, and Turkish. Of these, Spanish had no fewer than five versions, German and Japanese each had four, and French, Polish, Portuguese, and Turkish each had two. In addition, excerpts varying in length from a few lines to several pages had also appeared in translation, by other hands, in French, Galician, Hungarian, Italian, Japanese, Polish, Portuguese, Romanian, and Spanish.

Translations other than literary were evidently also envisaged by Joyce, who wrote to the young avant-garde American composer George Antheil (1900–1959) on 23 September 1930, "How are you getting on with the *Anna Livia* symphony?" (*L* 1, 293). If Antheil had indeed intended this project, it remained unrealized. Shortly afterwards, in 1932 or thereabouts, Stuart Gilbert, apparently with Joyce's support, was reportedly working briefly on a film scenario for *Anna Livia Plurabelle*, but this project too remained ultimately unrealized (Ellmann 1982, 654).

Bibliography

Joyce's works are cited parenthetically in the text by the abbreviations listed in section 1 below. The annotation "bilingual" in section 2 (which also includes Joyce's translations of his own work) indicates that the translation is accompanied by the original text.

1. Works by James Joyce

ALP Anna Livia Plurabelle. Preface by Padraic Colum. New York, Crosby Gaige, 1928; London: Faber and Faber, 1930, 1997. Corresponds to *FW* 196–216.

D Dubliners. 1914. Ed. Terence Brown. London: Penguin Books.1992.

FW Finnegans Wake. London, Faber and Faber; New York, Viking Press, 1939. Intro. John Bishop. 1999. Harmondsworth, UK: Penguin.

FW2 The Restored Finnegans Wake. Ed. Danis Rose and John O'Hanlon. 2010. London: Penguin Classics, 2012.

L 1 The Letters of James Joyce, vol. 1. Ed. Stuart Gilbert. London: Faber, 1957; New York: Viking, 1966.

L 2/3 The Letters of James Joyce, vols. 2 and 3. Ed. Richard Ellmann. London: Faber; New York: Viking, 1966.

P A Portrait of the Artist as a Young Man. New York: B.W. Huebsch, 1916; London: Egoist Press, 1917. Ed. Chester G. Anderson. The Viking Critical Library. New York: Viking, 1968.

SH Stephen Hero. Ed. Theodore Spencer. London: Jonathan Cape; New York: New Directions, 1944.

SI Scritti italiani. 1979. Ed. Gianfranco Corsini and Giorgio Melchiori. Milan: Mondadori. Includes "Anna Livia Plurabella," trans. James Joyce and Nino Frank, 197–214.

SL Selected Letters of James Joyce. Ed. Richard Ellmann. London: Faber and Faber, 1975.

U Ulysses. Paris: Shakespeare & Co., 1922. Ed. Hans Walter Gabler with Wolfhard Steppe and Claus Melchior. New York: Random House / Vintage Books, 1993.

2. Other Works Cited

Ackerley, C.J., and S.E. Gontarski. 2006. *The Faber Companion to Samuel Beckett: A Reader's Guide to His Works, Life, and Thought*. London: Faber and Faber.

Aixàs, Marissa [as Maria Lluïsa Obiols]. 2004. *Estudi del joc de paraules en* Anna Livia Plurabelle*: Anàlisi contrastiva de traduccions i proposta pròpia de versió*. Diss. Universitat Autònoma de Barcelona. Includes a Catalan version of *ALP*.

Alighieri, Dante. 1982. *The Divine Comedy of Dante Alighieri: Inferno*. Trans. Allen Mandelbaum. Toronto: Bantam Books.

Allen, Kim. 2000. "Beckett, Joyce, and Anna Livia: The Plurability of Translating *Finnegans Wake*." In *Translation Perspectives XI: Beyond the Western Tradition*, ed. Marilyn Gaddis Rose, 427–35. Binghampton, NY: Center for Translation Research.

Amarante, Dirce Waltrick do. 2009. *Para ler* Finnegans Wake *de James Joyce*. São Paulo: Editora Iluminuras. Includes a Portuguese translation of *ALP*.

Anevlavis, Eleftherios [Ελευθέριος Ανευλαβής], trans. 2013. *I agrýpnia ton Finnegan* [*Η* αγρύπνια των Φίννεγκαν][*FW*: Greek]. Athens: Kaktos.

Antip, Felicia, trans. 1996. "Veghea lui Finnegan: Anna Livia Plurabelle." [*ALP*: Romanian] *Vara* (Bucharest) 18:83–8.

Attridge, Derek, ed. 1990. *The Cambridge Companion to James Joyce*. Cambridge: Cambridge University Press.

Aubert, Jacques. 1967. "*Finnegans Wake*: Pour en finir avec les traductions?" *James Joyce Quarterly* 4 (3): 217–22.

– 1985. Introduction to "Anna Lyvia Pluratself." Trans. Samuel Beckett and Alfred Péron. In *James Joyce*, ed. Jacques Aubert and Fritz Senn, 417–18. Paris: Editions de l'Herne.

Aubert, Jacques, and Fritz Senn. 1985. *James Joyce*. Paris: Editions de l'Herne.

Ayto, John. 1991. *Dictionary of Word Origins*. New York: Arcade Publishing.

Bacigalupo, Massimo. 2009. "La lingua di Finnegan: James Joyce saggista e poeta italiano." *Scrittori stranieri in lingua italiana dal Cinquecento a oggi: Convegno internazionale di studi, Padova, 20–21 marzo 2009*. Ed. Furio Brugnolo. Padua: Unipress. 361–73.

Bahlow, Hans. 1980. *Deutsches Namenlexikon: Familien- und Vornamen nach Ursprung und Sinn erklärt*. Stuttgart: Deutscher Bücherbund.

Bair, Deirdre. 1978. *Samuel Beckett: A Biography*. New York: Harcourt Brace Jovanovich.

Banta, Melissa, and Oscar A. Silverman, eds. 1987. *James Joyce's Letters to Sylvia Beach, 1921–40*. Bloomington: Indiana University Press.

Baring-Gould, William S. and Ceil, eds. 1962. *The Annotated Mother Goose*. New York: Bramhall House.

Bartnicki, Krzysztof, trans. 2012. *Finneganów tren* [*FW*, Polish]. Krakow: Korporacja Ha!Art.

Beach, Sylvia. 1980. *Shakespeare and Company*. 1956. London: University of Nebraska Press.

Beckett, Samuel. 1929. "Dante ... Bruno . Vico .. Joyce." *transition* 16–17 (June 1929): 242–53.

– 1972. "Dante ... Bruno. Vico.. Joyce." In *Our Exagmination round his Factification for Incamination of Work in Progress*. By Samuel Beckett et al. 1929, 3–22. London: Faber and Faber.

Beckett, Samuel, and Alfred Péron, trans. 1985. "Anna Lyvia Pluratself." Ed. Jacques Aubert. In *James Joyce*, ed. Jacques Aubert and Fritz Senn. Paris: Editions de l'Herne, 418–22; rpt. Bosinelli 1996, 153–61. Corresponds to *FW* 196.01–201.21.

Beckett, Samuel, Alfred Péron, Ivan Goll, Eugène Jolas, Paul Léon, Adrienne Monnier, Philippe Soupault, and James Joyce, trans. 1931. "Anna Livie Plurabelle" [*ALP*, excerpts, French]. *Nouvelle Revue Française* 36 (1 May 1931): 633–46; rpt. Bosinelli 1996, 3–29. Corresponds to *FW* 196.01–201.20, 215.11–216.05.

Begnal, Michael H. 1975. "The Dreamers at the Wake: A View of Narration and Point of View." In *Narrator and Character in Finnegans Wake*. By Michael H. Begnal and Grace Eckley, 17–123. Lewisburg: Bucknell University Press.

Belyaev, Konstantin Aleksandrovich, trans. 2000. "Džejms Džojs, 'Anna Livija Pljurabell'." *Soyuz Pisatelei* (Kharkov, Ukraine). Online. Posted 19 January 2000. *FW* 196.1–5, 209.18–212.19.

Benjamin, Walter. 1969. "The Task of the Translator: An Introduction to the Translation of Baudelaire's *Tableaux parisiens*." *Illuminations*. Ed. Hannah Arendt, trans. Harry Zohn. New York: Schocken. 69–82.

Bennett, Arnold. 1929. "Review of *Anna Livia Plurabelle*." *Evening Standard* 19 September: 7.

Benstock, Bernard, ed. 1985a. *Critical Essays on James Joyce*. Boston: G.K. Hall.

– 1985b. *James Joyce*. New York: Ungar.

Bindervoet, Erik, and Robbert-Jan Henkes, trans. 2002. *Finnegans Wake* [Dutch]. Amsterdam: Querido. Bilingual.

– 2013. *Anna Livia Plurabelle* [Dutch]. Amsterdam: Rainbow. Bilingual.

Bíró, Endre, trans. 1964. "Finnegans Wake" [excerpts, Hungarian]. Includes excerpts from *ALP*. *Híd* 28 (11): 1241–56.

– trans. 1992. *Finnegan ébredése (részletek)* [*FW*, excerpts, Hungarian]. Budapest: Holnap Kiadó. Includes excerpts from *ALP*.

Bishop, John. 1986. *Joyce's Book of the Dark:* Finnegans Wake. Madison: University of Wisconsin Press.

Blanchon, Philippe, trans. 2016. *Anna Livia Plurabelle* [French]. Toulon: Éditions La Nerthe.

Bosinelli, Rosa Maria Bollettieri. 1987. "Joyce e la traduzione: Rifacimenti italiani di *Finnegans Wake*." *Lingua e stile* (Bologna) 22.4: 515–38.

– 1990. "Beyond Translation: Italian Re-Writings of *Finnegans Wake*." *Joyce Studies Annual* 1990:142–61.

– ed. 1996. *James Joyce, Anna Livia Plurabelle*. Intro. Umberto Eco. Scrittori tradotti da scrittori 8. Turin: Einaudi.

– 1998a. "Introduction: Anna Livia Plurabelle's Sisters." In *Transcultural Joyce*, ed. Karen R. Lawrence, 173–8. Cambridge: Cambridge University Press.

– 1998b. "Anna Livia's Italian Sister." In *Transcultural Joyce*, ed. Karen R. Lawrence, 193–8. Cambridge: Cambridge University Press.

– 2000. "Joyce on the Turrace of Babbel." In *Classic Joyce: Joyce Studies in Italy 6*, ed. Franca Ruggieri, 417–29. Roma: Bulzoni.

– 2001. "Joyce Slipping Across the Borders of English: The Stranger in Language." *James Joyce Quarterly* 38:395–409.

Bowker, Gordon. 2011. *James Joyce: A Biography*. London: Weidenfeld and Nicolson.

Budgen, Frank. 1972. *James Joyce and the Making of* Ulysses. London: Oxford University Press.

Burgess, Anthony. 1982. *Here Comes Everybody: An Introduction to James Joyce for the Ordinary Reader*. 1965. Feltham, UK: Hamlyn Paperbacks.

Butor, Michel. 1948. "Petite croisière préliminaire à une reconnaisance de l'archipel Joyce." *La vie intellectuel* 16.5 (1948): 104–35. Rpt. *Répertoire: Etudes et conférences 1948–1959*. By Michel Butor. Paris: Les Editions de Minuit, 1960. 195–218. Includes translation of *FW* 196.1–7.

Campbell, Joseph, and Henry Morton Robinson. 1961. *A Skeleton Key to* Finnegans Wake. 1944. New York: Viking Press.

Campos, Augusto de, and Haroldo de Campos, trans. 1957. [Excerpts from *FW*, Portuguese]. *Jornal do Brasil* (São Paulo) 15 September 1957; 29 December 1957. Seven fragments from *FW*, including from *FW* 196 (trans. Augusto de Campos) and 214–16 (jointly translated).

– trans. 1962. *Panaroma do Finnegans Wake* [*FW*, excerpts, Portuguese]. São Paulo, Comissão de Literatura do Conselho Estadual de Cultura. Eleven fragments from *FW*, including from *FW* 196 (trans. Augusto de Campos), 214–16 (jointly translated).

Carson, Ciaran. 2008. *The Táin: A New Translation of the Táin Bó Cúailnge*. London: Penguin Books.

Çelikyay, Umur, trans. 2015. *Finneganın Vahı* [*FW* I.1–8, Turkish]. Istanbul: Aylak Adam Yayınları.

Cerny, James W. 1971. "Joyce's Mental Map." *James Joyce Quarterly* 9:218–24.

Clark, Michael J. 1980. "Jean Itard: A Memoir on Stuttering." In *Psychology of Language and Thought: Essays on the Theory and History of Psycholinguistics*, ed. Robert W. Rieber, 153–84. New York: Plenum Press. https://doi.org/10.1007/978-1-4684-3644-0_7.

Colum, Padraic. 1928a. "The River Episode from James Joyce's 'Work in Progress.'" *Dial* 84:318–22.

– 1928b. "Preface." *Anna Livia Plurabelle*. By James Joyce. New York: Crosby Gaige. vii–xix. Appeared earlier as 1928a.

Coromines, Joan. 2012. *Breve diccionário etimológico de la lengua castellana*. Madrid: Gredos.

Costanzo, W.V. 1971. "The French Version of *Finnegans Wake*: Translation, Adaption, Recreation." *James Joyce Quarterly* 9:225–36.

Crémieux, Benjamin. 1929. "Le règne des mots." *Candide* 14 November 1929:3.

Crispi, Luca, and Sam Slote, eds. 2007. *How Joyce Wrote Finnegans Wake: A Chapter-by-Chapter Genetic Guide*. Madison: University of Wisconsin Press.

Cronin, Anthony. 1996. *Samuel Beckett: The Last Modernist*. London: HarperCollins.

Dai, Congrong, trans. 2012. *Fēnnígēn de shǒulíng yè*. Shanghai: Renmin Chubanshe [*FW* I.1–8: Chinese, first of 3 planned volumes].

Dante, *see* Alighieri, Dante.

Dauzat, Albert, Jean Dubois, and Henri Mitterand. 1971. *Nouveau dictionnaire étymologique et historique*. Paris: Librairie Larousse.

de Courcy, J.W. 1996. *The Liffey in Dublin*. Dublin: Gill and Macmillan.

Eastman, Max. 1931. *The Literary Mind: Its Place in an Age of Science*. New York: Charles Scribner's Sons.

Eckley, Grace. 1975. "Queer Mrs Quickenough and Odd Miss Doddpebble: The Tree and the Stone in *Finnegans Wake*." In *Narrator and Character in* Finnegans Wake. By Michael H. Begnal and Grace Eckley. 125–238. Lewisburg: Bucknell University Press.

Eco, Umberto. 1989. *The Aesthetics of Chaosmos: The Middle Ages of James Joyce*. Trans. Ellen Esrock. Cambridge, MA: Harvard University Press.

– 1996. "Ostrigotta, ora capesco." *James Joyce,* Anna Livia Plurabelle. Ed. Rosa Maria Bollettieri Bosinelli. Turin: Einaudi. v–xxix.

– 2001. *Experiences in Translation*. Trans. Alastair McEwen. Toronto: University of Toronto Press.

Edel, Leon. 1980. "The Genius and the Injustice Collector: A Memoir of James Joyce." *American Scholar* 49:467–87.

Ellmann, Richard. 1982. *James Joyce*. 1959. New York: Oxford University Press.

Epstein, Edmund Lloyd. 2009. *A Guide through* Finnegans Wake. Gainesville: University Press of Florida.

Ewen, David. 1963. *Encyclopedia of the Opera*. New York: Hill and Wang.

Fanzone, Leandro, trans. 2007. "Fragmentos de *Finnegans Wake*, de James Joyce" [*FW*, excerpts, Spanish]. *Seikilos* (Buenos Aires). Online. Posted 8 November 2007. Various excerpts, including *FW* 215.31–216.05. http://seikilos.com.ar/seikilos/traducciones

Ferrer, Daniel, and Jacques Aubert. 1998. "Anna Livia's French Bifurcations." In *Transcultural Joyce*, ed. Karen R. Lawrence, 179–86. Cambridge: Cambridge University Press.

Fordham, Finn. 2007. *Lots of Fun at* Finnegans Wake*: Unravelling Universals*. Oxford: Oxford University Press.

Frank, Nino. 1949. "Souvenirs sur James Joyce." *La Table Ronde* 23:1671–93.

– 1967. "L'ombre qui avait perdu son homme." In *Memoire brisée*, 26–94. Paris: Calmann-Lévy.

– 1979. "The Shadow That Had Lost Its Man." In *Portraits of the Artist in Exile: Recollections of James Joyce by Europeans*, ed. Willard Potts, 74–105. Seattle: University of Washington Press.

García Tortosa, Francisco, trans., 1992, with Ricardo Navarrete and José María Tejedor Cabrera. *Anna Livia Plurabelle* [Spanish]. Ed. Francisco García Tortosa. Madrid: Ediciones Cátedra. Bilingual. *FW* 196.01–216.05.

Gibson, George Cinclair. 2005. *Wake Rites: The Ancient Irish Rituals of* Finnegans Wake. Gainesville: University Press of Florida.

Gillet, Louis. 1941. *Stèle pour James Joyce*. Marseille: Sagittaire.

– 1979. "The Living Joyce." In *Portraits of the Artist in Exile: Recollections of James Joyce by Europeans*, ed. Willard Potts, 170–204. Seattle: University of Washington Press.

Glasheen, Adaline. 1973. Note. *A Wake Newslitter* 10 (1973): 80.

Golding, Louis. 1933. *James Joyce*. London: Thornton Butterworth.

Gordon, John. 1986. Finnegans Wake*: A Plot Summary*. Syracuse, NY: Syracuse University Press.

Gorman, Herbert. 1941. *James Joyce: A Definitive Biography*. London: John Lane/Bodley Head.

Goyert, Georg, trans. 1927. *Ulysses*. [German] Basel, Zurich: Rhein-Verlag.

– trans. 1946. "Anna Livia Plurabella" [*ALP*, excerpts, German]. *Die Fähre* (Munich) 1.6 (1946): 337–40. Also in *das silberboot* (Salzburg) 2.8 (1946), 139–41. *FW* 196–8, 213–15, 215–16.

– ed. 1970. "Anna Livia Plurabella" [*ALP*, German]. *Anna Livia Plurabelle*, ed. Klaus Reichert and Fritz Senn. Frankfurt: Suhrkamp. 141–66. *FW* 196.01–216.05.

Green, Miranda J. 1992. *Dictionary of Celtic Myth and Legend*. London: Thames and Hudson.

Grmela, Josef. 2004. "The Czech Reception of Irish Literature: The 1930s." *THEPES* (University of Masaryk) 2:36–42.

Grut, Mario, trans. 2001. *Anna Livia Plurabella* [*ALP*, Swedish]. Lund: Ellerström. *FW* 196.01–216.05.

Halper, Nathan. 1967. "Joyce and *Anna Livia*." *James Joyce Quarterly* 4:223–8.

Hamada, Tatsuo, trans. 2009. *James Joyce, Finnegans Wake (Parts I and IV)*. Abiko (Japan): Abiko Literary Press.

Hanks, Patrick, Flavia Hodges, A.D. Mills, and Adrian Room, ed. 2002. *The Oxford Names Companion*. Oxford: Oxford University Press.

Hart, Clive. 1962. *Structure and Motif in* Finnegans Wake. London: Faber and Faber.

– 1985. "The Elephant in the Belly: Exegesis of *Finnegans Wake*." In *Critical Essays on James Joyce*, ed. Bernard Benstock, 111–20. Boston: G.K. Hall.

Hayman, David, ed. 1963. *A First-Draft Version of* Finnegans Wake. Austin: University of Texas Press.

– 1990. *The Wake in Transit*. Ithaca, London: Cornell University Press.

Higginson, Fred H. 1953. *James Joyce's Revisions of* Finnegans Wake*: A Study of the Published Versions*. Minneapolis: University of Minnesota Press.

– 1960. *Anna Livia Plurabelle: The Making of a Chapter*. Minneapolis: University of Minnesota Press.

Hildesheimer, Wolfgang, trans. 1969. "Übersetzung und Interpretation einer Passage aus Finnegans Wake von James Joyce." *Interpretationen: James Joyce, Georg Büchner. Zwei Frankfurter Vorlesungen*. Frankfurt: Suhrkamp. 7–29. *FW* 196.01–197.33.

– trans. 1970. "Anna Livia Plurabelle." *Anna Livia Plurabelle*. Ed. Klaus Reichert and Fritz Senn. Frankfurt: Suhrkamp. 65–97. *FW* 196.01–216.05.

Hodgart, Matthew. 1978. *James Joyce: A Student's Guide*. London: Routledge and Kegan Paul.

Hoffmeister, Adolf. 1979. "Portrait of Joyce." In *Portraits of the Artist in Exile: Recollections of James Joyce by Europeans*, ed. Willard Potts, 127–36. Seattle: University of Washington Press.

Holmes, M.E. 2011. "Nino Frank, from Dada to Film Noir." Online. http://rememberninofrank.org/

Hooke, S.H. 1991. *Middle Eastern Mythology.* 1963. London: Penguin Books.

Jolas, Eugene. 1948. "My Friend James Joyce." In *James Joyce: Two Decades of Criticism*, ed. Seon Givens, 3–18. New York: Vanguard Press.

Jolas, Maria. 1949. "Traduttore ... Traditore?" In *A James Joyce Yearbook*, ed. Maria Jolas, 171–8. Paris: Transition Press.

Joyce, James, and Ettore Settanni, trans. 1940. "Anna Livia Plurabella; I fiumi scorrono." *Prospettive* (Rome) 4.2 (15 February 1940), 13–15; 4.11–12 (15 December 1940), 14–16. *FW* 196.01–201.21, 215.11–216.05. Rpt. in *James Joyce e la prima versione italiana del* Finnegan's [*sic*] Wake. By Ettore Settanni.Venezia: Edizioni del Cavallino, 1955; rpt. as "Anna Livia Plurabella." Ed. Jacqueline Risset. *Tel Quel* (Paris) 55 (1973): 59–62.

Joyce, James, and Nino Frank, trans. 1979. "Anna Livia Plurabella. Passi di *Finnegans Wake* tradotti da James Joyce e Nino Frank, 1938" [*ALP*, excerpts, Italian]. Ed. Jacqueline Risset. *Scritti italiani.* By James Joyce. Ed. Gianfranco Corsini and Giorgio Melchiori. Milan: Mondadori, 1979. 216–33; rpt. Bosinelli 1996: 3–29. *FW* 196.01–201.21, 215.11–216.05.

Kenner, Hugh. 1992. "Shem the Textman." *The Languages of Joyce: Selected Papers from the 11th International James Joyce Symposium, Venice, 12–18 June 1988.* Ed. Maria Rosa Bollettieri Bosinelli, Carla Marengo Vaglio, and Christine van Boheemen. Philadelphia and Amsterdam: John Benjamins. 145–54. https://doi.org/10.1075/z.54.14ken.

Kim, Chong-keon, trans. 1985. [*Anna Livia Plurabelle*: Korean]. Seoul: Jeong-eumsa.

Kitcher, Philip. 2007. *Joyce's Kaleidoscope: An Invitation to* Finnegans Wake. Oxford: Oxford University Press. https://doi.org/10.1093/acprof:oso/9780195321029.001.0001.

Knowlson, James. 1996. *Damned to Fame: The Life of Samuel Beckett*. London: Bloomsbury.

Lago, Eduardo, trans. 2016. *Anna Livia Plurabelle* [Spanish]. Online. http://www.enriquevilamatas.com/eduardolago/AnnaLiviaPlurabelle.html

Laman, Barbara. 2007. "ALP Goes to Germany." In *Joyce and/in Translation*, ed. Rosa Maria Bollettieri Bosinelli and Ira Torresi, 135–41. Rome: Bulzoni Editore.

Lavergne, Philippe, trans. 1982. *Finnegans Wake.* [French] Paris: Gallimard.

Lawrence, Karen R., ed. 1998. *Transcultural Joyce*. Cambridge: Cambridge University Press.

Lernout, Geert, and Wim Van Mierlo, eds. 2004. *The Reception of James Joyce in Europe*. London, New York: Continuum.

Levin, Harry. 1960. *James Joyce: A Critical Introduction*. 1941. New York: New Directions.

Linati, Carlo. 1926. "Da *l'Ulysses* di James Joyce." *Il Convegno* (Milan) 7.11–12 (November–December 1926): 813–28.

– 1940. "Ricordi su Joyce." *Prospettive* 4.2 (15 February 1940), 16.

Litz, A. Walton. 1961. *The Art of James Joyce: Method and Design in* Ulysses *and* Finnegans Wake. New York: Oxford University Press.

Lobner, Corinna del Greco. 1986. "Anna Livia Plurabella: La lavandaia antabecedariana di James Joyce." *Rivista di Studi Italiani* 4 (1): 84–91.

– 1989. *James Joyce's Italian Connection: The Poetics of the Word*. Iowa City: University of Iowa Press.

Loukopoulou, Eleni. 2013. "Upon Hearing James Joyce: The *Anna Livia Plurabelle* Gramophone Disc (1929)." In *The Aesthetics of Matter: Modernism, the Avant-Garde and Material Exchange*, ed. Sarah Posman, et al., 118–27. Berlin: Walter de Gruyter. https://doi.org/10.1515/9783110317534.118.

Lower, Mark Antony. 1988. *A Dictionary of Surnames*. Ware, UK: Wordsworth Editions. Originally published in 1860 as *Patronymica Britannica: A Dictionary of the Family Names of the United Kingdom*.

Macalister, R.A.S. 1919. "Temair Breg: A Study of the Remains and Traditions of Tara." *Proceedings of the Royal Irish Academy* 34 (C): 231–399.

McKenzie, John L. 1965. *Dictionary of the Bible*. New York and London: Collier Macmillan.

MacKillop, James. 1998. *A Dictionary of Celtic Mythology*. Oxford: Oxford University Press.

Malaparte, Curzio. 1940. "I giovani non sanno scrivere." *Prospettive* 4 (2): 3–6.

Mandelbaum, Allen. 1982. *The Divine Comedy of Dante Alighieri: Inferno*. Toronto: Bantam Books.

McCarthy, Patrick A. 2007. "Making Herself Tidal: Chapter I.8." *How Joyce Wrote* Finnegans Wake*: A Chapter-by-Chapter Genetic Guide*. Ed. Luca Crispi and Sam Slote. Madison: University of Wisconsin Press. 163–80.

McCourt, John. 2000. *The Years of Bloom: James Joyce in Trieste 1904–1920*. Dublin: The Lilliput Press.

– 2008. "His *città immediata*: Joyce's Triestine Home from Home." In *A Companion to James Joyce*, ed. Richard Brown, 123–36. Oxford: Wiley-Blackwell.

– 2013. "Joyce, *il bel paese* and the Italian language." *Joycean Unions: Post-Millennial Essays from East to West*. Ed. R. Brandon Kershner and Tekla Mecsnóber. European Joyce Studies 22. Amsterdam and New York: Rodopi. 61–79. https://doi.org/10.1163/9789401208826_007.

McHugh, Roland. 2006. *Annotations to* Finnegans Wake. 3rd ed. Baltimore: Johns Hopkins University Press.

Michel, Hervé, trans. 2015. *Veillée Pinouilles* [*FW*, French]. Online. https://sites.google.com/site/finicoincequoique/

Milesi, Laurent. 1998. "ALP in Roumanian (with Some Notes on Roumanian in *Finnegans Wake* and in the Notebooks)." *Transcultural Joyce*. Ed. Karen R. Lawrence. Cambridge: Cambridge University Press. 199–207. Includes Romanian version of *FW* 213.11–216.05.

Mink, Louis O. 1978. *A* Finnegans Wake *Gazetteer*. Bloomington: Indiana University Press.

Miyata, Kyoko, trans. 2004. *Finnegans Wake*. [Japanese, abridged] Tokyo: Shueisha.

Monnier, Adrienne. 1925. "James Joyce: From Work in Progress." *Le Navire d'Argent* 1 (5), 59–74.

Morel, Auguste, trans. 1926. "*Ulysse* (Fragment)" ["Calypso": French]. *900: Cahiers d'Italie et d'Europe* 1 (1), 107–31.

Morley, John. 1903. *The Life of William Ewart Gladstone*. 3 vols. New York, London: Macmillan.

Nishiwaki, Junzaburo, trans. 1933. "Anna Livia Plurabelle." *Joyce shishu* [Joyce's Poems; selections from the poems and from *ALP*: Japanese]. Tokyo: Daiichi-shobo. *FW* 196.01–19, 213.11–216.05.

Norris, Margot. 1976. *The Decentered Universe of Finnegans Wake: A Structuralist Analysis*. Baltimore: Johns Hopkins University Press.

– 1982. "Anna Livia Plurabelle: The Dream Woman." In *Women in Joyce*, ed. Suzette Henke and Elaine Unkeless, 197–213. Brighton, UK: Harvester Press.

– 1990. "*Finnegans Wake*." *The Cambridge Companion to James Joyce*. Ed. Derek Attridge, 161–84. Cambridge: Cambridge University Press.

– 2015. "Fluid Figures in 'Anna Livia Plurabelle': An Ecocritical Exploration of I.8." In *Joyce's Allmaziful Plurabilities: Polyvocal Explorations of Finnegans Wake*, ed. Kimberly J. Devlin and Christine Smedley, 133–48. Gainesville: University Press of Florida. https://doi.org/10.5744/florida/9780813061542.003.0009.

O'Brien, Edna. 2000. *James Joyce*. London: Phoenix.

Ó Corráin, Donnchadh, and Fidelma Maguire. 1990. *Irish Names*. Dublin: Lilliput Press.

O'Faoláin, Seán. 1928. "The Cruelty and Beauty of Words." *Virginia Quarterly Review* 4 (1): 208–25.

Ogden, C.K., trans. 1922. *Tractatus Logico-Philosophicus*. By Ludwig Wittgenstein. London: Routledge and Kegan Paul.

– 1930. *Basic English: A General Introduction with Rules and Grammar*. London: K. Paul, Trench, Trubner & Co.

– trans. 1931. "Anna Livia Plurabelle in Basic." *Psyche* 12.2 (October 1931): 92–5; rpt. as "James Joyce's Anna Livia Plurabelle in Basic English," *transition* 21 (March 1932): 259–62; rpt. Bosinelli 1996: 141–50. *FW* 213.11–216.05.

– 1932a. "James Joyce's *Anna Livia Plurabelle* in Basic English." *transition* 21 (March 1932) 259–62.

– 1932b. "Notes in Basic English on the *Anna Livia Plurabelle* Record." *Psyche* 12 (4): 86–95.

O Hehir, Brendan. 1965. "Anna Livia Plurabelle's Gaelic Ancestry." *James Joyce Quarterly* 2:158–66.

– 1967. *A Gaelic Lexicon for* Finnegans Wake. Berkeley: University of California Press.

O'Neill, Patrick. 2005. *Polyglot Joyce: Fictions of Translation*. Toronto: University of Toronto Press. https://doi.org/10.3138/9781442678620.

– 2013. *Impossible Joyce: Finnegans Wakes*. Toronto: University of Toronto Press.

Onions, C.T., ed. 1966. *The Oxford Dictionary of English Etymology*. Oxford: Clarendon Press.

Ono, Kyôko, Koike Shigeru, Junnosuke Sawazaki, Kenzô Suzuki, and Toda Motoi, trans. 1978. [Excerpts from *Finnegans Wake. Giacomo Joyce*]. Ed. Saiichi Maruya. Tokyo: Shueisha. Bilingual. Includes *FW* 206–7.

O'Rahilly, Thomas F. 1946. *Early Irish History and Mythology*. Dublin: Dublin Institute for Advanced Studies.

Osawa, Masayoshi, and Junnosuke Sawasaki, trans. 1968. Selections. *Sekai Bungaku Zenshuu 35* [Selected Works of World Literature, vol. 35]. Tokyo: Shueisha. Includes *FW* 206.29–207.20.

Osawa, Masayoshi, Kyôko Ono, Shigeru Koike, Junnosuke Sawasaki, and Kenzo Suzuki, trans. 1970–2. "Anna Livia Plurabelle." *Kikan Paedeia* [Paedeia Quarterly], nos. 7–11, 13, 15. Tokyo: Takeuchi-shoten. *FW* 196.01–208.05. Serialized in seven numbers of the journal.

Osawa, Masayoshi, Kyôko Ono, Shigeru Koike, Junnosuke Sawasaki, Kenzo Suzuki, and Motoi Toda, trans. 1982. *Anna Livia Plurabelle. Bungei-zasshi Umi* [Umi Literary Magazine] December 1982: 288–305.

O'Shea, Michael J. 1986. *James Joyce and Heraldry*. Albany, NY: State University of New York Press.

O'Sullivan, Carol. 2006. "Joycean Translations of *Anna Livia Plurabelle*: 'It's translation, Jim, but not as we know it.'" *Italian Culture: Interactions, Transpositions, Translations*. Ed. Cormac Ó Cuilleanáin, Corinna Salvadori, and John Scattergood. Dublin: Four Courts Press. 175–82.

Parrinder, Patrick. 1984. *James Joyce*. Cambridge: Cambridge University Press.

Pilling, John. 2006. *A Samuel Beckett Chronology*. London, New York: Palgrave Macmillan. https://doi.org/10.1057/9780230504837.

Potts, Willard, ed. 1979. *Portraits of the Artist in Exile: Recollections of James Joyce by Europeans*. Seattle: University of Washington Press.

Pozanco, Víctor, trans. 1993. *Finnegans Wake* [Spanish]. Barcelona: Editorial Lumen. Abridged and simplified.

Quigley, Megan M. 2004. "Justice for the 'Illstarred Punster': Samuel Beckett and Alfred Péron's Revisions of 'Anna Lyvia Pluratself.'" *James Joyce Quarterly* 41:469–87.

– 2015. "A Dream of International Precision: James Joyce, Ludwig Wittgenstein, and C.K. Ogden." In *Modernist Fiction and Vagueness: Philosophy, Form, and Language.*, 103–46. Cambridge: Cambridge University Press.

Rees, Alwyn, and Brinley Rees. 1989. *Celtic Heritage: Ancient Tradition in Ireland and Wales*. 1961. London: Thames and Hudson.

Reichert, Klaus, and Fritz Senn, eds. 1970. *Anna Livia Plurabelle*. Intro. Klaus Reichert. Frankfurt: Suhrkamp. Includes Wolfgang Hildesheimer, "Anna Livia Plurabelle" (65–97); Hans Wollschläger, "Anna Livia Plurabelle, parryotphrosed myth brockendootsch" (99–133); and Georg Goyert, "Anna Livia Plurabella" (141–66).

Reichert, Klaus. 1989. *Vielfacher Schriftsinn: Zu Finnegans Wake*. Frankfurt: Suhrkamp.

Rene, Andrey, trans. 2017. На помине Финнеганов (Na pomine Finneganov) [FW I.4, 7–8, Russian]. http://samlib.ru/r/rene_a/.

Reynolds, Mary. 1981. *Joyce and Dante: The Shaping Imagination*. Princeton: Princeton University Press.

Richards, I.A., and C.K. Ogden. 1923. *The Meaning of Meaning: A Study of the Influence of Language upon Thought and of the Science of Symbolism*. London: Kegan Paul.

Risset, Jacqueline. 1973. "Joyce traduit par Joyce." *Tel Quel* 55:47–58.

– 1979. "*Anna Livia Plurabella*: Passi di *Finnegans Wake* tradotti da James Joyce e Nino Frank, 1938." *Scritti italiani*, 216–233. Milan: Mondadori.

– 1984. "Joyce Translates Joyce." Trans. Daniel Pick. *Comparative Criticism* 6:3–21.

Rodríguez, Leopoldo. 1969. "Impresións encol do *Finnegans Wake* de James Joyce." *Grial* 26 (1969): 475. Includes Galician translation of *FW* 216.

Ruge, Elisabeth, Reinhard Schäfer, and Dirk Vanderbeke. 1990. "Digressions of the Book for Allemannen." In *Finnegans Wake: Fifty Years*. Ed. Geert Lernout. European Joyce Studies 2. Amsterdam and Atlanta, GA: Rodopi. 37–46.

Sage, Robert. 1928. "ETC." *transition* 14 (1928): 171–4.

– 1972. "Before *Ulysses* – and After." In *Our Exagmination round his Factification for Incamination of Work in Progress*. By Samuel Beckett et al. 1929, 147–70. London: Faber and Faber.

Sailer, Susan Shaw. 1999. "Universalizing Languages: *Finnegans Wake* Meets Basic English." *James Joyce Quarterly* 36:853–68.

Sandars, N.K. 1970. *The Epic of Gilgamesh*. Harmondsworth, UK: Penguin Books.

Schenoni, Luigi, trans. 1996. "Anna Livia Plurabelle" [Italian]. *James Joyce,* Anna Livia Plurabelle. Ed. Rosa Maria Bollettieri Bosinelli. Turin: Einaudi. 87–139. Bilingual.

– trans. 2001. *Finnegans Wake: Libro Primo V–VIII*. Milan: Mondadori. *FW*, I.5–8. Bilingual.

Schüler, Donaldo, trans. 2003. *Finnicius Revém* [*FW*, Portuguese]. Pôrto Alegre, Brazil: Ateliê Editorial. 5 vols. Bilingual.

Senn, Fritz. 1967. "The Issue is Translation." *James Joyce Quarterly* 4:163–4.

– 1984. *Joyce's Dislocutions: Essays on Reading as Translation*. Ed. John Paul Riquelme. Baltimore: Johns Hopkins University Press.

– 1995. *Inductive Scrutinies: Focus on Joyce*. Ed. Christine O'Neill. Dublin: Lilliput Press.

– 1998. "ALP Deutsch: ob überhaupt möglich?" In *Transcultural Joyce*, ed. Karen R. Lawrence. Cambridge: Cambridge University Press, 1998. 187–92.

– 2007. *Joycean Murmoirs: Fritz Senn on James Joyce*. Ed. Christine O'Neill. Dublin: Lilliput.

Settanni, Ettore. 1933. "Aria di Joyce." *Romanzo e romanzieri d'oggi*, 55–61. Naples: Alfredo Guida.

– 1937. *Les hommes gris*. Trans. Adeline E. Auscher. Paris: Éditions Rieder.

– 1939. *Amour conjugale*. Paris: Éditions Rieder.

– 1940. "Nota su Finnegan's [*sic*] Wake." *Prospettive* 4.2 (15 February 1940): 12.

– 1955. *James Joyce e la prima versione italiana del* Finnegan's [*sic*] Wake. Venezia: Edizioni del Cavallino.

Sevimay, Fuat, trans. 2016. *Finnegan Uyanması* [*FW*, Turkish]. Istanbul: Sel Yayınları.

Silva-Santisteban, Ricardo, trans. 1982. "Anna Livia Plurabelle" [Excerpts, Spanish]. *Cielo abierto* 7 (April–June 1982): 25–8. *FW* 196.01–197.17, 213.11–216.05.

– trans. 1991. "Anna Livia Plurabelle" [Spanish]. *Biblioteca de México* 3–4 (August 1991): 36–43. *FW* 196.01–216.05.

Słomczyński, Maciej, trans. 1985. *Anna Livia Plurabelle* [Polish]. Kraków: Wydawnictwo Literackie.

Soupault, Philippe. 1931. "A propos de la traduction d'*Anna Livia Plurabelle*." *Nouvelle Revue Française* 36: 633–6.

– 1943. *Souvenirs de James Joyce*. Paris: Charlot.

– 1963. *Profils perdus*. Paris: Mercure de France.

– 1979. "James Joyce." In *Portraits of the Artist in Exil: Recollections of James Joyce by Europeans*, ed. Willard Potts, 108–18. Seattle: University of Washington Press.

Spinks, Lee. 2009. *James Joyce: A Critical Guide*. Edinburgh: Edinburgh University Press. https://doi.org/10.3366/edinburgh/9780748638352.001.0001.

Stephens, James. 1918. *Reincarnations*. London: Macmillan.

Strzetelski, Jerzy, trans. 1959. "Noc opłakiwania Finnegana (Urywki)" [*ALP*, excerpts, Polish]. *Twórczość* 12 (1959): 62–64. Excerpts from *FW* 196–8, 206–07, 215–16.

Stündel, Dieter H., trans. 1993. *Finnegans Wehg: Kainnäh ÜbelSätzZung des Wehrkess fun Schämes Scheuss* [*FW*, German]. Darmstadt, Häusser; Frankfurt am Main: Zweitausendeins. Bilingual.

Szczerbowski, Tadeusz. 2000. *Anna Livia Plurabelle po polsku:* Finnegans Wake *Jamesa Joyce'a ks. I, rozdz. 8*. Kraków: Wydawnictwo Naukowe Akademii Pedagogicznej.

Tindall, William York. 1959. *A Reader's Guide to James Joyce*. New York: Farrar, Straus and Giroux / Noonday Press.

Tindall, William York. 1996. *A Reader's Guide to Finnegans Wake*. 1969. Syracuse, NY: Syracuse University Press.

Tymoczko, Maria. 1994. *The Irish Ulysses*. Berkeley: University of California.

Van Hulle, Dirk. 2004. "The Manner of Meaning: Ogden and Beckett Translating Joyce." *BELL: Belgian Journal of English Language and Literature* 2:75–84.

– 2007. "Dame Plurabelle: Joyce's Art of Decomposition and Recombination." In *Joyce in Trieste: An Album of Risky Readings*, ed. Sebastian D.G. Knowles, Geert Lernout, and John McCourt. Gainesville: University Press of Florida.

Weatherall, Maria, Vladimír Procházka, and Adolf Hoffmeister, trans. 1932. *Anna Livia Plurabella, Fragment: Díla v zrodu* [ALP, Czech] / *Anna Livia Plurabella, Fragment: Work in Progress*. Afterword by Adolf Hoffmeister. Prague: Odeon, 1932; Liberec: Dauphin, 1996. Bilingual.

Wilcock, Juan Rodolfo, trans. 1961. "*Frammenti scelti da* La veglia di Finnegan" [FW, excerpts, Italian]. *Tutte le opere di James Joyce*. Ed. Giacomo Debenedetti. Vol. 3. Milano: Mondadori, 1961. 1125–74. Includes Italian versions of *FW* 196.01–24, 206.29–207.14.

Wilson, Edmund. 1952. "The Dream of H.C. Earwicker." *The Wound and the Bow: Seven Studies in Literature*, 218–43. London: W.H. Allen.

Wollschläger, Hans, trans. 1970. "Anna Livia Plurabelle, parryotphrosed myth brockendootsch" [*ALP*, German]. *Anna Livia Plurabelle*, ed. Klaus Reichert and Fritz Senn. Frankfurt: Suhrkamp. 99–133.

Yanase, Naoki, trans. 1991. *Finnegans Wake* [Japanese] *I–II*. Tokyo: Kawade shobo shinsha.

Zabaloy, Marcelo, trans. 2016. *Finnegans Wake* [Spanish]. Buenos Aires: El Cuenco de Plata.

Zanotti, Serenella. 2001. "An Italianate Irishman: Joyce and the Languages of Trieste." *James Joyce Quarterly* 38:411–30.

– 2002. "L'italiano di Joyce nell'auto-traduzione di *Anna Livia Plurabelle*." In *Eteroglossia e plurilinguismo letterario*. Vol. 2, *Plurilinguismo e letteratura*. Ed. Furio Brugnolo and Vincenzo Orioles. Rome: Editrice Il Calamo. 277–307.

– 2010. "The Translator's Visibility: The Italian Translations of *Finnegans Wake*." *Mediazioni* (Università di Bologna) 10 (2010). Online. Posted 24 June 2010. http://www.mediazionionline.it/dossier/2006zanotti-print.htm.

Index

www.ingramcontent.com/pod-product-compliance
Lightning Source LLC
LaVergne TN
LVHW090157080826
844660LV00013B/850/J

* 9 7 8 1 4 8 7 5 0 2 7 8 2 *